Closed Seasons

CLOSED SEASONS

The Transformation of Hunting

in the Modern South

Julia Brock

THE UNIVERSITY OF

NORTH CAROLINA PRESS

Chapel Hill

This book was published with the assistance of the Wells Fargo Fund for Excellence of the University of North Carolina Press.

© 2025 Julia Brock
All rights reserved
Set in Chaparral and Bunday Sans by codeMantra
Cover art: The faunal motifs and stitching on the cover come directly from a quilt made in 1894–95 by Sarah Catherine Hunt and Martha Hunt Brock, my foremothers, in Cedartown, Georgia. The quilt was documented and stewarded by Alfred Brock, my great-uncle, of Atlanta, Georgia.

Library of Congress Cataloging-in-Publication Data
Names: Brock, Julia, author.
Title: Closed seasons : the transformation of hunting in the modern South / Julia Brock.
Description: Chapel Hill : The University of North Carolina Press, [2025] | Includes bibliographical references and index.
Identifiers: LCCN 2024051778 |
ISBN 9781469681450 (cloth) |
ISBN 9781469681467 (paperback) |
ISBN 9781469681474 (epub) |
ISBN 9781469681481 (pdf)
Subjects: LCSH: Game laws—Southern States—History—20th century. | Hunting—Southern States—History—20th century. | BISAC: HISTORY / United States / State & Local / South (AL, AR, FL, GA, KY, LA, MS, NC, SC, TN, VA, WV) | NATURE / Environmental Conservation & Protection
Classification: LCC KF5640 .B76 2025 |
DDC 346.7504/69549—dc23/eng/20241211
LC record available at https://lccn.loc.gov/2024051778

Portions of chapter 3 appeared earlier in somewhat different form in Julia Brock, "A 'Sporting Fraternity': Northern Hunters and the Transformation of Southern Game Law in the Red Hills Region, 1880–1920," in *Leisure, Plantations, and the Making of a New South: The Sporting Plantations of the South Carolina Lowcountry and Red Hills Region, 1900–1940*, ed. Julia Brock and Daniel J. Vivian (Lanham, MD: Lexington Books, 2015).

The author's royalties from the book are paid to the Minority Outdoor Alliance, Atlanta, Georgia.

For product safety concerns under the European Union's General Product Safety Regulation (EU GPSR), please contact gpsr@mare-nostrum.co.uk or write to the University of North Carolina Press and Mare Nostrum Group B.V., Doelen 72, 4831 GR Breda, The Netherlands.

For Jule Anderson

Contents

Introduction / 1

CHAPTER 1
   Game and Fish Laws and the Closing of the Commons / 9

CHAPTER 2
   Audubon, Alabama, and the Advent of Statewide Game
   and Fish Commissions in the Progressive Era Deep South / 35

CHAPTER 3
   Hunting Land, Hunting Labor: Charlie Young and
   the Growth of the Georgia Winter Hunting Colony / 77

CHAPTER 4
   Fannye A. Cook, the Federal Government, and the
   Maturation of Game and Fish Laws in the Deep South / 119

AFTERWORD
   The Outdoors Are for Everybody / 153

Acknowledgments / 161
Notes / 165
Bibliography / 193
Index / 209

Illustrations

Map

Mississippi, Alabama, and Georgia,
  with locations referenced in the text / x

Table

Hunting convictions in Alabama, 1907–1922 / 67

Figures

Hunter with dogs, ca. 1870s / 32

Woman's hat with plumage / 40

Portrait of John H. Wallace Jr. / 49

Charlie Young with hunting party, 1910 / 79

H. W. Hopkins and A. H. Mason, Susina plantation, ca. 1905 / 85

Charlie Young with family, ca. 1930s / 116

Fannye Cook, 1953 / 122

Workers in Mississippi natural history museum, ca. 1930s / 146

Fannye Cook memorial, Copiah County, Mississippi / 151

"Hunters Ask the Farmer First" sign / 155

Durrell Smith, 2021 / 157

Closed Seasons

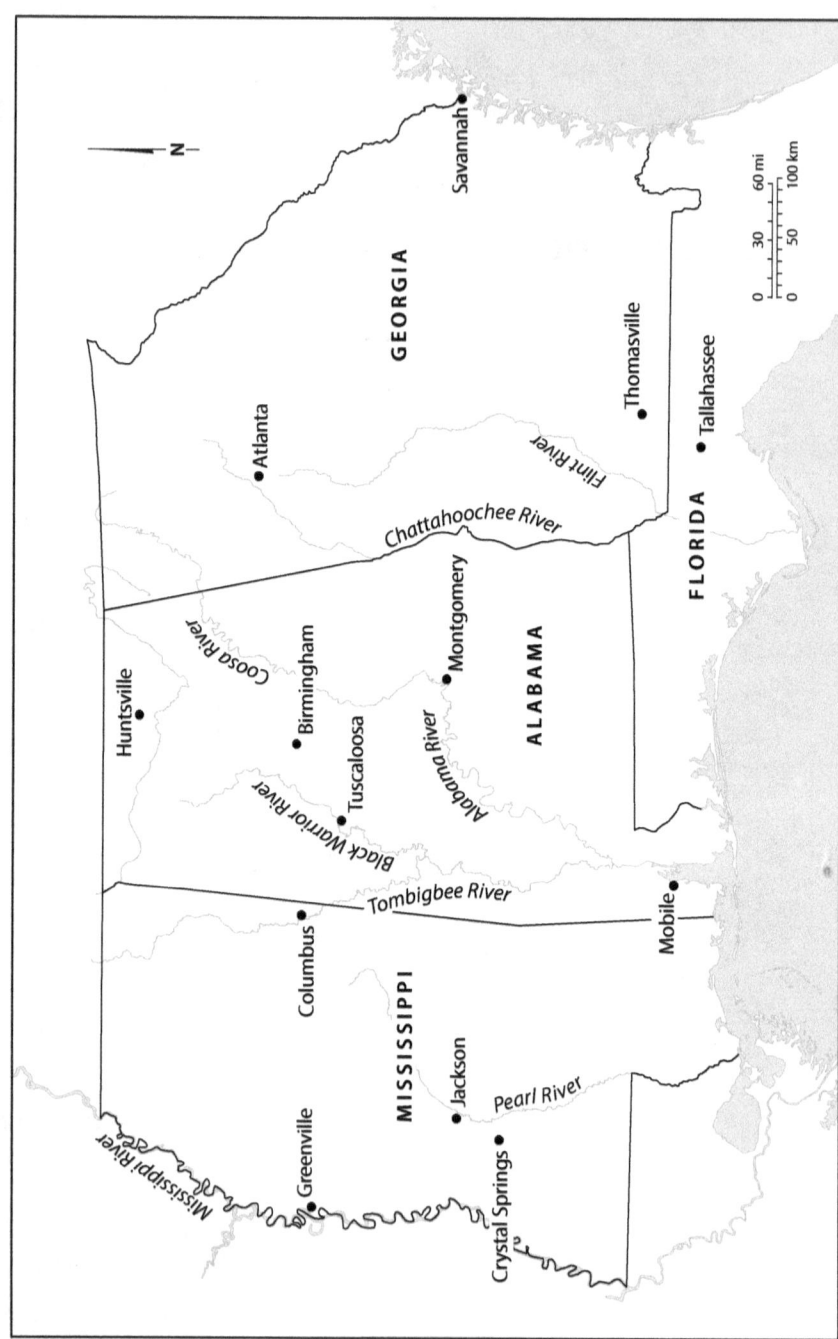

Mississippi, Alabama, and Georgia, with locations referenced in the text. University of North Carolina Press.

Introduction

Ellisville, Alabama, is a small hamlet just southeast of Centre, in Cherokee County, right next to the Georgia border. In the 1950s, it hosted a vital industrial cottonseed operation, owned and managed by two Ellises—A. W. Jr. ("Dub") and Jim, brothers born in the late 1920s, who had helped their father farm cotton, raise cattle, and operate a sawmill. The Ellis cottonseed business was a hallmark of the changing, post–World War II southern cotton economy—mechanized, land-intensive, and innovative. By the 1980s, Dub and his brother were experimenting with genetically modified seed, which bolstered the market for their Sure Grow Seed Company.[1]

My family, just over the border in Rome, Georgia, connected to Ellisville through the locally famous dove hunts hosted by the Ellises every September. Dub's son Shad (short for Shattuck) married my aunt Catherine, and Shad extended an invitation to members of our family to an event that, as my father remembers it, signified "the ritualistic end of summer and beginning of fall."[2] These were big events in the 1980s, with dozens of men parked at the edges of fields with plugged shotguns, waiting for birds to light.[3] After the hunt, nights brought revelry, with guests and their families enjoying the dove breasts, swaddled in bacon and grilled, and other food at an Ellis home on Weiss Lake, a 1950s-era impoundment of the Coosa River created by the Alabama Power Company. I was a child then, and my memories of the dove hunts are defined by one incident when my sister and I were offered the chance to fire a shotgun. We each remember the impact of the recoil.

The dove shoot as a white social/family occasion ran deep in southern hunting; in 1908, newly appointed Alabama game and fish commissioner John H. Wallace Jr. called it an "old fashioned southern custom."[4] But the dove hunt of the 1980s, on Ellis land, was also distinctly different from its earlier form. The Ellises, for starters, owned thousands of acres in Cherokee County, which undergirded their cotton business. A hundred years earlier, local hunters might have expected to be able to access that land, the uncultivated parts at least, in pursuit of prey. By the 1980s, these lands, when not in production, were the exclusive domain of owners, kinfolk, and friends to use during dove season, posted to prohibit trespassers. By the 1980s, too, doves were a protected species, included as they were in the Migratory Bird Treaty Act of 1918, which set bag limits, regional closed seasons, and stricter rules around harvest. Under the act's regulations, the Ellises would not have been able to bait their fields—a "baleful" practice that Commissioner Wallace despised—though they could expect harvested cornfields to attract the birds. And, the Ellises were aware of the presence of local enforcement; one year, Shad got word that game wardens would visit the hunt to check for licenses, and they did. Fortunately, my father and guests had purchased Alabama hunting licenses at a nearby Ellisville store. We can trace the dove hunt through two centuries, yet the circumstances surrounding access to land, hunting rights, the presence of law enforcement, and the protection of birds had changed dramatically over the course of seventy years. *Closed Seasons* follows the origins and maturation of that transformation in land, commerce, and social relations.

I begin with this personal connection as an entry into themes within these pages. In a region in which roughly 5.3 million people have hunting licenses, there exists a broad section of southerners (and not just men) whose annual calendar is defined by hunting seasons and related social events: the dove hunt, the dog trial, the night hunt, the hunting camp weekend. Hunting and fishing are cherished traditions in the South, enjoyed by people of all backgrounds; they are activities passed down from parents to children or elders to juniors. Hunters and fishers are storytellers, and tales of the hunt pervade southern lore and literature and, for those who participate in the sport, the dinner table, the Facebook group, the sporting podcast, and the workplace meeting room.

Popular media and hunting tourism outlets call these hunting and fishing practices "traditional," as I have, above. But to put what is now a set of largely recreational, not domestic, activities in the category of "traditional" masks a complex past defined by dramatic change in law, custom, and practice. This book charts the Progressive Era development of game and fish laws, the consequences of their implementation, and their transformation into the 1930s. The story is one of increased regulation that determined which southerners could access land and prey, and why. The laws offered limited protection to imperiled game and nongame species while reconfiguring human food systems and livelihoods and penalizing activity of diverse southerners that had long been customary.

Laws regulating hunting and fishing in the South were scattershot in the late nineteenth century; those that existed at all applied only to specific counties and had no arm of enforcement. Yet the late nineteenth-century conservation movement, combined with the growing, transregional identity of "sportsman," influenced some southerners to work for state-level systems of game and fish protection. The South was the last region in the nation to adopt these laws, and southern states did so against opposition from farmers, game sellers, and everyday southerners. This response resulted in an unstable legal landscape that was, initially, poorly funded and enforced. It took almost thirty years of race-baiting, state building, land enclosure, and federal intervention in wildlife protection for game and fish laws to mature and find purchase in the South.

This work builds upon an important body of historical literature that considers hunting and fishing in the South and beyond, as well as recent critical assessments of the Progressive Era conservation movement.[5] I offer a contribution that maps the development of game and fish laws in southern states, which is underexplored in studies that foreground cultural, social, or environmental aspects of hunting. These laws served as an early form of a conservation code in the South and reveal as much about shifting attitudes toward the environment, race, and gender as they do about the hunt or the chase.[6] In fact, the new laws defined how hunting would be transformed in the early twentieth century. They uprooted the tradition of access to unfenced hunting lands so that by the first two decades of the twentieth century, hunters and fishers were beholden to a rights structure that circumscribed movement in the fields and woods and access to rivers and streams. Although not strictly a legal history, *Closed Seasons* foregrounds law and the social impact of a penal conservation practice on ordinary southerners. Drawing on multiple voices, the work bridges social, cultural, and environmental history with that of policy.

I focus especially on the Deep South states of Alabama, Georgia, and Mississippi while offering thematic context of the entire region. Alabama is particularly important—it formed a centerpiece of regional efforts to create statewide policy protecting game animals, songbirds, and fish. Though not the first in the South to adopt a centralized protection system (that was North Carolina), Alabama was the first, in 1907, to create a comprehensive game and fish commission that would endure in spite of resentment from some public sectors. In contrast, Mississippi was the last southern state to adopt a consolidated game and fish commission. A sharper focus on this subregion of the South, then, allows for a chronological and thematic exploration of the changing strategies of conservationists and their allies to implement a protectionist overlay on the southern terrain often considered beyond the pale of state power.

Within the three states, debates over the passage of game and fish laws and resistance to their implementation allow us to plumb the sectional politics of a changing political economy. Historians who have charted the processes of enclosure in the nineteenth century see it begin in plantation districts and extend to the northerly mountains or the piney woods of the coastal plain—in essence, from the centers to the margins of agricultural production.[7] In the accounts that explore resistance to enclosure, the failure of localities to adopt fence and stock laws came from the farmers of the margins who refused to cede access to an open range for grazing, foraging, and hunting.[8] Game and fish laws have sometimes been included in these analyses, and for good reason. They formed another version of trespass law and extended the practice of posting land, a visual reminder of the emerging importance of private, landed property in the post–Civil War South. Though game and fish laws often followed the same pattern of dispersal—from plantation districts outward—the geography of acceptance or resistance to the new laws was more fluid. In plantation districts, as with laws to fence heretofore free-roaming stock, elites saw game and fish laws as a tool of the landowner to control labor and protect crops. But game depletion was a region-wide phenomenon by the late nineteenth century, and so supporters of the new laws motivated by wildlife protection were just as apt to represent mountainous areas as they were the richest agricultural belts. Advocates of the new laws were connected, however, by the surety that hunting and fishing were activities primarily of sport. They were buoyed by national wildlife and bird protection movements and experiments in game and fish laws in northern and midwestern regions. Like elsewhere in the country, the new southern laws curbed the right to sell and ship game and limited access to wildlife for sustenance. Indeed, "market hunter" and "pothunter" were epithets used repeatedly by advocates of the new laws to denigrate hunting for purposes other than sport. The class dimension of the laws left a broad field of rural resistance, from the top to the bottom of all three states. That resistance was guided by multiple motivations. Game and fish laws complicate what seems to be a linear story of transition from a "commons" to enclosure. Even small farmers might have supported trespass laws and requirements to post land, which gave them the right to exclusive possession of game on their property. But, some felt their rights were abridged when the state outlawed the selling of game. Farmers could assert possession of a resource but not free use—now controlled by a state that claimed ownership of natural resources. Farmer grievances remind us, then, of the multidimensional property rights structures that developed in the early twentieth century.

The fight for and ultimate adoption of a body of hunting and fishing laws with centralized police power illustrates the consolidation of the modern southern state. Progressive Era advocates argued that the central management of various functions of the state, including school systems, public health, and taxation, was the hallmark of a modernizing South. Conservation law, including hunting and fishing, forestry, and the management of oysters and seafoods, was key to efficient state management in both the protection and exploitation of natural resources.

As was the case in the Progressive Era South more generally, these efforts also meant to define and uphold a racialized state. Chandra Manning reminds us that state building is not simply the act of rationalizing state functions or amassing power but "the purposes for which that power is wielded . . . and the felt results of that power in the daily lives of people under the state's central governance."[9] The people who designed and heralded early twentieth-century game and fish laws clearly intended to render the fields, woods, and streams for white men (and sometimes white women) only. Drawing from nineteenth-century precedents, Progressive Era iterations of the game laws constructed the ideal hunter—the white sportsman—and cast a foil in Black men. The laws, in the rhetoric of their creators, would not only preserve game and fish but also control Black male bodies, keeping them immobile on farms and laboring for white landowners.[10] At least in intent, the laws would serve as a prop to transformations in the southern political economy.

The white smallholder was of equal concern to conservation advocates. Sometimes derided as clinging to customary hunting rights and sometimes heralded as an important frontline protector of wildlife, the white farmer preoccupied southern conservationists. Coming on the heels of late nineteenth-century agrarian resistance, it's no surprise that the architects of the laws in all three states were concerned about gaining the support of non-elite whites; they grew hoarse trying to convince ordinary white southerners that the laws would prove beneficial to their interests. But attempts to implement the laws had to contend with rural refusal. In fact, if we square intent with implementation, the new laws seem something of a failure. Letters from supporters poured into game commissioners' offices complaining of the lack of enforcement. Game wardens would not pursue violators; judges and grand juries repeatedly exonerated accused offenders. Conviction rates, where numbers are available for aggregation, are a minuscule fraction of those of other crimes. This widespread transgression can be thought of as a kind of "folk crime," a term sociologists have used to describe "violations" of laws in which a populace has no moral stake or sees as illegitimate.[11] If Black men escaped the worst of conservationists' penal intentions, it was because they were part of a broad-based resistance that manifested through noncompliance.[12] That's not to say the new laws were immaterial or inconsequential, however; as we will learn, license fees, middle- and upper-class preferences for guns and ammunition, enclosure, and Jim Crow custom all worked to bind Black men and poor whites in pursuit of prey.[13]

Though challenged politically, the game commissions of Alabama and Georgia remained intact in the first three decades of the twentieth century. By the 1930s, when Mississippi finally implemented a statewide conservation code, a confluence of changes helped to buttress game and fish laws. State game and fish commissions had reformed approaches to enforcement, for example, making game wardens a salaried position. Tourism by wealthy northern sportsmen and their southern compatriots brought attention to the vulnerability of game and fish resources of the South and catalyzed a new approach to game management. Wealthy hunters began to amass land by purchase and lease for hunting preserves, transforming how all hunters accessed land and prey. Biological study of wildlife and its habitats created advocates, besides sportsmen, to champion conservation law in the South. Importantly for Mississippi, white women's education and access to the vote brought women squarely into the field of conservation. Finally, federal interest in and management of conservation, activities that proliferated during the New Deal, transformed what southern game commissions could accomplish. By the 1930s, then, hunting and fishing and the laws regulating these practices prefaced the Ellis dove hunts of the 1980s.

The chapters unfold chronologically and thematically on five factors that shaped hunting and fishing in the South: the transformation of postbellum property law; the marriage of the national conservation and southern Progressive movements, built as they were on exclusive visions of the natural world; the rise of the transregional identity of "the sportsman"; the impact of land consolidation; and the muscle of federal law.

Chapter 1 surveys the broad changes in land use, labor, and law in the eighteenth and nineteenth centuries that underpinned the rise of conservation as an aspect of state police power in the early twentieth century. It revisits the end of Reconstruction and the resulting profound shifts in southern life by viewing those changes through hunting practice. The post-Reconstruction years saw the constriction of Black mobility and freedom and the emergence of a new agricultural regime that led to the shrinking of the southern commons. Game and fish regulation lay at the heart of changing property laws after the Civil War. Eroding access to the open range and emergent notions of private property and public protection paved the way for a modern game and fish commission in Deep South states by the early twentieth century.

Chapter 2 introduces John H. Wallace Jr. and the creation of Alabama's fish and game commission. Wallace was a political upstart from north Alabama, an aspiring writer, a staunch racist, and a committed conservationist who began to push for enforcement of game and fish laws in the 1890s. He drew upon decades of work by game and bird protection advocates in northern, midwestern, and western states to form Alabama's game and fish policy and, with the help of sportsmen and conservation advocates in the state and across the region, was successful in his cause by 1907. His example excited like-minded men in Georgia and Mississippi, the former founding its own state commission in 1911. Mississippi was not as successful; it would take another two decades before allies of conservation found their purpose there. This chapter traces the genealogy of statewide game and fish laws in the Deep South while contextualizing the movement in other parts of the South and beyond that provided important influence on Wallace. It considers how, by forming game and fish protection policy, Wallace and other lawmakers instantiated new notions of class and race by circumscribing access to game and fish for all except elite hunters and commercial fishers. Mandating new relationships to game and nongame animals and fish, Wallace and fellow policymakers illustrate how the "natural" world mirrored the Progressive Era social strictures of Jim Crow and the aftermath of the failed agrarian revolt.

The third chapter draws from the life of Charlie Young, an African American hunter and dog trainer who spent his life working for wealthy northern sportsmen in the winter hunting colony of the Red Hills region and authored his own autobiography of that story. Taking cues from Young, the chapter charts transformations in hunting practice wrought by sportsmen, and the consolidation of land in a small corner of the Deep South in South Georgia and North Florida. The enclosure of the Red Hills region presaged the trend across the Deep South of posting land and enforcing trespass and game and fish laws. Northern sportsmen of the Red Hills who sought to study and preserve quail vitality also embody the evolution of wildlife science that shaped what was to come in southern hunting law.

Chapter 4 moves to the 1930s, when federal policy grew robust in its support for wildlife and the preservation of public space in the South. Game and fish commissions, especially in enforcement, had matured, too. The warden system modernized, for example, with an application process and salary more akin to a civil servant's position. The southern populace, in a generation, applauded, accepted, or came to terms with the vision of natural resources as existing primarily for sport that was not-so-subtly mandated by game and fish laws. And while sportsmanship was a defining code of a certain type of masculinity in the early twentieth century, women became more visible as advocates of and actors in the pastime. No better example exists than Fannye A. Cook, a white woman and scientist from Mississippi who dedicated her life to the protection of wildlife. Cook's lobbying, fundraising, and education initiatives resulted in the first comprehensive state game and fish commission in Mississippi. She worked at a time in which federal protection of wildlife and conservation policy was strengthening and used federal funds during the New Deal to bolster her efforts to survey state fauna and continue educational outreach to the public. Cook looked to benefit from the insistence on individual property rights among farmers to further game protection—she chartered private game reserves and sanctuaries across the state, once again drawing from federal funds. Cook's story bends the arc of the book toward hunting in the modern South, and I conclude by casting forward in time to consider the legacies of legal transformation herein.

Conservation policy in the South, as elsewhere, expanded beyond regulation of hunting and fishing, but this study trains its focus on those activities, especially on hunting.[14] Perhaps because hunting centers on socially sanctioned violence and use of deadly weapons, or perhaps because of its centrality to premodern life, the debates that surround hunting laws and practices are emotionally charged. I chose to give it primacy because it offers such rich and underexplored terrain. The conservation regimes that emerged by the mid-twentieth century in the South are equally worthy of study. Much yet remains to be understood and written, and the sources used here (many that are digitized and freely accessible) are full of details awaiting illumination. I hope that hunters and fishers, policymakers, academics, and anyone with interest in these themes will extend the story.

1 Game and Fish Laws and the Closing of the Commons

So common across the nineteenth-century South, hunting and fishing tend to linger in the background of regional rural and agrarian histories. Yet laws regarding the capture and killing of prey for sustenance and sport saw profound change over the nineteenth century and connect to broader shifts in the political economy of the South. For many Black, white, and Native people in the South, hunting was essential to subsistence and required access—to guns or other technology (traps, nets), to prey, to time, and to the lands and waters beyond hearth and home. Land use, labor, and property rights thus underpin our understanding of how Deep South legislators, judges, and citizenry evolved a conservation code by the early twentieth century. That code could not have developed without a transformation of property rights in the late nineteenth century, when white elites who framed the law attempted to control access to the tools of survival, with some success, yet never without resistance. Laws that sought to control hunting and fishing began in the colonial era, continued into early statehood, and were transformed after the Civil War.

This story of hunting in the Deep South, then, opens with the forcible dispossession of Indigenous nations, many of whom had come to rely on commercial hunting for access to European markets and goods, and their replacement by settlers who would, in time, find themselves wrestling with social elites and government agents over access to and use of those lands.

The customary land regime's embrace of a traditional notion of the "commons," to which all had customary (if not unlimited) access, proved a field of struggle in the "frontier" states of Alabama, Georgia, and Mississippi. Black southerners, in particular, were targeted by laws and white extralegal violence to ever restrict their use of the open range and access to guns. By the end of the century, an emergent property regime moved toward enclosure in the plantation South and would in time encompass the non-plantation South as well. Alongside such structural and legal change, a budding conservation ethos appeared among some southerners, with disputes over hunting rights a central theme. This chapter surveys the broad changes that led to the rise of conservation as an aspect of state power in the early twentieth century.

In 1818, Thomas C. Hunter wrote from Tuskaloosa Falls to inquire of Alabama territorial governor William Bibb whether "the regulation with the respect to *Creek* Indians, whether friendly or hostile repairing to their own nation ought to be strictly enforced." Hunter was concerned because a "white man named Smith" had married a Creek woman and was living in newly formed Tuscaloosa County, where he had "in employ about 30 or 40 Indians for the purpose of hunting." The presence of Creek men and women alarmed Hunter not only because of racial boundary encroachment but also because of their alignment in the Creek War of 1813–14: "Those Indians have during the last war been unfriendly to the United States, but now profess peace—however they are suspected generally of giving aid and assistance not only to hostile and bad Indians but to rascals of every description."[1] Characterizing these Creek hunters as "hostile" Native men who had recently enacted violence on white settlers, Hunter suggested that armed Creek hunters posed a threat to recently arrived migrants. The hunters, of course, were operating within familiar territory, since the Black Warrior River watershed was an often-contested borderland among Choctaw, Chickasaw, and Creek Nations, who each saw these as traditional hunting grounds. Land between the Alabama and Tombigbee Rivers and north of the Tennessee River, too, featured multiple competing claims as hunting territory.[2]

Given their numbers, the hunters that so worried Hunter likely represented the last tatters of a commercial deerskin trade that had drawn the Deep South into the Atlantic world, a trade that served as the dominant economic activity for Native people of the Southeast across the seventeenth and into the eighteenth centuries. Commercial hunting of deer, bears, and enslaved Indians "lock[ed] the southeastern Indians into the global economy" as they flooded coastal markets of Charleston, Mobile, and New Orleans.[3] These commodities were traded for guns, powder, and shot and would become new fashions in breeches and hats, or forced labor in the Caribbean basin. The lucrative trade also provided diplomatic leverage for Native people situated amid imperial competitions among England, France, and Spain. Historian

Kathryn Braund estimates that by the mid-eighteenth century, individual Creek hunters, who dominated the southeastern trade, produced 100 pounds of deerskins annually, or "about 50 deer per man."[4] The high harvest rates demanded by the trade took a toll on deer populations, as did encroachment of white settlers into Native territory, as stock raising and field clearing eliminated deer habitat and sustenance.[5] Thomas Hunter's anxious complaint proved a forecast of the "logic of elimination" that settler-colonial regimes would soon employ.[6]

From the earliest colonial land negotiations with Indigenous nations, hunting grounds were clearly delineated in treaties, land cessions, and maps. Even as the federal government pushed Native peoples into its "civilization" project, in which Native communities were pressured to forgo the deerskin trade and build new livelihoods on agriculture, men, especially, fought to protect hunting lands, since agriculture was women's domain. Ethnohistorian Robbie Ethridge argues that "hunting . . . legitimated far-flung land claims" and that continued insistence on access to grounds, in this case for Creek hunters, "rested on . . . political implications about . . . land rights, national sovereignty, and access to commercial goods."[7] Indigenous understanding of land-use rights would shape resistance to white encroachment and federal attempts of curtailment. Hunting territory, for example, was central to Cherokee and Chickasaw competition for land in the Tennessee River Valley, struggles that featured in the negotiations of both nations with the federal government in the first decade of the nineteenth century. In the context of long-standing competition for control of hunting land, Chickasaw and Cherokee leaders mobilized Indigenous notions of sovereignty to claim territorial rights.

Commercial hunting, although enjoyed and exploited by colonial traders and governors, came to be disparaged by advocates of the United States' "civilization" policy and, later, by those who embraced removal. Beginning in the 1790s, the government employed a policy "of civilizing native people in place."[8] The "factory system," as imagined by Henry Knox, aimed to transform Cherokee, Creek, Choctaw, and Chickasaw men from hunters into yeoman farmers and Native women into spinners and weavers. This required, in the minds of advocates, reduced dependency on both subsistence and commercial hunting, as well as surrender of vast territorial claims. Hunting, in the rhetoric of federal Indian agents, fostered vice and idleness, while farming a typical fifty- or sixty-acre family plot would teach Indians discipline and attachment to the market. An agent to the Cherokee, William S. Lovely (presaging planter justifications of enclosure in the later part of the century), told Cherokee leaders in 1804 that too-expansive hunting ranges would prove to be "the

Seat of Idleness and horse Stealing." In Lovely's estimation, they allowed for "lazy" Cherokee to "hide themselves from cultivating their farms."[9] Benjamin Hawkins, the agent to the Creek Nation (present-day Muscogee [Creek] Nation), took up the "arduous work of protecting and civilizing the Indians" and, according to an encomium published after his death, "succeeded in advancing some of these people from the state of hunters to those of herdsmen, cultivators of the soil, and manufacturers."[10] Though the commercial trade in skins had caused Native people to intensify hunting activities and provided a boost to colonial and federal treasuries, federal agents now sought to quell activities that they characterized as an aspect of "savagery." Yet proponents for removal in the 1820s and 1830s would claim that Native nations in the Southeast remained culturally reliant on hunting (suggesting that Indians lacked the temperament for disciplined enterprise and that the "civilizing" process had failed); because land cessions had reduced hunting grounds and access to sustenance, so the argument went, it was their own cultural failings that required Native people to move westward. To one such report, editors of the *Cherokee Phoenix* curtly replied, "Whoever really believes that the Cherokees subsist on game is most wretchedly deceived and is grossly ignorant of existing facts. The Cherokees do not live upon the chase, but upon the fruits of the earth produced by their labour."[11] They rightly called out the misguided rhetoric of critics. The Cherokee were quick to refute the connection between Native people and "primitivism" ascribed by the advocates of removal. Indeed, many Cherokee, along with elites from other Native groups in the Southeast, had moved to agriculture, with some adopting chattel slavery; others had built expansive holdings in land and livestock.[12]

Forcible land cessions in the early nineteenth century would bring an end to the deerskin trade. The Treaty of Fort Jackson in 1814, which concluded the civil war between Creek peoples who aligned with the United States (the White Sticks) and those who fought for independence against white encroachment (the Red Sticks), spelled the end of large-scale commercial hunting. The terms of the treaty, dictated by Andrew Jackson, required that "all traders would operate strictly under American supervision," which would impose a severe circumscription to the trade.[13] The group of Creek hunters in Tuscaloosa County who so disturbed Thomas C. Hunter were by 1818 seen as trespassers on the landscape. The next year, 1819, brought statehood for Alabama (Mississippi's had come two years before) and new pressure on Native nations from white settlers who hastened to enter the newly created states of the lower South that had expropriated millions of acres of land that became, in Alabama and Mississippi, public land.

By the 1820s, the policy of "civilization" dissolved in the face of demands for removal from land-hungry whites in Georgia, Alabama, and Mississippi. Historian Claudio Saunt argues that, "with the exception of bayonets and rifles, the United States' most effective weapon in compelling people to move west was state law."[14] In the early 1830s, each of these states passed laws to extend, however illegitimately, jurisdiction over Native lands, sovereignty, and bodies— in Alabama's case, through control of the hunt. Tuscaloosa, Alabama's capital from 1826 to 1846, proved central to local efforts in the dispossession of Creek, Cherokee, Chickasaw, and Choctaw peoples in the 1830s. The Alabama state government pushed to take control of Indigenous lands, first by passing so-called extension laws in the late 1820s and early 1830s that claimed sovereignty over Creek and Cherokee allotted lands and forbade Creeks to hunt or fish in the state. Governor C. C. Clay characterized Creek resisters of extension laws as "deluded Savages" in correspondence with the US secretary of war.[15] For Clay and other Alabama whites, forced removal was "necessary to the permanent tranquility of the white population"—and for lands desired by aspiring white planters, who quickly began to establish an agricultural empire fueled by cotton and enslaved workers. The Indigenous "hunting ground" became the settler "commons," as white migrants imported customary and adapted forms of land use along with their families, possessions, and enslaved labor force.

Transformation came rapidly. A southern observer, writing in 1835, remarked on the vast changes of the previous two decades: "In 1816, nearly all Alabama, Mississippi, and Arkansas, and many of the most fertile districts in Georgia, Louisiana, and Tennessee, were a wilderness, the hunting grounds of savages." He concluded, however, that "such has been the prosperity of the country, that Indians have nearly all dispersed out of these regions, the terrors of emigration into the wilderness have vanished, settlements and civilization have extended over the country—canals, railroads and other useful improvements are rapidly progressing and banks and factors are ready to grant facilities to planters to extend their estates."[16] Such was the constitution of the writer's antebellum mind—wilderness and its "primitive" peoples were rightfully supplanted by robustly financed, labor- and land-intensive agriculture. The observation was correct to a point; state political leaders of the lower South, backed by the federal government, pursued Native dispossession to foster a "civilizing" wave of migration and monoculture. After the expulsion of the Choctaw and Chickasaw, about half of Mississippi's lands lay newly open to white settlers. Creek dispossession in Alabama added some 20 percent to what would become the state's total lands, while Georgia would add 12 percent from removal of the Cherokee.[17] Across the decade of the 1830s, cotton production soared in Georgia, Alabama, and Mississippi, nearly doubling as what were once Indian hunting grounds and cornfields went into monocropping. The newly opened lands impelled the wheels of the domestic slave trade, and the numbers of enslaved workers in the lower South grew exponentially. In Alabama, enslavers doubled the population of their captive labor over the course of the 1830s, importing 96,000 people. In Mississippi, the enslaved population increased "almost 200 percent" after white planters drove 100,000 enslaved persons into the state in the 1830s.[18] The federal government used monies from Native land sales to underpin the bank loans to these hungry settlers.[19] The spread of the planters' agricultural regime, driven by enslaved labor and destructive land-use practices, threatened the eco-diversity of former hunting grounds and imposed a new monocropping logic onto the most fertile parts of the southern terrain.

In the rush to move westward to cultivate new land, planters forced enslaved workers to clear fields, drain swamps, and plant arable property in cotton. Unlike counterparts in the Northeast and Midwest, planters did not fence in hogs and cattle. Rather, they allowed stock to forage in open terrain in order to maximize the labor and land use in cash crop production. As historian David Silkenat points out, "Slavery helped perpetuate open-range husbandry when the broader Western world had turned against it."[20] The plantation geography of cotton fields surrounded by open terrain extended the practice of keeping land in common in the fecund territories of the Georgia Piedmont, Alabama Black Belt, and Mississippi Delta.

The open range, however, extended beyond plantation districts. Grazing stock on unfenced lands was an adaptive practice that emerged in the earliest days of colonial settlement in the Chesapeake and farther south. Settlers found that, with relatively low initial costs in swine or cows, they could grow their herds on the forage in forests, canebrakes, and swamps that surrounded coastal settlements. By the late seventeenth century, laws in Maryland, Virginia, and South Carolina supported the practice by requiring landholders to fence in crops to keep out the destructive trampling, munching, and rooting of stock.[21] Open-range herding was adopted by Native groups, such as the Creek, as early as the 1750s and served as a viable economic alternative to the deerskin trade that dwindled by the late eighteenth century.[22] Just as the open range was closing in the northern regions of the United States, the southern open range spread westward with settler migration and was used by planters as well as yeomen, who continued to rely on herding as a livelihood with low investment costs and sustainable yields.[23] Though the 1850s and

1860s saw a dramatic decline in Deep South cattle and hog herds, thanks to the spread of cotton cultivation and the devastation of the Civil War, open-range herding persisted in the piney woods and hill and mountain regions into the late nineteenth century.[24]

The affordances of the open range shaped settler hunting practice in the South. State governments, by law and custom, allowed for hunting on "unimproved land," a nod to earlier colonial laws that rejected aristocratic protection of English hunting laws.[25] In 1808, for example, the Chatham County Superior Court in Georgia reaffirmed the right of access to and take of game in the forest. George Campbell had been indicted for "malicious shooting" and was tried under a Georgia law that drew from the 1722 "Black Act" of England. That act attempted to stop poachers (who sometimes blackened their faces with charcoal) in the forests of England by mandating that any form of armed disguise in the royal forests was punishable by death.[26] The State of Georgia argued that the Black Act, a form of which had been adopted by the colonial Georgia government, was sufficient precedent for the conviction of Campbell, who had been caught armed on another's property. The judge, Thomas Charlton, sided with the defense lawyers, who held that the English law had feeble purview in colonial and statutory contexts. Charlton concluded that the Black Act "was founded upon a tender solicitude for the amusement and property of the aristocracy in England. It was made to protect from the violation or profanation of the people, the forest of his majesty or the park of the peer. How then could it apply to a country which was but one extended forest, in which the liberty of killing a deer, or cutting down a tree, was as unrestrained as the natural rights of the deer to rove, or the tree to grow: and where was the aristocracy whose privileges were to be secured?"[27] Because there was no aristocratic interest to protect, reasoned the judge, usufruct extended to white southerners of any means.

Observers of hunting in the Deep South in the first half of the nineteenth century often noted white hunters' access to the open range. Philip Henry Gosse, an English naturalist, worked in the 1830s as a schoolteacher in Dallas County, Alabama, near the former state capital of Cahaba. Deer hunting on horseback was, according to him, preferred by some planters "in open ground, and even through the forest." He described "the excited planters [who] at such times dash boldly between the myriad trunks at full speed, and even plunge through the closer and more dangerous second growth, at the risk of limb and life" in pursuit of deer.[28] Gosse noted hunting of all types of prey as practiced by the eastern transplants in central Alabama—turkeys, feral hogs, squirrels, and deer. In his letters, he never noted obstacles like a fenced or posted land or of obtaining owner permission to hunt. Though landowners sometimes took out notices in papers that forbade hunting on specific acreage, in general, white antebellum hunters' only hindrance to the chase lay in the terrain itself.

The southern hunting range provided the backdrop for the creation and realization of a southern social order. Historian Nicolas W. Proctor sees the antebellum hunt as a "stage for the performance of the evocative drama of white manhood."[29] Hunting came to reflect an important ethos of the southern elite man: the woods and field set the stage for testing and proving prowess or hunting skill; self-control in the excitement of the hunt exemplified the feat of mind over physicality; and mastery, what Proctor calls a "multifaceted concept," "represented control over other people, animals, nature, and even death."[30] These "distinctively southern" qualities of hunting were reserved only to white men, who engaged in hunting as a way to reaffirm caste privilege and dominion over women and slaves. Elite men claimed these virtues in competition with one another. Harry W. from Mississippi, writing to the *Spirit of the Times*, an important early sporting magazine, began his deer hunting tale with an origin story: "In the first place let me premise that I was, as they say in the West, *raised* in South Carolina, and like every planter's son in that State, early learned to ride and shoot."[31] Harry suggested that his Carolina riding and shooting style became a test of prowess among hunters in Mississippi: the story turns on Harry trying a young, untested colt, Dare Devil. When at first he falters, his hunting partners taunt him: "Now Harry, you can shew us how you ride in South Carolina." Yet in the end, Harry and his horse best the team of hunters in pursuit of a legendary "Big Buck." He celebrated the "great rivalry" present in every "true sportsman." Hunting narratives enlivened the close connection between the practice and meaning of hunting and the intertwined values of manliness, competition, mastery, and power. Elite men found ways to separate their hunting practice from lower-class men through leisure time and accoutrements and, later, fealty to the ideal of the "sportsman."[32]

Some of what we know about antebellum hunting comes from commentaries offered by these men in their letters and diaries and, especially, their contributions (like Harry W.'s) to sporting periodicals, newspapers, and published books. Lower-class white hunters are also present in their accounts but often as caricatures—backcountry heroes, for example, or greedy market hunters. By the late eighteenth century, some writers and observers of the US South began to romanticize the frontiersmen of westward expansion, men like Daniel Boone who were the embodiment of the rugged woodsman and hunter. Kentucky settler John Filson, for example, published a biography of

Boone in 1786 to entice adventurous settlers to the frontier.[33] White men of fewer means often relied on hunting, trapping, and fishing to supplement family sustenance. They sold wild game at the market, even building livelihoods in the pursuit of game. Men who continued to hunt as a commercial activity, however, raised the ire of elite hunters, who railed against the wasteful excess of market hunting in antebellum sporting magazines and later in postbellum hunting and fishing periodicals.[34] The "pothunter," a term used to describe those who hunted for sustenance and for the market, represented an opposite to the "sportsman" and served as a foil to the rising interregional fraternity of elite hunters.

However stereotyped, lower-class men did rely on access to unenclosed land.[35] William Elliott, a South Carolina planter and famous author of sporting stories, complained in the mid-nineteenth century that "the right to hunt wild animals is held by the great body of people, whether landholders or otherwise, as one of their franchises, which they will indulge in at discretion; and to all limitations on which, they submit with the worst possible grace!"[36] That "franchise" depended on access to common land, and "the right to hunt on uninclosed lands, thus secured by usage, or in other words, by *our* common law," was to blame, according to Elliott—and so, especially, were politicians who refused to work against the will of "popularity" to protect rights of landowners.[37]

Mid-nineteenth-century laws regulating hunting and fishing reflect the complications that arose from the open range, particularly the tension in property identification and ownership created by common use. In 1856, several Alabama counties together passed a law that forbade hunting of wild hogs unless the hunter received the express permission of "three freeholders in the neighborhood." The Alabama legislature passed a statewide version of the code in 1868 and amended the law in 1871 to expressly identify "unmarked" wild hogs as those protected by the act.[38] A Macon County contretemps that unfolded in 1851 sheds light on motivation behind the law. A planter named James B. Hooten was accused by J. R. Lawson of using "two negroes continually in the woods looking out for flocks of unmarked hogs, and several others with their dogs following, catching and killing indiscriminately all unmarked hogs to make pork of."[39] Lawson had printed public notices to "all persons having fat or unmarked hogs in the woods." Hooten defended his honor by calling a meeting of his neighbors who swore testimony to his innocence and honesty, though one meekly offered that Hooten "stated that he thought all the old settlers should be entitled to all the unmarked hogs, and suggested we should all go and hunt them, but we never went." In the custom of free range, hogs were seldom fenced or were fenced with "slip gaps" so that they could leave pens and forage in the woods and swamps. Though some planters marked their hogs, others did not, and telling a "wild" hog from a feral one that belonged to a neighbor was more a matter of interest than judgment. The law against killing "wild" hogs unless notice was given was an attempt, then, to limit confusion of the open range. The law continued to be relevant into the twentieth century, when other trespass and game laws came into being, because, as explored below, the closing of the range was not an immediate or all-encompassing phenomenon.

If white men had access to unenclosed land, the same did not apply to Black hunters. Southern states criminalized the unsupervised use of guns by enslaved people, unless specifically deployed and under the command of white men. In Georgia, prohibition on gun use was included in the so-called slave code, which carried from colonial to state policy. The code made it illegal "for any slave to carry and make use of fire arms, or any offensive weapon whatsoever, unless there be some [white] person of the age of sixteen years or upwards in the company of such slave when he is hunting or shooting, or unless such slave be found in the day time, actually keeping off birds or killing beasts within the plantation to which such slave belongs, lodging the same gun at night within the dwelling house of his master, mistress or white overseer."[40]

Alabama and Mississippi state law, which drew from an earlier code passed in the Mississippi Territory, extended criminalization to weapons "offensive or defensive" used without consent from the enslaver.[41] In all three states, arms could be seized by anyone, and in Alabama and Mississippi, conviction of the crime brought thirty-nine lashes. In those states, neither enslaved men nor women could keep dogs.[42] In Mississippi, free Black men and women could not keep guns or ammunition unless they received a license from the county court, which could be repealed at any time.[43] On the eve of the Civil War, laws remained essentially the same, with the exception in Georgia that an enslaved person could hunt with a license, renewed each week, from "his" enslaver (the law imagined enslaved hunters as male, though, as we'll see below, women hunted and fished).[44] And laws criminalizing ownership and sometimes the use of arms by enslaved people were echoed in other southern states.[45] The code was not apt to change, given white fear about armed resistance of the enslaved, made manifest by uprisings led by Denmark Vesey in 1822 and Nat Turner in 1831.

Despite having such laws on the books, however, historian Scott Giltner argues that enslavers, not legislatures, were the final arbiters of access to guns by enslaved people.[46] Whites sometimes relied on enslaved men to act as guides or huntsmen in the field, to shoot animals considered pests (raccoons, squirrels, and bears, for example), and to supplement rations on the plantation. The latter was especially important as the quantity and quality of food provided varied widely between plantations and farms. Allowing some leeway for the enslaved population to trap, hunt, and fish saved money for planters and granted privileges that kept "good order and docile labor" in place.[47]

Whatever practical considerations might have been at play for enslavers, hunting and fishing proved essential to the well-being of enslaved families and communities. Historians such as Giltner, Mart A. Stewart, David Silkenat, and Ras Michael Brown have drawn from accounts of formerly enslaved people, plantation records, and archaeological evidence to argue for the multiple ways that hunting and fishing served bodily and psychic needs of slaves.[48] Catching fish and game with a gun, traps, nets, and snares provided a modest economy for some individuals who sold or traded at markets or within their own plantation community.[49] Activities that took enslaved people away from the farm or plantation allowed for exchange of information with others met in the woods or by the stream; as Giltner argues, hunting and fishing provided a distance, physically and mentally, from the direct orbit of the enslaver.[50]

Interviews with formerly enslaved men and women by those working for the Federal Writers' Project add texture to the hunting and fishing within enslaved communities. Georgia Baker, who was enslaved near Crawfordville, Georgia, by Alexander H. Stephens, the Confederacy's vice president, remembered that "George and Mack" were the hunters who "brought back jus' evvything: possums, rabbits, coons, squirrels, birds, and wild turkeys." She clarified that by "birds," she meant partridges (or quail, she acknowledged, as they were commonly called by the 1930s).[51] Hunters and fishers could sometimes find time and energy after long days toiling in the field to leave plantation grounds but also used weekends, when enslavers might grant customary time off. Jim Allen, enslaved near Columbus, Mississippi, told an interviewer that "some went to chu'ch an' some went fishin' on Sunday."[52] According to John Cameron, enslaved near present-day Jackson, "They got off from de fiel's early on Satu'd'y evenin's, washed up an' done what dey wanted to. Some went huntin' and fishin', some fiddled an' danced an' sung, while de others jus' lazed round de' cabins."[53] Women fished as well and helped prepare game and fish captured in the field for meals. Rachel Adams remembered that when possums were caught and carried home on her Putnam County, Georgia, plantation, her mother "would scald 'em and rub 'em in hot ashes" to clean them in preparation for cooking.[54] Archaeological evidence from the cooking quarters of enslaved workers suggests that wild game was a regular part of the diet of enslaved men, women, and children.[55]

Black men and women drew material and spiritual sustenance from the practice of catching wild game and fish. Although spatial mobility and access to guns varied widely from one enslaver to the next, enslaved men could and did enjoy gendered approval derived from hunting prowess. A formerly enslaved man recounted to W. Irwin MacIntyre, who collected stories of nineteenth-century Thomasville, Georgia, that one of the most respected enslaved men in his "quarter" could "sker up a drove of partridges, and ketch two 'fore they lit."[56] That the man hand-caught the birds serves as a reminder that laws barring slaves from owning and using firearms required that they sometimes used other means to ensnare prey. In a world where family units were ever vulnerable to separation, hunting proved a conduit for fathers to pass down skills and share time with sons. And hunting and fishing provided connections to African forebears. Historian Ras Michael Brown argues that methods of hunting with traps in the Lowcountry of South Carolina and Georgia represent connections to African hunting practices. The use of a particular bird trap, for example, was derived from a similar Kongo device, the *kulula*.[57] Brown's research also reveals that Lowcountry enslaved communities continued to use Kongo, Mande, and Atlantic language words for certain birds and game.[58] Enslaved people imbued their time in woods and near water, in pursuit of and in proximity to wild animals, with lessons of spiritual import. Hunters in the Lowcountry looked to the assistance of ancestors and spirits for a successful hunt, for example, and curated certain animal parts of their kill, known as "stones," for the spiritual powers they held.[59] Hunting practices in the South, which employed guns, dogs, traps, and bait, derived from multiple cultural influences but hint at cultural continuity for some enslaved people of African descent.

Once granted, enslaved men and women cherished the privileges of hunting and fishing as natural, if not legal, rights. And even when forbidden by enslavers, men hunted surreptitiously, refusing to give up a chance to supplement food, sell and barter, and find physical distance from sites of forced labor.[60] Giltner frames this as a form of resistance or a subversive act "that stretched the bounds of what slaves could and could not do." The "antiauthoritarian element" of hunting and fishing, which remained among hunters and fishers of the "lower-orders" in the South, surfaces in interviews of formerly enslaved people who told stories of hunting despite the master's prohibitions and who used hunting as excuse for other illicit activities (for example, to plan dances) or as a pretext for running away.[61] Though excluded from any formal rights enjoyed by white southerners who accessed the commons, enslaved hunters nonetheless claimed space in southern woods and waters. Certainly, enslaved hunters and fishers were always at risk from laws that restricted mobility and use of guns, patrollers, the changing whims of enslavers, and the ire of whites beyond the plantation. Because the enslaved were severely circumscribed in their mobility and access to firearms, the capacity to hunt in the full array of cultural expressions and to draw from the tropes of manhood that hunting offered whites would remain strictly limited. Even in freedom, after a bloody war that transformed the southern landscape, Black men and women wrestled with enduring efforts to control their movement and access to hunting grounds in the form of extralegal violence and then of game and fish laws.

The Civil War dramatically recast land use and agricultural production and in turn social relations among Black and white southerners. After the legal destruction of slavery, land became even more valuable, posted, and protected. Before the war, wealth in the South was not held in real property but in enslaved people, whom southern law categorized as a form of property. Emancipation destroyed the concentration of wealth in humans, shifting the focus of southerners to the value, real and potential, in land.[62] Planters looked to the formerly enslaved laboring class to continue to supply agricultural labor; formerly enslaved men and women looked to define laboring modes in alignment with their newly gained freedom, which included control over their own mobility and labor and some form of compensation. What resulted, the land tenure system, grew after the war with contracts between landowner and worker, the planter providing the land and often tools and implements and seed. Over time, the system trapped most non-landholding farmers, Black and white, in debt and poverty, and late nineteenth-century southern legislatures fortified landowner control over agricultural workers with new laws that forbade enticement (or landowners attracting workers to other farms with promises of better conditions) and penalized perceived vagrancy. Landowners also became more protective of the land itself in what historian Susan Eva O'Donovan has called "cotton's newer ground" and began pushing for laws that curtailed trespass and required the fencing of stock.[63] The shift in labor relations and new forms of property laws, combined with an emerging commitment to conservation by the end of the nineteenth century, laid the groundwork for game and fish laws in the early twentieth-century South.

The war left burned fences and crops, abandoned homes and fields, and livestock pillaged for rations. Demand for fortification matériel and fuel destroyed an estimated 4 million acres of southern forests, though the rapidity of new growth could quickly cover visible scars.[64] More lasting was the destruction of livestock populations and the labor shortage, which resulted in a shrinkage of improved land. But historian Erin Stewart Mauldin argues that "southerners' antebellum system had forged the preconditions" for environmental devastation in the war's aftermath.[65] The agricultural practices made possible by enslaved labor—cutting, clearing, planting, harvesting, and plot cycling—had eroded soils, a reality made worse by involuntary neglect after the war. Southern forests grew back in pines, leaving needles on the ground that cast off fewer nutrients and more acidity than hardwood shed. Environmental change accompanied efforts by southerners to rebuild lives, or begin them anew, after the war's end.

In the years during and after the Civil War, white and Black southerners, as well as Union soldiers, took to hunting to supplement provisions. In the wake of emancipation, however, southern legislatures passed a nexus of laws that restricted Black men, women, and children, including laws that forbade gun and dog ownership and hunting on Sunday and new trespass laws that protected privately held lands from foraging for timber, berries, and flora. Black Codes passed by southern states in the immediate aftermath of the war limited or outlawed Black access to arms and ammunition.[66] Outside of these codes, which Congressional Reconstruction dismantled, states passed general laws that began to curb the hunt. Georgia, for example, passed laws in 1866 that forbade hunting with firearms or dogs on Sunday; historian Charles L. Flynn Jr. points out that these laws applied only to counties that were predominantly Black. The state also limited foraging for timber or foodstuffs on private land, enclosed or not.[67] Efforts like this by Georgia to control land and labor prefigured what would come in game and fish and trespass laws in the later decades of the nineteenth century.

Whites employed extralegal violence to control newly freed Black southerners. Gun ownership featured in the terror unleashed by the Ku Klux Klan and other authors of racially motivated violence during Reconstruction. The report of the Joint Committee to Inquire into the Conditions of Affairs in the Late Insurrectionary States, a congressional committee that collected testimony from victims and witnesses of racial violence, reveals how common hunting practices both informed terroristic activity and made targets of Black men. Hezekiah Bush, in northern Alabama, gave testimony that a group of masked men with "white hoods over their heads and dark gowns over the other parts of their persons" demanded Bush surrender the shotgun he used for squirrel hunting and fire any rounds left in it; when the gun wouldn't discharge, one of the men used it to club Bush in the head. The men then took turns whipping him and, when finished, asked Bush "if I ever would go hunting after squirrels again. I said no. They left me, carrying off my gun."[68] William Coleman gave witness to multiple accounts of violence against Black landowners in Winston County, Mississippi, from where he had fled after being beaten by men dressed in horns and masks. One assault he recounted was predicated on controlling a Black man's access to the hunt—Robin Coleman (the relation to William is unclear) was met in the woods by white men while hunting at night and warned from doing so again. Hunting, a sanctioned form of quotidian violence, provided an easy metaphor for William Coleman to describe his own beating at the hands of the costumed Klan in Winston County. After dodging their bullets, he wrestled with the eight men until they pinned him down: "Some had me by the legs, some had me by the arms and neck and anywhere, just like dogs string out a coon."[69]

Indeed, the common practice of hunting and the widespread use of guns buttressed campaigns of terror led by white vigilantes and provided for defense by Black men in some cases. M. H. Whitaker, a witness before the congressional inquiry from Meridian, Mississippi, recounted a series of violent incidents between Black and white men. When asked, "Have the people in the country generally got guns?" he replied that both Black and white households commonly kept guns. When pressed for what purpose, Whitaker noted, "For hunting; common shot-guns, bird guns, that is all I have seen." He argued that most guns were employed for bird and squirrel hunting, though whites accused Black gun owners of killing livestock.[70] Violent raiders featured their own traditional, collective hunting practices and accoutrements in terroristic campaigns. One Alabama eyewitness described the "hideous" getup of Klan riders, adding that marauders signaled to each other using "common hunting whistles."[71] Another eyewitness noted that Klan costumes were made of "something like an old-fashioned hunting shirt, as they have them in this southern part."[72]

A. S. Lakin, a northern Methodist minister who came south after the war and who briefly served as the president of the University of Alabama, gave lengthy testimony to the congressional committee. In his work as a circuit preacher, he kept notes on assaults and murders in various Alabama counties. He himself was the target of intimidation in Tuscaloosa, when he was chased from the city, and of arson in Huntsville, his home base. The burning of his home, he told committee members, began with a shot fired through his window. After back-and-forth about the marksmanship of the shooter—committee members were inclined to think that the shot was fired in warning—Lakin gave them a lesson in common hunting practice: "It is a well known fact with all marksmen—perhaps you are not so well acquainted with hunting—that in shooting in the night, all men, unless they are experts, always shoot over. In shooting a deer at night, or a turkey . . . a marksman is pretty sure to shoot over . . . and allows for the darkness of night."[73] Hunting practice is threaded through the unstable years of Reconstruction; the commonness of gun ownership heightened propensity for bloodshed in a region rife with political and social turbulence.

The volatile politics of Reconstruction accompanied changing labor and land regimes. Black freedom reconfigured the intensive, centralized land cultivation methods of the antebellum years, replacing them with a decentralized pattern of family-run farms.[74] The land tenure system that undergirded the new agricultural regime was initially the result of negotiation among freed people and planters. Black men and women refused to return to forms of labor, like the gang system, that evoked the bodily memory of slavery. They pushed for farmwork with a modicum of independence, structured around the family. Planters, for their part, had no wages to pay workers and no access to credit to shore up agricultural expansion. In the years after the war, labor contracts attest to the variety of agreements between freedmen and planters, revealing the ways in which Black families shaped their lives within the bounds of a postwar agrarian society.

The tenant system that emerged over the course of the 1860s and 1870s, however, came to be a hallmark of the southern caste structure. As the last decades of the nineteenth century unfolded, tenancy dragged many southern freedmen and their descendants into cycles of debt and stasis. Though the system could be fluid for those with capital in stock, implements, and land, by the early twentieth century Black farmers made up a disproportionate number of farmers and laborers who did not own land—that is, share tenants (those who furnished stock or tools and rented land in return for a portion of the crop), sharecroppers (those with little or no physical capital who were legally considered "a wageworker paid with a share of the crop"), and wageworkers (often young men with no stock or land and who worked under direct supervision of the planter).[75] The farmers in these categories made less money, were more indebted to furnishing merchants and planters, and had less freedom from the landowners' control than those on a fixed rent and, of course, landowners. By 1900, only 11 percent of Black farmers in Alabama and Georgia and 14 percent in Mississippi owned their farms outright, compared with 54 percent, 51 percent, and 65 percent, respectively, of white farmers in the same states.[76] Black agricultural landownership hit its peak in 1920 and declined precipitously throughout the twentieth century, while the number of Black families farming on shares increased in the 1920s and 1930s until World War II and mechanization shifted the South's economy.[77] These broad demographic trends underpin the way that southern legislatures perceived and managed labor by the late nineteenth century, when attention turned to new forms of property law.

Though whites also farmed as tenants and as sharecroppers, the "labor question"—concerns almost solely focused on the quantity and quality of Black agricultural workers—became consuming for white landowners, who argued that Black men and women would not work without coercion and the threat of violence. One planter wrote to Georgia's *Banner of the South* in 1870 that "the freed Negro, instead of being the willing and steady laborer, has become a skulking loafer by day, and a prowling thief by night."[78] Such racialized characterizations became the muttered refrain of landed white southerners faced with a laboring population that they could no longer confidently control. Immediately after the Civil War, southern state legislatures turned to the law to reinforce control over freedmen's mobility and independent economy.

Historians debate the length to which change in postbellum property laws were motivated by attempts to control Black agricultural labor. New stock laws (requiring farmers to fence in stock as opposed to the older customary practice of fencing crops), trespass laws, and game and fish laws made up a new body of code that limited access to unenclosed lands in the last decades of the nineteenth century and into the twentieth. Steven Hahn argues that poor southerners, Black and white, "derived special benefits from common rights" and relied on customary use of unenclosed land for subsistence in the form of hunting, fishing, and foraging stock.[79] New laws curtailed these rights and worked as a form of economic and social control by planters over Black farmers and lower-class whites. Struggles over their passage reveal how Black and non-elite farmers were bound in changes to use rights they could not control.[80] Planters, in turn, could use the laws as a means to keep workers in the field. Shawn Everett Kantor and J. Morgan Kousser, however, employ economic data to refute that fence laws necessarily had a racial motive and were more about the cost of fencing livestock versus crop acreage.[81] J. Crawford King Jr. and Brian Sawers concluded that new property laws included multiple motivations but that control of Black labor and economy played an oversize role.[82] The same might be applied to game and fish laws in the postbellum Deep South. In experimentation with new laws, southern legislatures drew from decades of legal precedent that sought to limit the access of nonwhites to the bounty of the natural world. The patchwork of codes passed in Deep South states also reveals concern about certain species of game and fish that many thought were being depleted by the end of the nineteenth century. The budding conservation ethos in the South grew from this unequal struggle for access.

Game and fish laws correlated geographically with the other forms of evolving property law, particularly the movement for stock laws. Alabama offers a revealing example. J. Crawford King looked closely at the stock laws in Alabama and Mississippi, exploring how they were adopted at the county level—through legislative act, through appointment of a local commission, or through a local election option. In his analysis, counties (or parts of counties, known as "beats") that adopted a stock law had shared characteristics. These places, on average, were more densely populated, had more land in cotton cultivation and more farmers working as tenants or on shares, and had a high Black population. Counties that left an open range were less populated, had more landowning farmers, featured a population still dependent on livestock herding and the open range, and were predominantly white.[83] Though the statewide closing of the range took decades (until 1951, in Alabama), patterns of fence law adoption suggest it was a mechanism motivated by a consideration of economy that included cost and labor control.[84]

Alabama had but few statewide game laws on the books until after the Civil War: no hunting on Sunday, no killing wild hogs without notification of local landowners, no hunting by use of fire at night, and regulation of gun ownership by enslaved and free Blacks. The period following the war in Alabama, Mississippi, Georgia, and elsewhere in the South featured a spate of countywide laws regulating hunting and fishing. The laws were patchwork at best—some reflected local concerns about camp hunting, for example; some created seasons for deer and fowl; some required landowner permission before a hunt. But, taken together, they reflect a growing concern in the late nineteenth century with unchecked access to land and prey. In that way, the new laws represented a wider concern about continuing the customary commons and made up the strategies, along with fence laws and trespass laws, by which it was limited after the Civil War. King divided Alabama counties into those that had passed some form of fence law by 1880 and those that had not. The state was evenly divided; among its sixty-six counties, thirty-three passed laws that required stock to be fenced and thirty-three remained open range.[85] By the same time, 48 percent (sixteen out of thirty-three) of stock-law counties and 42 percent (fourteen out of thirty-three) of open-range counties had a game law on the books.[86] Given that stock-law counties were generally those with a predominantly Black population, game laws could certainly have impacted the Black population disproportionately in relation to whites. In 1879, for example, a game law was passed in nineteen counties of south and central Alabama and in counties heavily concentrated in the Black Belt. Of those nineteen counties, twelve (or 63 percent) had a Black majority.[87] The tally of open-range counties that adopted some form of game law by 1880 does not take into account the spate of repeals in the later nineteenth century. Of the seven open-range counties (that were predominately white) included in the 1879 law, four repealed the law in 1881 and one dismantled it in parts of the county in 1885.[88] Geography and environment played some role in the adoption and repeal of game laws, yet, as we'll see, labor control also motivated lawmakers. So, too, did the concern over the depletion of game and fish.

Holdovers of prewar laws regarding public access to unimproved lands, whether public or private, reflect the lingering shadows of prewar geography and demography. The plantation counties of the Deep South were under cultivation by large forces of enslaved labor and more populated generally, and they had more land in cultivation. As the volatile political terrain of Reconstruction hardened into the Jim Crow South, Black men and women continued to farm lands in these soil-rich counties. Many planters in these regions, and elsewhere in the South, had long hoped to see a reform in law regarding the open range—they would save thousands if they did not need to fence their crops. As one writer from Putnam County, Georgia, complained in 1873, "The protection of crops from marauding stock is becoming every year a matter of greater and greater importance."[89] He and others who owned larger acreages and had to fence in their crop to protect from foraging stock urged state legislators to change laws that protected the open range. They complained about the expense, especially with depleted timber resources, made so by years of use for fencing and by the devastation of the Civil War. Another farmer wrote of the unjust burden put on landowners, who he argued could not make use of what would otherwise be fine farming land (but without timber) and who paid an extra tax on their farm by having to fence in crops: "A stock law would not only be a just law, but we believe it would be beneficial to this country. There are many valuable places that will soon have to be abandoned, for the lack of rail timber. Some may say hedge, ditch, or build a wire fence. Perhaps the parties are not able to go to so great an expense. And if they are, why tax them to the bottom dollar to fence out their neighbor's stock."[90] Southern agricultural journals filled with similar rhetoric from landowners who saw the protection of the open range as a costly reality. It's no surprise that plantation counties, still dominated politically and socially by planters, voted for some form of stock law. There was plenty of economic motivation to fence in cattle and hogs.

Racial ideology also guided arguments for laws that curtailed access to unenclosed (and enclosed) lands. Planters blamed Black hunters for the need for new laws, or the enforcement of existing ones, that protected land and crops. "Can you not," one self-identified planter moaned to the *Southern Cultivator* in 1869, "urge the adoption of some remedy for the indiscriminate destruction of stock by thieves and vagrants?" He argued for the passage of a law that forbade hunting on private property, though acknowledged a similar bill had suffered defeat in his home state of Georgia. "What then is the duty of the planter?" he asked. To continue to advocate for such a law would stop "the unlimited privilege that vagrants and idlers enjoy, of hunting on enclosed and unenclosed lands," which he blamed for the destruction of stock. Enforcement of the law would benefit the state "by the convict labor" that would result. He argued that those who supported rights to hunt on others' property—"negroes, idlers about little towns, and those who ride into office on the votes of such a class"—would try and defeat such bills, but "let the planter do *his* duty."[91] The *Southern Cultivator* editors responded by reprinting a Georgia newspaper editorial with a more dire warning: "Hunting has become a mania among negroes, and in this way they have become an annoyance and a nuisance." Not only were Black hunters a threat to stock and crops, but "the privilege of hunting induces them to obtain fire-arms, which they might use *for other purposes besides hunting*, and even when hunting they are likely to kill domestic animals as well as ordinary game." The writer acknowledged that "we cannot deprive them by law of the privilege of hunting" (laws that limited hunting seemed a step too far even in the face of purported "mania") but suggested that states could enforce existing trespass laws to stop unwanted hunting. The authors hearkened back to the power of planters in the South, urging readers to remember that "the landowning power is almost omnipotent in any country, and if we sit still with folded arms and allow ourselves to be outraged it is our own fault."[92] The answer would be found in planters moving to post lands and to pressure states to impose trespass laws.

Trespass laws existed in the South before the Civil War to enforce the consequences of stock breaking fences and damaging crops (the law put the responsibility upon the fence builder to keep out wandering hogs and cattle). That version of trespass law continued in the later nineteenth century and lay at the center of debates about the stock law. But trespass laws came to encompass other forms of encroachment, including foraging timber and sometimes food on private property, nearing or entering a residence without permission, and being on government or school grounds without permission.[93] Legal historian Brian Sawers, in an analysis of trespass laws after the Civil War, notes the correlation between the new laws and labor control; six southern states (Louisiana, Georgia, South Carolina, Florida, Alabama, and North Carolina) passed new trespass laws in the immediate aftermath of war during Presidential Reconstruction.[94] After so-called Redemption, when white southern Democrats wrested control of state legislatures from Republicans, southern states began to tie trespass laws to hunting.[95] By 1873, for example, Georgia's code included a section on "Crimes and Offenses Relative to Property," which forbade "illegal hunting," defined as hunting within enclosed spaces where sheep were confined and without the consent of the landowner. In 1895, the law required landowners to post enclosed lands on the property and at the county courthouse.[96] In Mississippi's 1892 code, hunters were forbidden from hunting on the lands of another, enclosed or unenclosed, provided the landowner had hung three "posted" notices for every mile.[97] Certain states allowed individual counties to enact trespass laws, and Sawers found that majority-Black counties in Mississippi (1867), Tennessee (1870), Alabama (1889), and Virginia (1866) adopted some form of trespass law that forbade hunting at a greater rate than majority-white counties. Economic historian Shawn Kantor, in his research on the correlation between postbellum property law and labor control in Georgia, concludes that "the greater the black population, the more likely it is that a county would have implemented a law restricting hunting rights."[98]

Legislatures also took notice of what was becoming a popular summertime activity for southerners—camp hunting. Some Alabama counties passed laws against camp hunting, making it illegal. "A complainer" wrote to a Marion, Alabama, newspaper in support of outlawing camp hunting. Camp hunters, they argued, overkilled young deer and let hunting dogs destroy local livestock. Even worse, "they assume the authority of camping in our church houses and abusing their floors, seats and yards by greasing the floors, carving their meat on the seats, making fires in the yard, feeding &c."[99] By the 1890s, as noted above, some counties required landowner permission before hunting. This provision, in particular, would become central to Alabama's efforts in the early twentieth century to pass statewide game and fish laws.

Laws regulating hunting and fishing also reflected a new and growing consciousness about preservation and a concern for diminishing game. This, in part, was tied to the outbreak of pests, like the cotton caterpillar, and the possibility of birds as natural agents of destruction. Some farmers in the South came to hail the benefits of "insectivorous" birds for protecting crop fields against pests. In doing so, they reflected a growing interest in "economic ornithology," or the study of birds for their practical use to farms and orchards. By the 1850s, ornithologists were examining the contents of birds' stomachs and conducting field observations to determine what birds might be "useful" or harmful to farmers.[100] The promise that such examination would be of economic use led the American Ornithologists' Union, whose members were spearheading the study, to press for congressional support. The result was the creation of the Division of Economic Ornithology within the US Department of Agriculture's Division of Entomology.[101] The unit would become the Bureau of Biological Survey, which would prove critical to the passage of southern game and fish laws, as detailed in the next chapter. In 1873 newly elected South Carolina governor Franklin J. Moses Jr., a Republican leading an integrated legislature, called for legislators to pass a law that would help suppress the army worm: "The only mode of checking and subduing these pests is to respect the order of nature, and preserve the small birds to meet and conquer them. I earnestly recommend the passage of an act providing for the punishment, by moderate fine and imprisonment, of any person who shall wantonly kill or injure any insectivorous bird at any season of the year."[102]

The legislature took heed and authored code that protected "bats, whippoor-wills, fly-catchers, thrashers, warblers, finches, larks, orioles, nut-hatchers, wood-peckers, hummingbirds, blue-birds, and all other species and varieties of land birds, whether great or small, of every description, regarded as harmless in their habits, and whose flesh is unfit for food."[103]

More often, however, when southerners began to echo the cry for the preservation of "useful" birds, there was no consensus on which birds *were* "beneficial." Calls for preservation of insectivorous birds seldom delineated what birds were to be protected. In 1874, the Grange chapter of Mobile County in Alabama applauded a game law passed there in 1871 but requested additional measures to protect, and even import, "beneficial" birds, though without naming specific species. Generally, "beneficial" or "insectivorous" birds referred to small songbirds and never included owls, hawks, or any bird that preyed upon smaller birds; raptors, in fact, were often expressly singled out for destruction in game law. Sometimes, the designation of a "beneficial" bird and game bird overlapped; Alabama, for example, would pass a law to import and protect the ring-necked pheasant in 1893, a bird popular with sportsmen and farmers.[104]

The economic argument for bird protection proved one aspect of calls for broader game and fish protection by the American Ornithologists' Union and would direct the energy of the Bureau of Biological Survey until the early twentieth century. Justification provided by economic ornithology also supported the efforts of southerners to create game and fish commissions, as will become apparent in subsequent chapters. As historical geographer Matthew D. Evenden argues, however, the "science" behind economic ornithology was based on imperfect and limited methods, and, with few exceptions, ornithologists who argued for the economic importance of birds never gave clear instruction to farmers on how to apply the findings in their own fields (beyond building birdhouses and staving off predators). Within the US Department of Agriculture, economic ornithology was all but abandoned by the 1930s as pesticides became more widely available.[105]

Other nods to preservation had less to do with the possibility of pest control and more to do with concern about overhunting. By the late 1870s, supporters of a general game law wrote to local newspapers lamenting the "rapid extermination" of game through overhunting.[106] Likewise, sport hunters became aware that certain species—doves, quail—were under threat, and by the 1880s laws often included closed seasons for the small birds. Increasingly, men of a certain class regarded themselves as "sportsmen" and appealed to a growing fraternity across the state and across regional lines, a phenomenon that the following chapters explore. The game laws proved one aspect of sincere attempts at preserving game and bird species, and arguments that drew from the growing conservation movement became louder in the early twentieth century.

Yet with all of the energy given to the passage of new laws, a law passed is not a law enforced. Historians who study changes in postbellum property law have considered motivation, but there remains a need for analysis of implementation. A thorough survey and synthesis of county circuit court records would be a prodigious (though worthy) effort, yet not all of these records are extant or accessible. It is clear, however, that at the time of their passage, supporters of new laws recognized the disparity between intent and action and grumbled about the lack of enforcement. Contemporaneous publications are peppered with complaints. "Ex. Confed" wrote to the *Southern Cultivator* to moan that Sumter County, Alabama, juries would not convict anyone who violated the county's new stock law (which required stock owners to fence grazing pastures). He blamed the lack of enforcement, not surprisingly, on the political power of freedmen and their allies: "This is a righteous law if it

A man poses with gun and hunting dogs in Montgomery, Alabama, ca. 1870s. Alabama Department of Archives and History, Montgomery.

only could be enforced—but, alas! . . . Whenever a suit under it is brought before a jury of 'Busters,' a black and tan jury, the owner of the stock is bound to win."[107] The South Carolina editorial that urged landowners to post lands to keep unwanted hunting off their property, and especially to control Black hunters, recognized that traditions of the commons made trespass laws hard to enforce. "True, strictly speaking," the author argued, "notices are unnecessary, for trespass is always supposed to be prohibited; but the custom of the country to the contrary, has also the force, of common law, and to *insure* the success of prosecution and also to stimulate land-owners themselves to institute legal proceedings, the publication of notices will be valuable."[108]

The same was true of game and fish laws; as states or counties began to pass new codes, southerners remained suspicious, or simply disregarded them. Across the late nineteenth century, county game and fish laws were repealed as quickly as they were passed, revealing the contested nature of a code that curbed customary hunting and fishing practices. Those that did remain do not appear to have been widely enforced. State attorney general reports to the legislature, for example, are telling. Alabama's reports helpfully include summaries of arrests and convictions in county circuit courts, and these records suggest that there existed little will to arrest and convict those in violation. In 1886, three years after Winston County in north-central Alabama passed a new law against camp hunting, the courts accused ten people of the crime. Four of the accused were convicted and fined and six were "nol prossed," or the charge was terminated without a conviction.[109] In 1888, the Winston County circuit court prosecuted no camp hunting cases but convicted one person of hog hunting and one person of Sunday hunting; both cases were terminated.[110] From 1892 to 1894, only three cases of camp hunting came before Alabama courts; two parties were found guilty, one was acquitted, and no one was sentenced to hard labor.[111] Two people were accused of hunting on lands of another without written permission and tried in Montgomery city courts; one person was convicted and fined, one acquitted.[112] Six people stood accused of killing wild hogs, but only one was convicted. One was acquitted and the other four cases were "nol prossed."[113] Few people in Alabama were charged with breaking game laws, and even fewer convicted. Perhaps the threat of the law was enough to elicit intended consequences, or perhaps the advocates of the game and fish laws had not yet convinced the southern populace of the benefit of the code. That work would come in earnest in the early twentieth century.

Across the nineteenth century, hunting and fishing practices composed an unstable yet shared aspect of the lives of Native, Black, and white people in the South. Nonetheless, access to land, guns, and prey proved contested and divisive as Deep South legislatures used laws, from the beginning of the century, to curtail and limit who had the privileges of the hunt. Game and fish regulation intertwined with changing property laws after the Civil War. Erosion of the commons and emergent notions of private property and public protection prepared the field for a modern game and fish commission in Deep South states by the early twentieth century. We will see a new identity emerge, fostered by an ever-widening sporting culture that appealed to middle- and upper-class white men nationwide. The interregional rise of the sportsman brought new status and state regulation to hunting and fishing across the South. A growing national conservation and bird protection movement undergirded and inspired southern advocates of game and fish laws, and the consolidation of state power in the Progressive Era South offered the theater for enactment of a new regime in natural resource protection. The chapters that follow delineate each of these threads to offer a fully interwoven understanding of the transformation of southern hunting.

2. Audubon, Alabama, and the Advent of Statewide Game and Fish Commissions in the Progressive Era Deep South

When southerners set out to create statewide game and fish laws and attendant enforcement regimes, they did so in the aftermath of an agrarian insurgency, in the context of a new regime in property law that worked to close the open range, and during an era in which politicians and civic leaders pushed for statewide reforms to expand public schools, public health, better working conditions, and political change. This swell of reform, a hallmark of the Progressive Era nationwide, resulted in uniquely southern policies that reflected an enduring white supremacist ideology, which had been shaken briefly by the dim possibility of biracial cooperation in the 1890s. The Progressive Era in the early twentieth-century South would see the entrenchment of Jim Crow laws and disenfranchisement in Alabama and across the region. White reformers argued that to segregate Black and white people and to control Black political action was the key to uncorrupt politics and uninterrupted white rule.

The move to centralize fish, bird, and game protection meshed well with southern Progressivism. To attempt a new kind of regulation of natural resources, one that might infringe upon traditional use rights of southerners, required political acumen, persuasive messaging, and wholehearted belief in a cause. John H. Wallace Jr. (1874–1922) was the architect of Alabama's comprehensive game and fish bill, and he fit the mold of a southern reformer. As the Progressive movement gained traction, he campaigned for a new form of consolidated state action in the South—conservation. The game and fish commission that Wallace created showcased his ideological commitments. He believed that hunting was the province of a certain type of white man and that white men should control African American laboring populations. He knew that, despite its political defeat in the 1890s, the "agrarian class," or "agricultural class," as he called it, was central to the success of statewide hunting and fishing laws. While shaped by national trends in wildlife protection, southerners' adaptation of the laws fit the conditions of a region shaken by political revolt and whose leaders wished to bind it back together with the tight weft of inequality.

Wallace drew upon several decades of experimentation in game and fish regulation in the Northeast and Midwest. When he drafted legislation, he could borrow from policies already in place in the Adirondacks and in states like Pennsylvania, from the guidance of newly created government agencies like the Bureau of Biological Survey, and even from failed attempts at passing game and fish laws elsewhere in the region.[1] His efforts built upon judicial assertion of state ownership of wildlife alongside a newfound emphasis on private property protection in the South, shifts that seem incongruous but aligned to Wallace's purposes. He also received critical direction and financial support from organizations pushing for game, fish, and bird laws. None proved more active on the behalf of Wallace and other southerners than the National Association of Audubon Societies (NAAS), an organization in its infancy in the early twentieth century. NAAS leaders were sportsmen, bird lovers, and men of influence, and they easily blended campaigns for bird and game regulation in the South, which was bereft of meaningful protective policies. The NAAS was especially attuned to the South—southern coasts were important resting stops for migratory birds, and southern hunters provided much of the raw supply for trade in bird feathers (for hats) and meat (for restaurants). Game, fish, and bird regulation in the South was key to the NAAS's aim to stop the sale and shipment of nongame and game birds.

The NAAS was especially active in coastal southern states, and Alabama, whose game and fish policy was a centerpiece of joint efforts, takes the stage in this chapter. John Wallace would benefit from NAAS support yet ultimately had to craft legislation that won agreement not just of sportsmen but of rural white hunters and fishers, groups that did not necessarily share goals in a broader conservation movement. To that end, he was bolstered by the campaign in Alabama to create a new state constitution in 1901, one that routed the US Constitution's Fourteenth and Fifteenth Amendments and that put an end to the rash of local (or countywide) game and fish laws. Both features of Alabama's new constitution served Wallace well—he argued to Alabama audiences that the game and fish laws would further entrench white control over the southern landscape and that he was free of legislative obstacles to establish uniform code across the state. The state, he contended, was a key actor in the protection of wildlife and natural resources; indeed, the state was morally obligated to use its police power to such ends. After establishing the game and fish commission in Alabama, Wallace undertook to work with lawmakers in the neighboring states of Georgia and Mississippi to craft and deploy similar legislation with mixed success. Georgia would create a commission very similar to Wallace's; Mississippi would not. What follows reconstructs the genealogy of game and fish laws in the Deep South, from the influences of the bird protection movement in the Northeast, to North Carolina, where the NAAS first experimented with game and fish regulation and enforcement, and finally to Wallace's successful, lasting legislation in Alabama that was tangled with social and legal inequality and that created a movement in other southern states. We end with Wallace's move into federal bird protection via the Migratory Bird Treaty Act, portending the ways in which southern conservationists would look to a growing federal intervention in wildlife regulation to support their own aims in the South.

Men like Wallace considered themselves arbiters of a sportsman's ethos that circulated widely in periodicals like *Forest and Stream*, *Field and Stream*, and *Sportsman's Review*. Wallace corresponded with editors of these national magazines, before and after he became game commissioner in 1907. His attitudes and later policies aligned with the construction of the ideal sportsman and, by extension, with his relationship to the natural world and to others who might compete for its resources. In this cosmos of belief, prejudice, and priority, men who hunted and fished for sport, and not for sustenance or commercial gain, were the true protectors of wildlife. At the end of the nineteenth century, there was an outcry about an environment depleted of animals and fish and about the slaughter of nongame birds; nowhere was that lamentation louder than among sportsmen. There existed clear villains, too, whom sportsmen could blame for the kill. The "pothunter" and "game hog" were common bogeymen vilified in the sporting periodicals and bird protection literature—the pothunter either hunted for his own pot or for the commercial market (or both), and the game hog was one whose kills knew no limits. There was also the hunter or fisher who was simply "other"—the non-white man (or woman, sometimes) who could not be trusted to steward the earth's resources and whose competition threatened to limit the sport enjoyed by men like Wallace. White wildlife advocates characterized Native Americans, African Americans, and immigrants as lazy (hunting when they should be working), irresponsible (ignoring bag limits and hunting seasons), greedy (overkilling for commercial markets), and dangerous (possessing weapons, like military-issue rifles, that sportsmen considered inappropriate for hunting).² In the minds of sportsmen, pothunters, game hogs, and nonwhite hunters did not simply break the law (laws were scant in the first place) but transgressed firm boundaries of social hierarchy in American society.

This caricature of heroes and varlets permeated hunting narratives in sporting periodicals and the rhetoric of game and bird protection advocates, and eventually found its way into policy. Some species were undoubtedly overhunted for hats, meat, and specimen collection. But the classification of humans into categories with fixed relationships to the natural world proved specific and stark; sportsmen and game and bird protection advocates styled themselves as "stewards," while other hunters and fishers became racialized parasites who depleted populations of birds, game, and fish. These assumptions cut across the people and organizations—game protective associations, the bird protection movement, individual sportsmen and scientists interested in wildlife populations—from which southerners like John Wallace drew to build their own campaigns for game and fish laws. William Hornaday, who was famous by the late nineteenth century as an advocate for wildlife protection, was an ally to Wallace in the bid to protect migratory birds and used language in his plea for game laws that would become a refrain in the castigations of sportsmen. In his influential *Our Vanishing Wildlife*, in a section titled "Special Work of the Southern Negroes," he argued that "the pot-hunting negro has all the skill of the Indian, has more industry in his loafing, and kills without pity and without restraint."³ Stratification based on race, ethnicity, citizenship status, and class defined beliefs that would shape, in ways explicit and implicit, the justification for and implementation of game and fish laws in the South, and elsewhere, by the early twentieth century.

The National Association of Audubon Societies in the South

In his memoir, *Adventures in Bird Protection*, Thomas Gilbert Pearson recalled 1907 as a year full of possibility. "The legislatures of more than forty states," he offered, "held sessions and into their hoppers were poured many bills having for their purpose the liberalizing of the modest restrictive laws on hunting then existing."⁴ The movement to protect birds, game, and fish was growing, and Pearson stood at the heart of it. He then served as the secretary of the newly founded National Association of Audubon Societies, "the only membership organization trying to work on anything like a national scope" of game and bird protection laws, in his estimation.⁵ That year, the NAAS was busy helping Texas fund a movement for state game wardens, advancing the

Michigan Audubon Society's efforts to stop a bill that would permit the killing of meadowlarks, and providing financial and human resources to Alabama's John Wallace, then lobbying for a statewide game and fish commission. The NAAS provided "literature, news-releases and correspondence" for Wallace's cause and sent its vice president, T. S. Palmer, to speak at the Alabama legislature on the importance of wildlife preservation.[6] Palmer, an American zoologist who worked for the Department of Agriculture during these boom years of game and fish legislation, led a department in the Bureau of Biological Survey focused on game preservation.[7] Pearson had already proven his organizational and political muscle by establishing a game and fish commission in North Carolina in 1903 under the auspices of the state's Audubon Society. National networks of sportsmen, scientists, and wildlife protection advocates served as tailwind for Wallace and other southerners working to pass protective legislation in the South by extending the substance for policy and inspiring the rhetoric that Wallace and others used to sway southern audiences.

The steady increase in statewide game and fish laws in the late nineteenth century reflected a growing will to legislate the kill rate of game animals. At the same time, not unrelated, a movement emerged to protect "nongame" birds that were vulnerable to market hunters who sourced for the hat trade, especially in New York City. The Victorian era craze for naturalia—collecting and displaying items from the natural world—manifested in fashion. The hats in question, some of which can be seen in digital collections, are startling in their eerie contrivance. In one example from the Metropolitan Museum of Art, three taxidermied parakeets adorn a bonnet of chocolate velvet, each dumbly posed with beaks resting on beaded trim.[8] Au courant women who wore these feather-adorned hats and the millinery trade that produced them became the object of scathing attacks by an emergent bird protection movement that saw its beginnings in the 1880s and an upswing in the late 1890s.[9]

The American Ornithologists' Union (AOU) propounded a strong bird protection platform that set a foundation for the later work of the NAAS. Its founding in 1883 was a move by ornithologists to professionalize the field. As historian Mark V. Barrow Jr. documents, the AOU promoted reform of technical nomenclature of birds and worked to create "occupational space" for ornithologists in museums, zoos, and governmental agencies. The organization walked a blurred line between its "scientific" and "amateur" constituents. It created a hierarchical structure, wherein power resided with a central council and a small group of "active" membership designees. The vast majority of ornithology enthusiasts were considered "corresponding" members. Men were

Hats with bird plumage were popular among elite women of the late nineteenth and early twentieth centuries. The hats, in part, inspired the bird protection movement. The Metropolitan Museum of Art, New York.

the predominant members of the organization; in its early years, no women were nominated to "active" members, though women proved critical to the bird protection movement in later years.[10]

The AOU drove bird protection through the early twentieth century. To that end, it created a bird protection committee, a body that in 1885 proposed language for legislation that would later be influential in the southern game and fish protection movement. Supporters of the recommended legislation, "An Act for the Protection of the Birds and Their Nests and Eggs," came to call it the "Model Law" of bird protection. The Model Law would lie at the heart of the policy promoted by the southern game and fish movement. Its chief purpose was to protect nongame birds and, in doing so, to define what birds would be categorized as game: "The Anatidae, commonly known as swans, geese, brant, and river and sea ducks; the Rallidae, commonly known as rails, coots, mud-hens, and gallinules; the Limicolrae, commonly known as shore birds, plovers, surf birds, snipe, woodcock, sandpipers, tatlers, and curlews; the Gallinae, commonly known as wild turkeys, grouse, prairie chickens, pheasants, partridges, and quails."[11] Other species—with the exception of the house sparrow (*Passer domesticus*), reviled as an intrusive threat to native birds—were protected, and the proposed legislation made the acts of killing, catching, and selling nongame birds a misdemeanor. The second tenet of the proposal allowed for collection of protected species for scientific purposes. A collector could obtain a certificate from an authorized body—after securing recommendation from "two well-known scientific men" and a bond of $200—and take nests, eggs, and bird specimens for study. The provision underscored the importance of collecting to the growing ornithological field and attempted to claim the field from the amateur. As Barrow notes, "The permit clause—with its demand to differentiate legitimate scientific collecting from other forms of bird slaughter—became a source of tension between scientific ornithologists and the collectors, taxidermists, and natural history dealers who had once been closely allied with them."[12] The clause came under fire, too, as the bird protection movement gained in momentum; some advocates considered any kill to be part of the widespread problem of bird destruction. The tension over collecting eventually led the AOU to repudiate the bird protection movement that, by the early 1900s, was led by Audubon societies.[13] Nonetheless, the Model Law established an important vehicle for supporters of game and fish protection in the South—it often preceded, as was the case in Alabama, Georgia, Louisiana, and Mississippi, the creation of more robust statewide game and fish regulation.

By the turn of the twentieth century, William Dutcher, a businessman and sportsman from New Jersey, was "the engine that powered the bird protection movement through its early crucial years," according to Barrow.[14] Dutcher began as the AOU's treasurer, and in 1895 the organization appointed him head of its bird protection committee. The group had been largely inert since the push for and publication of the Model Law, which one state—Pennsylvania—had adopted in 1889.[15] At the same time that Dutcher took the helm of the committee, Harriett Lawrence Hemenway and Minna B. Hall founded the Massachusetts Audubon Society to advocate for the end of the plumage market. West Virginia and Pennsylvania followed suit. Dutcher was encouraged by the renewed invigoration of the Audubon Societies, and, to help coordinate state Audubon initiatives, he "orchestrated" the organization of the National Association of Audubon Societies in 1905.[16]

Public education was an important element of the work for Dutcher and other advocates. At the beginning of his tenure on the bird protection committee, Dutcher vigorously promoted the adoption of a national Bird Day. Designed by C. A. Babcock, a school superintendent of Oil City, Pennsylvania, Bird Day was intended as a program of avian devotion and study in public schools, modeled on Arbor Day.[17] John Wallace would become a staunch advocate for Bird Day in Alabama, where he oversaw its adoption in schools using his *Alabama Bird Day* book as a curriculum guide.

In the rhetoric of the bird protection movement, fashion-crazed women were not alone to blame for the killing of songbirds. Immigrants, African Americans, poor white southerners, and slingshot-packing boys received the vitriol of advocates. Early in the life of the AOU, founder J. A. Allen published a supplemental piece in *Science* magazine decrying the "wholesale destruction of bird-life in the United States." Allen reprinted an observer's notes that "colored vendors" of market stalls in the South sold strings of small birds that were likely "captured by the same class."[18] In 1903, almost twenty years later, William Dutcher reported on the work of the AOU bird protection committee, noting that while the movement had yet to take hold in the Gulf South, bird protection was needed "especially near the great cities and towns having a large foreign element among their citizens who kill anything that flies, be it large or small."[19] In 1905, the Delaware Audubon Society assured readers of *Bird Lore*, the NAAS's flagship publication, that "the foreign bird-shooting elements is being looked after sharply." In this case, an Italian man was accused of killing nineteen songbirds, arrested, and sentenced to ten days of hard labor as punishment, which had a "decided and wholesome influence" on the rest of the immigrant community there.[20] The alarms sounded by bird protection advocates mirrored those of game protectionists in sportsmen's periodicals; all wanted protection and enforcement of new laws and found ideal scapegoats outside of the sportsman class.

The legislative advocacy of the AOU and state Audubon Societies took on new momentum after the passage of the Lacey Act of 1900. That law established, among other provisions, the federal government's ability to control the importation and propagation of wildlife in the United States and to outlaw the interstate sale of game.[21] Its successful enactment showcased the cooperative power of sportsmen, bird protection activists, ornithologists, and federal policymakers, many of whom embodied these varied identities. The League of American Sportsmen, founded by G. O. Shields in 1898, for example, put its shoulder into the campaign for the act, which endured four years of debate before it finally passed. In Shield's *Recreation* ("a monthly magazine devoted to everything the name implies"), an early engine of the League of American Sportsmen, he celebrated that "10,000 letters have been written to Senators and Representatives by League members and at the instigation of League members' praying for speedy and favorable action on the Lacey bill."[22] As historian John F. Reiger argues, sportsmen advanced the passage of the Lacey Act, and in many cases sportsmen constituted the ranks of bird protection groups; John F. Lacey, the author of the famed bill, was a hunter and fisherman as well as a bird lover.[23] Such was the case with many leaders of the movement for wildlife protection—including men in the South, like Pearson and Wallace.

The momentum created by the Lacey Act extended to enforcement in eastern states, including those in the Southeast. In 1900, naturalist Abbott Henderson Thayer joined with William Dutcher, on hiatus from leading the AOU bird protection committee after 1897, to create a fund that would hire game wardens for bird protection. The Thayer Fund employed wardens in states along the Atlantic and Gulf Coasts—including Maine, Virginia, North Carolina, Louisiana, and Florida.[24] The earliest dedicated, paid wardens in the South were not employed by counties or states but by investment from the bird protection movement. Dutcher led an effort to reinvigorate and unify state Audubon Societies and to persuade state legislatures to pass the AOU Model Law. To this end, supported by allies in the movement, he followed T. S. Palmer by visiting legislatures across the Eastern Seaboard, promoting the importance of bird protection. Palmer, who had helped draft the Lacey Act, was assistant chief of the Department of Agriculture's Bureau of Biological

Survey.[25] He became the vice president of the NAAS in 1905 and, later, an important ally to Wallace in Alabama. In their efforts, Palmer and Dutcher turned their attention southward at a strategic moment.

Dutcher formed a partnership with Thomas Gilbert Pearson in North Carolina. Pearson, who moved with his family to Florida as a child, developed a love of birds inspired by the tropical species of the state. He later moved to North Carolina to teach biology at the State Normal and Industrial School for women in Greensboro.[26] In the early twentieth century he published *Stories of Bird Life*, a collection of short essays based on his observations in the field.[27] The book's reviews caught the attention of Dutcher, prompting him to send a letter to Pearson that, as Pearson said, "had much to do with my future work." Dutcher, then in the midst of his campaign to promote passage of the Model Law, hoped to recruit Pearson to the work of NAAS and suggested he form a society in North Carolina to advocate for the law. Pearson offered a mixed response. He wanted more stringent protection but "had a mild prejudice against [NAAS], having seen a disparaging reference to it in some publication." His suspicions were not helped by literature from NAAS supporters that seemed to show the presence of "extremists in the field of bird protection, whose writings could serve to mislead the uninformed, and would hurt our cause with thinking people." He had a distaste, for example, for provocative claims that "birds designed for the millinery trade were skinned alive so their feathers would not fade . . . and that all species of American birds soon would become exterminated."[28] Nevertheless, after convening with other concerned North Carolinians in March 1902, Pearson helped to found the Audubon Society of North Carolina and became its first president. "'Bird protection,'" he observed, "was a new note in North Carolina, the idea was novel." The organization, through press coverage, drew supporters from across the state. Pearson soon joined the NAAS as secretary and became a member of the AOU bird protection committee.[29] This professional network would bolster his work in North Carolina.

Pearson knew that, even if the Audubon Society of North Carolina could successfully lobby for protective legislation, the improbability of North Carolina dedicating state money to an enforcement division was unavoidable. He devised another plan. After vetting the idea with T. S. Palmer, "as he knew more about the practical workings of game-law than any man in America," Pearson collaborated with supportive lawyers and politicians to write and propose a bill that the state Audubon Society administer a state game and fish agency and establish a warden system to enforce protective measures. The bill was successful. In 1903, the Audubon Society established a warden system in North Carolina through a cooperative partnership with the state. Pearson hoped that the partnership between the society and state government would be "entirely divorced from politics."[30] As part of the system, the state extended authority to the society to enforce the new state law and to collect funds raised by license purchases.[31] The Audubon Society of North Carolina had the extra income of membership dues, which it circulated to its enforcement arm. In his memoir, Pearson recalled the optimism of his early years as chief enforcer: "Within twelve months from the date of its founding the Society had aroused a lively interest throughout the State in the subject of bird protection, and had been granted unheard-of legal powers. . . . The world seemed very bright. We were going to save the wild birds of the State."[32] But Pearson's plans and hopes proved naive: the Audubon Society would confront powerful local resistance to the new order in coastal North Carolina.

The Currituck Sound in the northeastern corner of the state had not always been a favored stop on the route for migratory freshwater ducks. Only after a storm closed the last inlet in 1828 were ducks increasingly drawn to a new abundance of freshwater in the sound.[33] By the late nineteenth century, the northeastern coastal landscape of marshes and grassy plains, including Currituck, Albemarle, and Pamlico Sounds, also attracted growing numbers of hunters looking to sell ducks and plumage to urban markets outside of the South.[34] "Next to the bobwhite," Pearson wrote, "water-fowl long produced more revenue to the state of North Carolina than any other bird or group of birds."[35] Market hunters, and area politicians who wanted to protect the livelihood of constituents, were especially vociferous in their opposition to the new game laws in North Carolina. Pearson and Audubon wardens pursued violators of the new law with fervor. Yet wardens secured only 245 convictions by 1908. In 1909, opponents from eastern counties and elsewhere rallied enough support to remove fifty-four out of ninety-eight North Carolina counties from the Audubon's purview. Able to enforce the law in a patchwork of only forty-four counties, the Audubon Society was rendered ineffective.[36] Pearson subsequently advocated for the state to nullify the partnership and create a state game and fish commission at every legislature thereafter for sixteen years. In 1927 the state did so, though coastal counties did not fall under the commission's jurisdiction until 1935.[37]

Pearson's efforts to establish code and enforcement regimes in other southern states initially seemed promising. The South Carolina Audubon Society formed a similar partnership with the state in 1907 but made slower progress there. In January 1908, Pearson visited the state to bolster the work of enforcement. He was discouraged that even though the state Audubon

Society had been working for ten months, it "had secured only eleven convictions, and many rumors of law violations were reaching me."[38] The source of at least some of the problems came from the tourist centers like Aiken, near the Georgia border, and the coastal cities Charleston and Georgetown. By the late nineteenth century, Aiken and its surrounds had become one of several popular destinations for northerners and midwesterners coming south for leisure, convalescence, and sport.[39] In Aiken and nearby North Augusta, Pearson found that hotels were not abiding by the new state law that restricted the sale of game. One hotel, Hampton Terrace, had quail on its menu and did not hide from Pearson that its chefs kept 3,000 refrigerated birds on hand. The hotel, in fact, employed hunters to replenish its fare. Pearson duly reported the violation and was subsequently accused by the owner of unethical behavior, as Pearson was a guest of the hotel ("a paying guest," Pearson reminded his readers). In Georgetown he found northern hunters who refused to purchase out-of-state licenses (because the law was not being enforced anyway, they cried), and in Charleston he found game birds for sale in restaurants and city markets.[40] In 1909, the state Audubon Society began to lobby the South Carolina legislature to create a state game and fish commission, much as it had done in North Carolina. South Carolina established a state warden system in 1911, though the state did not supply adequate appropriations for its work. The warden system remained ineffective in the 1910s until, motivated by John Wallace's success in Alabama, the state passed a law to establish a game and fish commission in 1915.[41]

Pearson set sights on Florida, Louisiana, and Georgia in the hopes of encouraging like-minded residents to work for game and fish laws. For Pearson and others, Florida was especially important in the fight for wildlife protection as hunters ravaged bird populations for the millinery trade. By 1904, the Thayer fund employed four wardens, one each at Pelican Island, Cape Sable, the Dry Tortugas, and nearby Sand Key Lighthouse.[42] President Theodore Roosevelt had bolstered the work of enforcement the year before by creating the first national wildlife refuge at Pelican Island. The pressure to end the plumage trade and the presence of wardens proved a dangerous mix. In 1905, hunter Walter Smith shot and killed warden Guy Bradley on Pelican Island. Bradley had arrested Smith's son for continuing to shoot plume birds to sell in the North.[43] Supporters of Audubon work made a national martyr of Bradley, using his death as a way to shame women who continued to buy feather-festooned hats. The state was the first in the Southeast to pass the AOU Model Law in 1902; afterward, the Florida Audubon chapter called upon the legislature to create effective enforcement.[44] A *Tampa Tribune* editorial cautioned after Bradley's death that "the subject of providing Game Wardens is a serious one, for few men are willing to accept a position, for which the State will not guarantee the law will protect them. There are 46 counties in Florida and 13 Game Wardens, 33 depending on an over-busy Sheriff to see that the game laws are enforced. May we not ask for better legislation?"[45] Another editor lamented the ineffectiveness of the county system of wardens established in 1897 by the state legislature: counties could opt into the warden system when seventy-five "freeholders" petitioned for a warden.[46] But, "few men" risked the job without state protection. Florida would not create a state department of game and fish until 1925.[47]

Like Florida, Louisiana's coast was vulnerable to market hunters. The NAAS found a leader there in Frank M. Miller, who helped to establish the state society in 1902. Two years later, the society successfully lobbied for the passage of the Model Law.[48] As part of his duties as president of the state society, Miller began to tour coastal Louisiana to inspect bird breeding grounds. There he found that hunters shot seabirds for millinery feathers and for eggs, shipping the latter to St. Louis to use in the production of photographic plates.[49] Miller discovered that some of these islands were owned by the federal government and hatched a plan to designate them as bird refuges. After gaining support from T. S. Palmer of the Bureau of Biological Survey's game protection unit and William Dutcher of the NAAS, he appealed to President Roosevelt, who listened. Roosevelt created the Breton Island Bird Reservation in 1904 on Breton Island and the Chandeleur Islands.[50] The NAAS continued its support of Miller's efforts in Louisiana; in 1908, it underwrote a successful drive to create a statewide game and fish law. The state passed two bills to that effect: one created a Board of Commissioners, empowered to create protective laws and employ state game wardens, and the other established a licensing fee structure.[51] Miller became the first state game and fish commissioner. For all of the early support of the laws, the state would not go so far as to include robins and cedar waxwings as protected species, since attempts to do so met with resistance from some Louisianans who considered the birds a delicacy.[52]

Georgia seemed to promise a model like that of North Carolina, in which the state gave the Audubon Society chapter the ability to enforce game and fish laws.[53] Pearson established the Georgia Audubon Society in 1903. Initially, the society was energetic in its work and used social and political influence to successfully advocate for the passage of the Model Law in 1903.[54] In Georgia, birds protected regardless of season included barred owls, finches, vireos, cranes and herons, warblers, robins, nighthawks, screech owls, shrikes (or "butcher birds"), grosbeaks, swallows, scarlet tanagers, orioles, kingfishers, and mockingbirds, or, as one newspaper account summed, birds categorized as "Useful, Insect-eating, or Songbirds."[55] Georgians could shoot swans, geese, ducks, quail, plover and other shorebirds, turkeys, and doves in open season. At risk of gun or snare in any season were birds considered pests by farmers: great horned owls, English sparrows, crows, Cooper's hawks, sharp-shinned hawks, larks, crow blackbirds, jackdaws, and "rice birds," which commonly referred to bobolinks.[56] In addition, the law required that superior court judges appoint county wardens to enforce the law. The Georgia Audubon Society's ally, the Society for the Prevention of Cruelty to Animals, circulated the new law in pamphlet form as an easy guide for Georgians to abide the restructuring of relations between humans and birds. At the same time, in 1903, another "general" game law passed in the Georgia legislature; if the Model Law primarily focused on songbirds, the general law, introduced by a Chatham County legislator, focused on regulating the take of game animals, birds, and fish. The laws set closed seasons, mandated licenses for market hunters, and outlawed the dynamiting and poisoning of streams as a mode of taking fish. In addition, county residents could petition to create a game warden.[57] Soon after these legislative victories, however, the state Audubon Society lost its momentum, and the NAAS became active in attempts to sustain the state chapter.[58] Efforts to create a Carolina model failed in the legislature. When Pearson again picked up the fight to create a consolidated game and fish commission in Georgia, he would do so with the assistance of John H. Wallace Jr., who brought colorful character and ample passion to the ring.

Alabama, Audubon, and the 1907 Department of Game and Fish

John H. Wallace Jr. was born in northern Lauderdale County, Alabama, in 1878, the son of a farmer and Confederate veteran. He studied at the State Normal College in Florence, the precursor to the University of North Alabama, before passing the bar in 1896. Wallace moved to Huntsville to practice law and then entered politics as a young man, serving as a state representative for Madison County in 1898–99 and again in 1900–1901.[59] Before his death in 1922, he would run for state senate and for the governorship of Alabama, but these attempts to formally reenter politics were unsuccessful. Instead, his life's work, and oblique point of entry into politics, became the protection of wildlife.

Wallace was an author of fiction, and his writerly efforts provide an unusually intimate window into both man and movement. He published his only book-length work in 1904, three years before the creation of the commission and as his advocacy for bird, game, and fish protection was growing in the

John H. Wallace Jr., here photographed as part of the Alabama House of Representatives, ca. 1900. Alabama Department of Archives and History, Montgomery.

state. The novel, *The Senator from Alabama—A Romance Treating of the Disfranchisement of the Negro and Including a Scathing Arraignment of the White House Social-Equality Policy*, is, like its title, wordy and zealous. Fittingly for a fox hunter, Wallace opened his tale with a fox hunting scene, in which the protagonist, George Jarman, bests his opponent in love and politics by capturing the bushy tail of the fox and presenting it to the woman who is one part of the titular "romance." The other enthrallment is a political one. The young Jarman, styled as an "Adonic" man and paragon of "honesty" and "virtue," dedicates his life's work to reform the corrupt world of late nineteenth-century state politics. In a drawn-from-real-life plot, Jarman witnesses the gubernatorial defeat of Reuben F. Kolb ("Rufus Knobb" in the novel), a leader supported by Populists, by the will of Alabama's Black Belt "princes." Because Democrats used ballot-stuffing and the harvest of African American votes (registering all Black votes as Democratic, whether Black men voted or not) to claim victory, Jarman crusades to "eliminate the negro [from politics] by imposing such restrictions on the right to vote as will practically disfranchise the entire colored voting population."[60] The novel ends with Jarman's election to the state senate and his successful push to ratify the 1901 Alabama Constitution, which, barring the character at the heart of the story, is no fiction. The constitution became the lever by which Alabama routed the Fifteenth Amendment and formally disenfranchised its Black citizens.

The themes that emerge in Wallace's novel offer us a lens into his political footing around game, fish, and bird protection. Wallace rehearsed the rise of the Populist Party in 1890s Alabama that took shape thanks to earlier joint efforts by organized labor and agricultural associations like the Agricultural Wheel and Farmers' Alliance. Even after the Democrats defeated the Populists, an "unusually long-lived farmer-labor alliance" continued in the state until the 1940s, according to historian Matthew Hild.[61] If the political threat to the Democratic Party did not extend past the elections of 1896, dissent against elite interests did. Wallace understood that dissatisfaction from former Populists remained, now within the ranks of a reunited Democratic Party, which had usurped parts of the Populist platform in the 1896 gubernatorial election. In fact, many former Populist strongholds, especially in northern and central Alabama, voted against the ratification of the 1901 state constitution, knowing well the impact that Black disenfranchisement had on marginal white men.[62] Wallace understood, when campaigning for a new state agency that promised to shape access to resources, including real property, that he would have to win the support of what he called "the agrarian class," white smallholders who did not align with Black Belt elites. He did so, as covered in more detail below, by appealing to what he saw as smallholders' natural interest in protecting the bounds of their property from roving hunters, thus implicitly emphasizing the closing of the range. He credited the success of his platform on his ability to convince white farmers that the laws were in their best interest, and he blamed other states when they failed to take seriously the demands of landowning rural whites. Farmer outreach became a signature strategy of Wallace's efforts.

Wallace entered politics in the late nineteenth century, just as the game and bird protection movements were gaining ground in the Northeast. As a House representative in 1898, he proposed two bills: one that created a state game and fish commission of three governor-appointed commissioners and another that created regulation to protect game, fish, and birds.[63] The bills made it out of the Judiciary Committee; the former was "taken up" but "indefinitely postponed."[64] The second bill, however, became law. William D. Jelks, who would become governor in 1901 and support Wallace's reintroduction of a game and fish commission bill in 1906, wrote florid praise of Wallace's efforts in 1898. Reporting on the state legislature, he wrote that Wallace's bill excited debate and elicited mockery in the Judiciary Committee. A lengthy text, the bill "provide[d] for county and precinct wardens for the preservation of song birds, game birds, and fish and provides a penalty for slaughtering the first at any time and the others out of season."[65] The cynicism of some legislators, however, was no blight on Wallace. Jelks opined that "there are not a sufficient number of the tender and aesthetic in this world and Wallace, why, I shall call him our High Priest of beauty and song."[66]

T. S. Palmer later reported that Wallace's early bills "[were] evidently based on the Pennsylvania Game Law of 1897."[67] That Pennsylvania law came on the heels of an 1895 statute establishing a board of game commissioners that was empowered to employ "game protectors" to enforce law. Pennsylvania's 1897 code established penalties for violation of the game law; enlarged the category of nongame birds protected (the legislature had adopted the Model Law distinctions of game and nongame birds in 1891); set new seasons for game birds, deer, elk, and other quarry; established a protocol for certificates to collect specimens (in keeping with the Model Law); and outlawed the sale and shipment of game, among other limitations.[68] It is hard to know how closely Wallace's law followed suit, though presumably it included Model Law language, given Jelks's gentle gibe that the "the technical name for two dozen birds is mentioned" in the bill. It likely also established uniform closed seasons, and it certainly repealed local laws in favor of a statewide code. Given that the bill to create a board of commissioners failed, it is not clear whether

Wallace's law created an enforcement system for the new code. To outsiders, it did not seem that the second bill had the support to move forward in the legislature. Jelks lamented that "the bill will never become law. Once it is too late our people will wake up to find our forests denuded of their bright plumage and our fields innocent of the sweetest sounds capable of coming from delicious throats."[69]

Contrary to Jelks's belief, legislators in the Alabama House of Representatives passed the protection bill. The state senate approved it with heavy amendments, removing fifty-nine counties from the bill (which left only eight within its scope). By the next legislative session, seven other counties passed local game laws that "emasculated" the general law. In 1901, only Madison County—Wallace's home—remained within the purview of the law.[70] By then, the rash of local lawmaking was ended by the 1901 state constitution that augured a newly repressive state and that bolstered Wallace's next effort.

After the Populist defeat in 1896 and the end of the potential for biracial and labor cooperation it seemed to portend, state leaders in Alabama "chose the one-way street that led through decades of reaction, injustice, recurring violence, and sectional stagnation."[71] By the late nineteenth century, calls for a constitutional convention to ensure Black disenfranchisement grew louder. Governor Joseph F. Johnston tried to stave off the swell of support for the convention. The Democrat from north Alabama, who had absorbed aspects of Populist reform in his gubernatorial bid in 1896, was concerned that Black disenfranchisement would in time lead to poor white disenfranchisement. The debates came to a head when Johnston challenged General John Tyler Morgan's bid for reelection to the US Senate and the campaign became a referendum on the convention.[72]

Wallace, in both life and fiction, was a strong supporter of the convention movement. As a state representative, he broke with his constituents on the issue. Charley Lane of the *Huntsville Enterprise* lamented Wallace's support of John Tyler Morgan against Joseph Johnston—"Question[:] will John [Wallace] get with the people, or the people with John, who is the biggest?" The editor of the *Courtland Enterprise* reprinted Lane's assessment but tepidly reassured readers that "John [Wallace] is a good fellow. He is misguided in his choice for United States Senator, but he will come around alright in due season. Johnston will carry Morgan county and John [Wallace] will be on the bandwagon with him."[73] Wallace never came around. In 1899, he voted in favor of a bill to establish a statewide vote to call a convention. After the bill was narrowly repealed, Governor Johnston circulated a letter to certain representatives, including Wallace, soliciting opinions on the convention; Wallace confirmed he would continue to support and vote for a convention.[74]

Johnston and anti-convention forces lost ground in April 1900 when Johnston lost in the Democratic primary to Morgan for the US Senate nomination and to William J. Samford, who was pro-convention, for the gubernatorial nomination.[75] The state legislature again approved a bill to cast a popular vote for a convention and delegates. On May 21, 1901, 155 delegates met in Montgomery to "turn back the clock."[76]

The Alabama Constitutional Convention of 1901 left a detailed record of its proceedings, thanks to political leaders who fought to hire a stenographer to document each day's events. Historian R. Volney Riser argues that convention delegates were well aware such a record could be damning and could rouse the pushback of the federal judiciary, given that a main purpose of the new state constitution was to obstruct the Fourteenth and Fifteenth Amendments of the US Constitution.[77] Though legislators debated the methods of disenfranchisement—the details of which can be found in the convention proceedings (now digitized)—political leaders settled on the so-called grandfather clause as a way to curtail Black votes while ostensibly preserving those of poor whites.[78]

John Wallace stood solidly behind all efforts to disenfranchise Black men. And the constitution of 1901 served his agenda in another way. Among the initiatives on the conventioneers' docket was the curtailment of local laws in favor of general laws, in certain cases. Aligned with the broader Progressive movement then taking hold nationwide, some Alabama politicians argued that certain issues—such as public education and public health—were most effectively reformed through the state.[79] The initiative to create statewide code could serve Wallace's hopes to finally get a general law for game and fish. But legislators were not convinced that game and fish laws were effectively a matter of state law, and the exhaustive transcript of convention proceedings recorded the debate. Given that broader discussion of Wallace's earlier legislation does not exist in Alabama House journals from the late nineteenth century, the exchange below lends flavor to arguments about the need for statewide game and fish laws and the kinds of resistance Wallace's bill would face in 1907.

Legislators argued about what kinds of issues should be regulated by local versus general (or statewide) law, and game and fish laws proved a point of contention among some members of the convention. The debates tied to what would become Section 104 of the new constitution—"Special, private or local laws—Prohibited in certain cases." When delegate Hubert T. Davis from Etowah County in east Alabama introduced an amendment "regulating or catching the hunting of game" to be included in the section, Emmett O'Neal voiced opposition. O'Neal, who chaired the Committee on Local Legislation, reported that the committee decided against any game law as a general law based on the particulars of geography and habitat. "Some counties have no game," he argued, "and some have a great deal of game, and . . . to secure a general law would be a matter of great difficulty. . . . There are some communities in a county desiring game laws while probably the balance of the county are indifferent on the subject, we thought it proper if there was a community that desired to protect game to allow them to do it, other counties having no game would oppose any law of that sort."[80] Another delegate agreed—regulating diverse "beats and parts of beats and certain boundaries would be too difficult for a general game law."[81] T. M. Espy from Henry County in south Alabama spoke up in opposition. The amendment to regulate hunting was "one of the best provisions contained in this section of the article." He refuted the argument that a general law would prohibit the protection of game where it was wanted. By leaving hunting regulation to special law while moving issues such as public education and stock law to general code, Espy argued, "they will say that the birds and game of this country are of more importance and entitled to more protection under the laws of this State than the children and the stock."[82] Game regulation, he argued, like the creation of separate school districts or stock districts, should be included in a general law that gave power to a county "Commissioners' Court or the Board of Revenue" to enact such provisions (indeed, the Alabama legislature passed a 1903 law that gave counties the purview of establishing local stock statutes).[83] In essence, Espy's argument kept in place the local designation of certain kinds of laws that had geographic resonance (some species needed protection in certain counties but not others) while removing the constant swing of passage and repeal that hounded these laws in the legislature. Espy also pointed to the gutting of Wallace's law, passed initially as a general law but reduced to the sole purview of Madison County: "That one law . . . has never been worth 5 cents to anybody and it never will be." In response to protestations that no other state constitution considered game and fish, Espy urged Alabama to "have some originality" in the new constitution by including protection.[84] He failed to persuade his peers and the amendment was tabled.

Wallace was surely disheartened to see the transcript of this day's proceedings published in the *Montgomery Advertiser*.[85] But the convention did include a provision in the final constitution that would ultimately allow his and others' work toward a general game law to gain energy. Section 111 established that "no bill introduced as a general law in either house of the legislature shall be so amended on its passage as to become a special, private, or local law."[86] As T. S. Palmer would write, this amendment saved Wallace's next bill from meeting the same fate as that of 1899.[87] When Wallace revived the push for a general game law a few years later, he would have an alliance of seasoned advocates behind him.

Wallace left the Alabama House of Representatives to run for a state senate seat in 1902. He lost the bid to Robert E. Spragins, who had been a delegate to the 1901 convention.[88] Never one to be humbled by defeat—he was sometimes maligned by the Alabama press for his political ambition—Wallace remained active in Alabama and national politics, traveling as a speaker for the Democratic National Convention in the presidential campaign of 1904 and considering a bid for Alabama House speaker in 1906. He also wrote and published his novel, heralded by Alabama reviewers as "intensely southern" and "the antithesis of George W. Cable," the novelist from New Orleans known for his sober and realistic depiction of southern race relations.

Even with setbacks in his political ambitions, Wallace continued to advocate for a general game and fish code. In 1906, he helped to form the Alabama Game and Fish Protective Association to renew the push for statewide game legislation that he had begun in his first term as a state representative in 1898. As the Protective Association's first president, he became the mouthpiece for the interests of white sportsmen in the state. Four months after the association was founded, Wallace announced in newspapers the intent of the group to push for new laws.[89] He knew well the uphill fight for a statewide bill in a region in which the custom of local lawmaking was paramount. But much had changed in the eight years since his first attempt as a lawmaker. Wallace built upon the growing recognition that game and fish were becoming scarcer in parts of the state. He took every chance he could in the press to lambaste market hunters who shipped quail from Alabama (in 1906, he reported that 500,000 quail were shipped to restaurant markets elsewhere). Wallace now had bird protection organizations, legal precedent, and a shifting awareness about the threat to game animals and wild birds on his side. The Alabama Game and Fish Protective Association hosted T. S. Palmer and T. Gilbert Pearson—both leaders in the national effort to push for protective laws—as well as other speakers at the Alabama legislature when it convened for the 1906–7 session.[90] Wallace rallied sportsmen in the state through letters and speeches (in turn reprinted in the newspapers) to use their influence in politics to see that the Democratic Party included game, fish, and forestry protection in its 1906 platform.⁹¹ Forest protection was necessary, Wallace argued, to stop the destruction of Alabama's woodlands, which provided important habitat for game.⁹² In 1908, he supported the passage of an act to protect forests and then served as secretary on the State Commission of Forestry.⁹³ In these lobbying efforts, Wallace received support from Governor William Jelks, the newspaper editor who had earlier lauded Wallace for his tenderness toward bird protection.⁹⁴ With support from the top of Alabama's government, Wallace took advantage of the shift in political winds created by the 1901 constitution that called for centralization of certain aspects of public life. The Progressive Era, ushered in by Alabama's new, repressive state constitution in 1901, created the backdrop for the bill that Wallace wrote and that was sponsored by the Alabama Game and Fish Protective Association.

National networks like that of the NAAS were critical to the movement for game and fish laws, but southern policymakers understood that any sort of statewide law had to conform to southern power structures. The tension in conforming to a code considered to be far-reaching by conservation advocates and the realities of southern politics emerged clearly in response to Wallace's bill for game and fish regulation, drafted in 1906. He shared the bill with William Dutcher, then president of the NAAS, who in turn shared it with T. S. Palmer of the Bureau of Biological Survey. Both men made extensive changes in pencil to the draft and sent Wallace thirteen pages of comments that went through the code section by section.⁹⁵ Though the draft sent by Palmer and Dutcher does not completely match the law in its final form, it is clear by comparison where Wallace was influenced to make changes and where he was not.

Dutcher and Palmer, for example, had reservations about the dates of open seasons proposed by Wallace. In the original draft, Wallace designated separate open seasons for game birds such as quail and turkeys—in this case, the turkey shooting season extended from November until April. The men cautioned him against a later closing date for turkeys. If hunters were allowed to kill turkeys later in the spring, they might feel inclined to shoot other game birds, like quail, while in the fields and woods.⁹⁶ Turkeys would be nesting before the season closed, they reminded Wallace. In this case, Wallace heeded advice; in the 1907 code, Wallace set the turkey season to open December 1 and close March 1. The quail and dove season ran from November 1 to March 1, and most wildfowl were open for shooting from November 1 to March 1 (except plover and snipe, which weren't protected until May 1).⁹⁷

In some cases, Dutcher and Palmer thought Wallace was going too far. They argued that penalties for violating the law were much too high, counseling

Wallace, "Our experience has been, especially in the South, that Judges and juries will not enforce a very high penalty" (in the final code, many violations were fined at $25; it's unclear if Wallace lowered the figure based on comments).[98] They criticized the structure of the new bureaucracy, arguing that probate judges would resent having to fill hunting licenses; that the game and fish commissioner should be appointed by the governor; and that the commissioner should not make above $2,000 a year, lest the job become a "political plum"—but Wallace changed none of these points (the commissioner would be first appointed by the legislature and then elected every four years) and gave the commissioner a $2,500 salary.[99]

Dutcher and Palmer were unsupportive of any regulation they imagined would cause Alabama legislators or other lobbyists to defeat the bill. Wallace, for example, had included penalties for using a "pump gun," a firearm that would allow for multiple, rapid rounds of fire. "Do not under any circumstances," warned Dutcher and Palmer, "put in those two words, for if you do you will have all of the gun manufacturers in the United States sending down special delegations to Alabama to kill your bill."[100] The final code mentioned nothing of guns, illustrating the power of the manufacturers. Wallace also included laws protecting fish against seining, dynamiting, and other kinds of fishing except for hook-and-line. But Dutcher and Palmer strongly urged Wallace to remove all sections pertaining to fish regulation to avoid political snafus: "There are many men who will take interest in a fish bill who will not take an interest in your game bill and vice versa, and the man who is interested in fish will antagonize your bird bill if you do not do as he wishes about fish."[101] They then decried his inclusion of an anti-pollution statute that would have penalized dumping into rivers and creeks. "Pollution of a river," they argued, "is a matter that has nothing whatever to do with the protection of birds or game."[102] The men's thinking illustrates a narrow schema of species habitat; whereas they did not see a need for protecting flowing water, they did urge Wallace to name all game wardens "forest wardens" to watch for and control fire (a more nuanced ecological understanding of habitat would develop in the decades to come). Wallace kept fishing regulations—and the bill passed with them intact—but he removed the anti-pollution statute. He would continue as commissioner to push a bill that penalized polluters, particularly the coal and timber industries that dumped "coal-wash and saw-dust" in rivers and creeks, but later admitted to a constituent that "the mine operators in the vicinity of Birmingham have fought the measure so vigorously that at each session . . . they have succeeded in defeating it."[103]

In other instances, Palmer and Dutcher thought Wallace had not gone far enough. They worried over Wallace's intention to allow hunting on one's own land without a license or with written permission on another's land but conceded to him that such a provision was probably necessary in the South: "In a great many states a citizen is not allowed to hunt anywhere without a license, but as a concession to the sentiment in the south persons are allowed to hunt on their land without a license."[104] The political and cultural realities of the South tamed Dutcher and Palmer's vision, particularly the expectation of access to hunting lands.

They were especially insistent that Wallace go further in banning certain types of people from hunting. Whereas in speeches Wallace promised control of Black labor through game and fish laws, the final 1907 code—much like the Alabama Constitution of 1901—did not mention race explicitly but kneaded inequality into its statutes in other ways, discussed below. Dutcher and Palmer, however, urged Wallace to consider banning "aliens," or hunters who did not have US citizenship, from procuring a hunting license in the state. They explained,

> In the North, we have a great deal of alien labor such as Italians, Poles, Hungarians, and foreigners of this class who roam about the country shooting all classes of birds whether they are game or non-game. Some of the northern states are taking very drastic measures regarding these people and always class them as non-residents and make them pay a non-resident fee. . . . While you may not have many aliens in Alabama at present, yet you sooner or later will find that they are moving into the State, especially where large public or private improvements demand cheap labor and you might just as well anticipate their arrival and provide against their shooting without procuring a non-resident license.[105]

The comments of Dutcher and Palmer came in the wake of the murder of a Pennsylvania game warden, L. Seely Houk, by Italian immigrants in April 1906.[106] The murder of Houk led to a pitched rhetoric among game and bird protection advocates that immigrant hunting to degenerate behavior and lawlessness. The men were correct that Alabama had a small foreign-born population (.08 percent of the total population in 1900), though the coal and steel industry of the New South had grown Birmingham's immigrant population to 4.3 percent by 1910.[107] Wallace invoked another scapegoated class, African Americans, and did not see the need for the exclusion of "alien" residents as suggested by his northern allies.

The 1907 Alabama Game and Fish Laws and Local Reaction

The Alabama legislature passed Wallace's "Act Relating to the Preservation, Propagation, and Protection of Game, Animals, Wild bird, and Fish" in January and February of 1907.[108] Wallace infused the final code with priorities that befitted the Progressive Era South. In Alabama, these priorities emerged in a few key ways: First, the commission would not be approved unless it was a self-supporting entity. Alabama's state government was not going to spend "public" money to fund this work. Second, it had to appeal to and appease landowning farmers. Third, it had to fit squarely in the state's new political economy, including the effort to control Black movement, labor, and access to land. With these caveats in place, the laws were designed to create a relatively exclusive field for sport, one that was especially accessible to sportsmen, who, from Wallace's perspective and that of many others, were the South's key stewards of wildlife.

Wallace solved the problem of budget by drawing from models elsewhere in the country. He included in the bill a tiered licensing system, monies that went into a game and fish protective fund that supported the department's work. In this aspect he was successful, and in the first year his office generated enough so that it was in essence self-supporting (though it did not, for example, supply warden salaries, a key misfire).[109]

Second, he created a requirement that licensed hunters had to solicit written permission to hunt or fish on another person's property. This was not an unusual provision—earlier countywide laws in the South and game commissions in the North, for example, included caveats like this. For Wallace, the provision was key to eliciting the buy-in of the so-called agrarian class. Farmers, Wallace reminded readers of his first biennial commission report, "are citizens of conservation and discretion." The farmer "[owns] the domain over which hunting is done [and furnishes] the provender on which the State's game subsists, and he should have a right to elect who his guests shall be."[110] By emphasizing the principle of private property and a landowner's sovereign privilege, Wallace argued that farmers were game wardens in their own right, and if the written permission clause was left out of the law, "the farmer would often be discredited in courts by unscrupulous persons" who would lie about receiving verbal permission.[111] He credited the written permission statute with controlling Black hunters, whom he blamed for boundless destruction of wildlife. As soon as he was appointed commissioner in 1907 he crafted a press release that highlighted the point: the written permissions clause would "put out of business each hunting day in Alabama not less than five thousand negroes, who are the greatest game destroyers extant. Proceeding upon the theory that this great black horde will only kill ten birds per day, they will destroy in one year nine million quails and will kill thirty six million before the next legislature can assemble."[112] Wallace evoked the specter of Black hunters to assure readers that the written permission clause was the state's best "labor law" because, he argued, it effectively limited the mobility of Black agricultural workers. Like many sportsmen of the time, Wallace cast Black hunters as one of the bogeymen of conservation. In a short guide he wrote for new game wardens, Wallace reminded the wardens that the laws were meant to "[take] out of the fields and forests the vast black hoard [sic] of negroes that formerly slaughtered game in many sections of the state."[113] No veils hid the rhetoric regarding intent of the new code. Wallace was passionately committed to both white supremacy and conservation, a blend of loyalties that encompassed changing ideas about human access and rights to the natural world and provided yet another frame through which racialized hierarchies took shape.

The laws excluded Black hunters and pothunters in other ways, according to Wallace. Local licenses cost one dollar, though one could hunt one's own land without a license. Tenant farmers could hunt without a license on the property they farmed with the landowner's permission, which buttressed the powers of private landowners. Some landowners transferred that right seasonally to tenants, Black and white. But in Wallace's estimation, the one-dollar fee to hunt elsewhere in a locality was just pricey enough to be out of reach for poor Black and white farmers, and the provision for tenant farmers meant that they would be relegated to the lands upon which they were laboring. He bragged to an admirer of the law that of all those licensed to hunt by 1910, 98 percent were white.[114] In addition, by outlawing formerly customary ways of capturing food—like the use of fish traps, which were a more efficient way to fish—the laws targeted poor people, including women, as pothunters who aimed not for sport but sustenance. Wallace assumed that these arguments, especially those that claimed racial control, would make conservation laws more palatable to white rural Alabamians across the state.

Alabama's new code, and those adopted by other southern states thereafter, vested ownership of wildlife in the state. The state ownership doctrine was upheld in the Supreme Court's *Geer v. Connecticut* decision of 1896, a case that centered on a state's right to outlaw the shipment of legally acquired game across state lines.[115] The court ruled that the state could claim ownership of wild game insofar as it held game in trust for the people as their sovereign representative. The state thus had the authority to extend police power to "secure [game's] beneficial use in the future to the citizens."[116] The court drew from the legal treatises of English jurist William Blackstone to trace common ownership of "wild and untamable" animals; individuals had only a qualified or transient, not permanent, property right in game in the liberty to hunt and kill.[117] Instead, the public held ownership in common. John Wallace reassured readers in his first report as game and fish commissioner that the state "occupies the attitude of guardian and custodian of the people's welfare" and would "restrain the hands of the wanton and reckless, whose vandalism would annihilate every visible thing of fin, fur or feather, to gratify their savage instincts."[118] The state ownership doctrine, which established a common interest in game and fish, did not infringe upon the larger region's shift to a closed range. As one guide to game and fish law argued, "No other person has a right to go on [the landowner's] premises, without permission, to take game. Subject to regulations imposed by the State the owner of the land has a right to control the game on his lands." Representative of a qualified interest, the game found on private property was the right of the landowner to access and use.

The 1907 Alabama code was thus comprehensive for its time: it established the state's ownership of wildlife; created standard seasons for game animals; protected certain nongame birds; banned particular modes of hunting and fishing; and established a warden system, the state's police power in enforcing the new laws. It was soon heralded, by Wallace and others, as a law worthy of adoption in other southern states. An editor for the *Charleston News and Courier* observed that "if so much could be accomplished and so quickly in Alabama, it seems similar results might be hoped for in South Carolina if a John H. Wallace were available to draft a statute and enforce it after its enactment."[119] The president of NAAS, William Dutcher, announced that the Alabama law was "the most advanced and drastic game law now in the country."[120] Wallace himself did not shy from self-congratulation; he called his creation "the most perfect statute on the continent for the preservation and protection of game and fish."[121] He borrowed from the northern states, including the licensing structure that funded his department, the permission clause that appeased landowners, and the Model Law that protected nongame birds.

Wallace hailed the new laws as being "directly beneficial to the common masses" of Alabama. Because they protected game and fish "near at hand," the laws, he argued, protected resources against the "money-king." He reassured readers of his first report that "the idea that game laws are statutes made for the benefit of the rich is an exploded theory."[122] The defensiveness there is telling, and, despite his race-baiting rhetoric noted above, responses from ordinary Alabamians show that not everyone was convinced of the value of the new laws.

Alabamians were confused and sometimes angered by the laws, and letters poured into Wallace's office asking for copies of the laws and clarification about their purview. These letters are revealing about the ways that the laws impacted what had been traditional hunting and fishing practice. J. M. Boshart wrote from Woodville, Alabama, to inquire about continuing the tradition of a Christmas squirrel hunt: "We have never bin in any trouble in court and dont want to get in any but we have always hunted with one another of a Christmas (which is about all we hunt) and want too this Christmas if we can it would seem verry hard for us to pay three dollars $3.00 for just what we hunt we own most of the land and what we dont those [that] does will give us permits now."[123] The license requirement that seemed "verry hard" to Boshart may not have applied to him; landowners did not have to buy a license to hunt on their own lands. His question, however, speaks to the general confusion created by the new laws. Wallace responded diligently to inquiries, which represented a variety of questions and concerns:

"Can we fish in the Ala[bama] River with fish baskets or not. Please let me hear from you."[124] (The answer: no.)

"Please inform me if seining minnows in running branches or streams is a violation of the law."[125] (No, as long as he used a "minnow seine" under four feet wide and twelve feet high, and only to be used for catching minnows as bait.)[126]

"Wish to inquire whether you had game laws so amended that you could permit me to ship more than ten pairs of 'Bob Whites.'"[127] (No.)

"I have been informed that the Supreme Court of the State has *held* the law unconstitutional prohibiting seining so far as it relates to navigable streams. Pleas inform me."[128] (Wrong: "You are advised that the Supreme Court has not nor is there any probability of its declaring unconstitutional the law which prohibits seining in navigable streams.")[129]

In addition to questions, Wallace received numerous requests for the new game laws, which were published as a small pamphlet, and solicitation from probate judges for license blanks. Wallace and his secretary responded in kind. The volume of correspondence in the first several years of the commission reveals a population adjusting to a new regime of hunting and fishing regulation.

Unsurprisingly, people complained about the laws. At least a few probate judges were displeased with the added workload created by the new laws (probate judges sold licenses, reported monthly sales to Wallace, and, in some counties, impaneled jurors to hear violations in court).[130] Judge Emmett Crook of Calhoun County wrote to Wallace that he was generally happy with the laws with the exception of his role in enforcing them: "You know the legislature considers the Probate Court dumping ground for all laws where there is no pay, and we are expected to be enthused, and employ extra labor at our own expense, but you and I can't help this and we must carry out the law just the same as if we were being paid. I shall see that the law is obeyed in this county so far as my authority extends."[131]

Judicial burden was one kind of complaint, but a more serious genre came from Alabamians whose livelihoods were curtailed by the new laws. John Hughston, a lawyer friend of Wallace's from Florence, wrote to him about the toll that the laws took on individual economy. He warned Wallace that the "law prohibiting fish traps in rivers is . . . rendering the entire game and fish laws unpopular." Reminding Wallace of his local connection, Hughston urged him to "recall that almost since the settlement of this country, fish traps have been built, operated, and sold on the Shoals, like property." Arguing for the economic importance of fishing, he told Wallace of a man who owned "about $1,500 worth of traps, which represents practically everything he owns; and is his only support for himself and family."[132] Wallace conceded that he had initially thought of leaving out the section of the code that prohibited traps in navigable waters, but he was overridden by Alabama's Code Commission. He shot back to Hughston, too, that "only those who actually run traps are in favor of them," pointing out that most Alabamians opposed the "wholesale destruction of fish."[133] Another writer, a disabled Confederate veteran from Lincoln, wrote Wallace seeking a permit to fish with nets. E. B. Tuck had been "wounded four times" in the war and, at sixty-seven, eked a living on a small farm and fished with nets as a way to supplement income.[134] Wallace wrote back that "I deplore the fact that, under the law, I have no right to grant permits to anyone to use nets . . . in any stream of the State."[135] New restrictions meant hardship for some Alabamians, but, in his responses, Wallace stood fast in his belief that most saw benefit in the laws.

Unfortunately, the wardens, once appointed and on duty, sometimes reported differently. Wardens were Wallace's eyes and ears and in letters to him and in monthly reports (submitted on a standardized form) they related arrests, convictions, observations of animal life, and attitudes of the people. The warden from Elmore County, A. H. Chrietzberg, warned Wallace in 1907 that "there is so much dissatisfaction [about the new laws] in this county among the farmers." Such a statement no doubt caught Wallace's attention; he had repeatedly sold the laws as the friend of the landowning farmer in his appeals. Chrietzberg did not suggest the reason for the unpopularity, only that he felt that "when [farmers] thoroughly understand the law, they will approve it."[136]

Another measure of response to the laws can be found in complaints that they were not being enforced. Wardens wrote to Wallace about public response, and the public wrote to Wallace about wardens and their relative commitment to enforcement. The wardens were local men who, like the foresters in historian Karl Jacoby's study of game laws in the turn-of-the-century Adirondacks, were pulled between allegiance to the state and to local pressure to ignore the laws.[137] In Mobile County, the warden was reported to Wallace in 1908 for violating the law.[138] J. B. Stickney wrote to Wallace in 1910 to tell him the game laws in Hale County were "a farce," as "most people have ceased to buy licenses and very few even get permits [to hunt on another's land]." Stickney blamed the warden who "pays no attention to his job."[139] In 1912, as Wallace sought reelection for his position as commissioner, a supporter wrote that the game laws were good and "the only thing necessary is to enforce them."[140] One warden, W. D. Cuthbert, defended himself and fellow wardens by pointing out to Wallace the serious structural deficiencies in the role. Asking a warden, even with the help of several deputy wardens, to cover an entire county (like Mobile County, where Cuthbert was based) was "a monstrous absurdity," and "add this to the fact that he is supposed to do this at his own expense and without adequate remuneration!" Cuthbert warned Wallace that "there can be no improvement [in enforcement] unless the wardens should be paid a fair monthly salary and traveling expense money."[141] Wallace and his successor, I. T. Quinn, agreed, and wardens would receive salaries after 1922.[142]

Regular pay could not solve a larger problem of public resistance to the laws. As historian Richard W. Judd argues in his study of conservation in northern New England, "game laws violated rural prescriptions for egalitarian access" to game and fish.[143] Many Alabamians initially did not comply—they broke the laws or refused to identify those who did. Cuthbert noted in his report to Wallace that without local people ready to identify violators of the law, he could not do his job effectively. "No one seems willing," he told Wallace, "to lose time by bringing offenders to court or willing to incur their animosity."[144] Another warden from Perry County wrote to Wallace to resign (to run for office) and noted the reluctance of justices of the peace to help enforce the law; the JPs were simply not willing to "bind neighbors and friends over."[145] A concerned supporter from Marion County in west Alabama wrote to report that "the law is not verry popular here in some places and there cannot be a grand jury drawn that will notice any testimony in regard to the game law."

Grand juries just would not indict, the writer told Wallace. Local elected officials, too, shied away from public support of the law "as they think there is more people opposed to the law than there is for it."[146] In his response to this letter and others like it, Wallace urged the writer to find a suitable man to nominate as warden and reminded whistleblowers that his hands were tied without "the co-operation of our law-abiding citizens."[147]

The reality of nonenforcement is borne out in conviction numbers, which Wallace and his predecessors included in biennial and quadrennial department reports. In the course of Wallace's tenure as commissioner (1907–22), the agency averaged roughly 149 convictions per year. Some years convictions were especially low; in 1917 and 1918, for example, county courts convicted only 30 people, likely due to US involvement in World War I and the onset of the flu epidemic. These numbers, pointed out I. T. Quinn, Wallace's successor, "do not take into consideration cases brought into court, but lost through technicalities or through the hostility of the neighborhood towards the enforcement of the law." Nonetheless, convictions of game and fish laws were a tiny fraction of total convictions statewide. During Wallace's tenure, county courts convicted 74,047 people of a range of crimes; the 2,663 game law violations brought to conviction over the same period make up 0.04 percent of the statewide total.[148] Though Wallace continually maintained the success of his agency in his reports and in letters to supporters, enforcement was inconsistent and undermined by popular sentiment in the first years of the new laws.

The code, however, withstood challenges in the court. The first case to travel to the Supreme Court of Alabama struck at the constitutionality of the state ownership doctrine. The challenge emerged after Bibb County warden C. L. Cleveland arrested brothers John and Tom Hyde and their friend Andrew Reach in early 1908 for violating the written permission clause—that is, the men were trespassing in order to hunt.[149] The Hydes lived in Bibb County, southwest of Birmingham, and worked as coal miners near Blocton, Alabama.[150] They were not landowners, and under the new laws they would have to purchase a county hunting license and ask for permission to hunt on the property of others. They were convicted and each fined ten dollars but appealed their case, which was heard by the state supreme court in April 1908.[151] The lawyers of the men argued that the arrest warrant "fails to allege that the hunting was of some birds or animals protected by the game law" and that section 44 of the code, which forbade hunting on another's land without permission, was outside of the purview of the state in its use of police power and therefore unconstitutional.[152] Justice N. D. Denson upheld the conviction, citing the *Geer* case: "Speaking generally . . . it may be said that the right of the State, in the exercise of police power, to make regulations for the preservation of game and fish ... is recognized not only in the common law of England but by the decisions of the courts of last resort in many of the States, as well as by the Supreme Court of the United States."[153] One of the central tenets in Wallace's code thus remained unadulterated.

Indeed, the centrality of the written permission clause becomes clear in successful convictions of game violations across the state. During Wallace's tenure, hunting on another person's land without permission made up 32 percent of all such convictions. In five of those years, trespassing violations made up close to, exactly, or just above 50 percent of convictions for the year (see table 2.1). Hunting without a license proved the second largest category of infraction after trespassing. Trespassers were perhaps easier to catch, given that property owners had interest in reporting the crime, and easier to convict, as a local grand jury or judge may have been more sympathetic to penalize the violation of private property rights embedded in this part of the game and fish code. Given its prominence in catching violators of the new game and fish laws, Wallace had been correct that the written permission clause was a key feature of them; he saw it as a rallying point for farming landowners. Landowners clearly benefited from the new code, and the written permission clause fit squarely into a region in which laws were shifting to close the range and in which landowners were increasingly putting up fences and posting lands.

Any racial disparity in conviction of the new laws is less clear. Despite bragging about the laws' success in keeping Black tenant farmers out of the woods and fields, Wallace did not report convictions by race. Yet warden reports show that when Black men and women were arrested for violating the laws, penalties could be heavier. In 1909, warden L. P. Hutchinson arrested a Black man accused of shooting bats near Enterprise, in south Alabama. The man pleaded guilty and was convicted, though after the hearing he employed a lawyer to appeal the case. The lawyer argued that because the man did not actually kill a bat, he should not be convicted under the law.[154] Wallace wrote back to Hutchinson declaring that the lawyer "had no right at this time to reopen the case" and that Hutchinson should "proceed at once to collect the fine or to have the county sentence the negro to hard labor."[155] The records do not reveal whites being threatened with the same fate of hard labor, which was in keeping with patterns of Alabama's carceral system in the early twentieth century, when Black men and women made up "95 percent of county prisoners and 90 percent of state prisoners."[156] Wallace reminded constituents in a reelection circular of 1912 that, under his watch, "the great army

Hunting convictions in Alabama, 1907–1922

Dates reported*	Hunting without written permission	Hunting without a license	Total convictions
Feb. 27–Dec. 31, 1907	81	26	176
Jan. 1–Sept. 29, 1908	36	26	109
Sept. 30–Dec. 31, 1908	41	15	78
Calendar year 1909	90	30	182
Calendar year 1910	27	12	70
Calendar year 1911	54	45	175
Jan. 1–Sept. 29, 1912	51	41	151
Sept. 30, 1912–Sept. 30, 1913	112	75	351
1913–14	25	22	121
1914–15	57	26	152
1915–16	79	19	146
1916–17	45	16	99
1917–18	15	6	30
1918–19	31	40	118
1919–20	35	35	156
1920–21	61	101	304
1921–22	20	92	245
Total	860	627	2,663

Sources: The Alabama Department of Game and Fish (later the Department of Conservation) tabulated data from convictions and reported them in biennial and quadrennial reports, 1907–22. Wallace, *First Biennial Report*, 65–66; Wallace, *Second and Third Biennial Report*, 123, 129, 135–36, 142; Wallace, *Fourth Biennial Report*, 167, 173; Quinn, *First Quadrennial Report*, 63, 66, 70, 73.

*Wallace sometimes reported convictions by calendar year and later, after 1912, by fiscal year, which started on September 30.

of pot-hunters and negroes that at one time patrolled the State, in quest of game, has practically been disbanded."[157]

Wallace's Work beyond Alabama

Soon after the passage of the statewide game and fish laws, Wallace began to consult with other states; he often traveled to speak in front of the legislative bodies of southern states and closely advised sportsmen and interested policymakers on how to organize allies and harness political will for the passage of statewide laws. In 1912, he boasted to one supporter that the laws he crafted for Alabama had "been copied by twelve states since their passage."[158]

Despite his boast, and the model provided by Alabama, the path forward in other southern states was not immediate—though the passage of Wallace's laws did unleash the energy of southern conservation advocates. He immediately turned his attention to neighboring Georgia, after reporting to William Dutcher that "I have been receiving large number of letters from statesmen and game protectionist[s] of Georgia who have sought my opinion relative to some legislation which they contemplate for their state." Wallace wrote to representative S. H. Striplin, encouraging Striplin to invite him to consult: "When your bill shall have been introduced, have a joint legislation passed inviting me to address a joint session of the House and Senate on subjects of game, fish and forestry protective legislation." He connected Striplin to Frank I. Stone, a business owner in Atlanta who pushed for a general game and fish law by "promulgating educational propaganda" and who was in touch with Wallace during the 1908 push for a bill.[159] Stone, Striplin, and others indeed welcomed Wallace for a visit to the legislature, a trip supported financially by Audubon leaders Dutcher and T. Gilbert Pearson. After the visit, Wallace reported to Dutcher with supreme confidence that the bill would pass and stressed his own influence: "There is no question about this bill being passed at this session. It is a splendid one and an exact copy of the Alabama law. . . . I never saw such a wave of enthusiasm as there is in Georgia on the subject of better bird and game legislation. Never in my life have I ever received such an ovation as was accorded me in Georgia. The gallery was packed with game law advocates when I spoke and the press has taken up the fight and the matter is being pushed in every possible way."[160]

The bill failed in 1908 by four votes. In an exchange with Wallace, Pearson lamented that "our bill" did not pass, signaling the joint effort in promoting legislation so closely aligned with Alabama's law. Echoing the advice he received and ignored from Dutcher and Palmer, Wallace argued that, when the legislature next met, the bill's sponsors should "separate the fish proposition from the game provision, because there are many who will object to some parts of a combined law, but would favor a bill designed for a single purpose."[161] Wallace's supposition, which echoed Dutcher's and Palmer's suggestion for Alabama's bill, might have been based on observations while in the Georgia state house. Georgia sportsmen were not entirely convinced that Alabama's commission served as the best model for adoption.

There was disagreement, too, in the provision, borrowed from Alabama, that required landowner permission. In 1909, supporters of game protection planned to submit the bill once again. Frank Stone, Wallace's ears on the ground, wrote that requiring written permission was simply too great a burden on urban hunters. In his reasoning, farmers would be better protected under a different code:

> I do not object to the requirement of a written permission of the farmer, but think it should be in a separate act and not incorporated in the Game Law. This feature will work a very great hardship on many a worthy sportsman, especially from the cities. It protects hunters in small towns and villages to the exclusion of a great many good people, who can only get off for a day at the time to indulge in this sport. . . . [Charles] Davis's idea is that it will more thoroughly protect the game and draw a stronger support from the farmers. Perhaps, it will, but a separate act under the Trespass Law would have practically the same effect.[162]

In Stone's logic, strengthening trespass laws would be more effective in protecting landowner rights than the hunting law, though this argument was self-serving for him, a city-dwelling sportsman. And, Georgia already had a law, passed in 1895 and extended in 1903, that forbade hunting and fishing on land that was posted in two places, whether it was fenced or not (though the burden was on the landowner to register his name and land boundaries with the county ordinary).[163]

The disagreement illustrates the ways in which Wallace's "agricultural class" was on the minds of advocates. Wallace, in an earlier letter to Stone, held firm on the mandate:

> Permit me to insist that the written permission feature will do more towards preserving your game than any other single provision. We have found that this clause has won the hearts of the agricultural class in this State, who are generally hostile to game laws, regarding statutes of this character as being in the nature an infringement on their personal

rights and an abrogation of their individual liberties. By all means, insist that the written permission feature be included in your bill. It may seem to appear to be a hardship on sportsmen residing in large cities, but this can be easily overcome by the securing of written permission during the non-shooting season, which will hold good until revoked.[164]

Wallace was sure of the need for the measure to win over Georgia's landowning farmers who threatened to stop the law in the wake of losing "individual liberties"; we'll see in the next chapter that he was correct about this point of resistance to the law by Georgia farmers.

When the Georgia game protection bill finally passed in 1911, the landowner permission clause was in place, though watered down. The law did not require written permission of the landowner, just that evidence that permission was granted in some form.[165] In 1912, a year later, a Georgia appeals court ruled the law would allow the pursuit of prey to continue onto another's property, as long as the chase began on land on which the hunter was allowed.[166]

The Georgia law hewed closely to Alabama's in other ways. It set up the same licensing structure—one dollar for county hunters, three dollars for state coverage, and fifteen dollars for out-of-state hunters—and a game protection fund that would support the work of the new game and fish commission. The law allowed Georgians to hunt in their own militia district without license and required tenant farmers to seek permission of the landowner. It banned the sale and shipment of game and established uniform closed seasons for game. Most importantly, it established an enforcement regime—a game and fish commissioner, appointed by the governor (Alabama's was an elected position), who had power to designate county wardens. Georgia was more generous in its compensation of wardens; like Alabama, it did not give a salary but offered partial fees from convictions and from the sale of licenses (the latter was not the case under Wallace). After a decade of work in Georgia—speechifying across the state, circulating educational materials, and sending Audubon "agents," including Wallace, to advocate on the law's behalf—T. Gilbert Pearson celebrated that "the passage of the Georgia game law is the longest step forward in bird protection which has been taken in the southern states in many years, and an immense amount of good must result."[167] For Pearson and Wallace, songbird and game protection were linked, and the joint campaign made the push for the statewide law more successful.

If Alabama and Georgia were (faux) feathers in the caps of Wallace and Pearson, Mississippi would prove an elusive catch. As Frank B. Vinson noted in his unpublished study of conservation in the South, "A sharp contrast existed between the wildlife legislation in Alabama and the lack of advancement in this field in Mississippi."[168] Chapter 4 recounts the 1930s creation of the Mississippi State Game and Fish Commission—the last southern state to adopt such a regulatory code. Wallace spent the second decade of the twentieth century lobbying for its passage.

He also, in 1913, announced his campaign for the 1914 gubernatorial election. Wallace's platform reflected his southern Progressive commitments to white supremacy and natural resource protection. For example, he declared openly his support for a more robust education for white children, and white children only—he even gave a stump speech to northern benefactors of Booker T. Washington's Tuskegee Institute lamenting the neglect of "mountain children" who were "free of mixed blood" and in need of public education.[169] He argued for railroad regulation, more equitable credit standards for farmers, curtailment of industrial child labor, and more transparent operation of government agencies (and that virtue he could claim as a skilled manager of the Department of Game and Fish). He also argued for an expanded conservation regime in Alabama's government, including a new Public Utilities and Conservation Commission that would supervise "all public utilities and natural rights of the state, belonging to the people in their sovereign capacity." In the same vein, he argued for state control of hydroelectric plants, as "no private individual or corporation has the right to monopolize water-power," which "belonged to the race."[170] Presciently, he foresaw the limits of coal in powering Alabama homes and predicted a day when coal was depleted and "the people will be driven to the necessity of depending on electricity to furnish them with heat and light."[171] The future dominance of and dependence on electric power required, in his argument, ownership of electric production by the state. Finally, in this bid for office and in his continued role as game commissioner, he urged the creation of a state-based commons in the form of animal refuges. Specially protected habitat would be the place of "last stand for birds and game of this country." Pointing to the growing number of national parks in the West, Wallace urged that "all government lands in Alabama be declared Federal forest reserves and game refuges."[172] Reflecting on these policy commitments to the "purest strain of pioneer Americans" and conservation, the *Richmond (VA) Journal* celebrated that Wallace was "as deeply in earnest of the saving of this breed of American citizenship as . . . game protection."[173] Wallace's message, so rooted in an idyllic racial past, blended elements of conservative ideology and forward-thinking action, but it did not convince Alabamians, who elected fellow Democrat Charles Henderson.

In the midst of his campaign and his continued work to spread a conservation message to neighboring states, Wallace turned his attention to national, and international, matters concerning bird protection, which joined his energy more closely with federal efforts. As reflected in Wallace's argument for game refuges, Deep South advocates for game and fish protection embraced federal support and intervention in the cause of conservation. Beyond relying upon and consulting with federal agencies like the Bureau of Biological Survey, Wallace became a champion for increased federal regulation, going on in the 1910s to take a larger role in service to its implementation.

By 1913, Wallace served on the advisory committee of the American Game Protective Association, along with Theodore Roosevelt, Henry Ford, Henry L. Stimson, W. A. Wadsworth (the president of the Boone and Crockett Club), and George P. McLean and John W. Weeks (authors of the Weeks–McLean bill, described below).[174] The association called upon his service for continued advocacy of state game laws—he spoke to the Virginia legislature in 1914 to support the Hart–White bill working its way through legislation, a "comprehensive protective measure" that ultimately did not pass.[175] The association publicized Wallace's work, noting that he "fully sustained his reputation as a speaker on wild life conservation."[176] He was heralded (and not only by himself) for bringing uniform game code to Alabama and took greater prominence in national organizations.

Wallace lent his voice to a matter that seemed increasingly urgent to conservation supporters, that of protecting migratory birds. Ornithologist and bird protection groups had, since the 1883 founding of the American Ornithologists' Union, devoted themselves to bird migration study and brought an increasingly hemispheric perspective to the issue. That work was continued in the early twentieth century through its second decade by the Bureau of Biological Survey.[177] The National Association of Audubon Societies, which had supported Wallace and other southern states in creating protective laws, had always been keenly interested in southern Gulf states as the wintering places for migratory birds and had early employed wardens to protect vulnerable rookeries and designated bird refuges. But by the early twentieth century, sportsmen's groups and bird protection advocates were lamenting the variations in (or complete lack of) state law regulating the shooting of migratory birds. One sportsmen's group in Nebraska argued, "We believe such restrictions [on shooting migratory ducks] by the central and northern states unfair, inasmuch as our neighbors in the southern states are permitted to shoot until the birds begin their northern migration." The group called for protection against the "wholesale destruction and threatened extermination of many valuable species of said game birds."[178] These sportsmen in Nebraska were part of a national turn toward attention to vulnerable bird species, and laments about declining birds were coupled with calls for federal action.[179] Sportsmen were joined by nationally renowned conservationists, including William T. Hornaday and Theodore Roosevelt, and major conservation organizations. According to historian Andrea L. Smalley and biologist Henry M. Reeves, "National protections were necessary, many argued, because birds' biological migrations when alive and economic mobility when commodified had proved impossible to contain within the jurisdictional control of individual states."[180] Or, as John Wallace argued, "Birds know no State lines, and, so far as the preservation and protection of those that belong to the migratory family is concerned, it is a national and not a state question."[181] Wallace stood firm throughout the 1910s for migratory protection legislation. In 1904, George Shiras III of Pennsylvania introduced "A Bill to Protect Migratory Game Birds of the United States," not so much to push its passage, as he reflected later, but "to have the entire country carefully consider the same before asking action."[182] The bill authorized the Department of Agriculture, which housed the Bureau of Biological Study, to assign and enforce closed seasons for migratory birds across the country.[183] In 1913, John W. Weeks, a congressman from Massachusetts, and George P. McLean, senator from Connecticut, reintroduced a version of the bill, this time including protection for songbirds and "the addition of migratory insectivorous birds."[184] The act passed, and birds, but not other game, came under federal jurisdiction.

The Weeks–McLean bill superseded the state ownership doctrine of wildlife, a provision that drew legal precedent from the 1896 *Geer* decision.[185] Wallace defended the Weeks–McClean bill in press statements and in department bulletins, as he continued to legitimize game and fish laws among everyday Alabamians. He embraced the federal law as an appointee by the Department of Agriculture on an advisory committee "to cooperate with the Bureau of Biological Survey in fixing regulations for the closed seasons."[186] For the South, the new bill prohibited springtime shooting, when birds were overwintering, and set other kill regulations by species. Wallace took to the newspapers to explain to Alabamians the conflict between national and state law—whereas the law previously set the season for waterfowl ("swans, geese, brant, rails, duck, coots, mudhens, and shorebirds") opening September 1 and closing March 15, federal law changed the season for most waterfowl to open November 1 and close February 1 and, for woodcocks, to November 1 through January 1. He reminded readers that the law forbade any shooting of songbirds and "insectivorous" birds. He stressed finally the supremacy of federal law: "In all cases where a conflict occurs between the federal and state statutes, the federal statute takes precedence, and therefore governs."[187]

The arguments of Wallace and other advocates of federal migratory law did not sway the minds of some hunters. Opposition to the law, particularly by recreational hunters now prohibited from spring shooting, began in the Midwest, with hunters from Kansas and Missouri forming the Interstate Sportsman's Protective Association—western Missouri "border ruffians," as William T. Hornaday would call them in a letter to Wallace.[188] Hunters quickly defied the law and ended up in the federal court system. Two back-to-back cases in federal district courts in Arkansas and Kansas City, US v. Shauver (1914) and US v. McCullagh (1915), respectively, declared the law unconstitutional, both citing Geer v. Connecticut.[189] These cases, and the refusal of the US Supreme Court to hear the Shauver case, allowed hunters to declare that the Weeks–McLean bill was null and void.

Supporters of the federal law, including a characteristically committed Wallace, turned to other options to cement uniform protection of migratory birds. In 1913, Wallace began working with Senator John Bankhead Jr. of Alabama to lobby for US treaties with those countries in the migratory fly zone in order to protect the birds. In a 1919 letter to the New York Sun outlining his work in this regard, Wallace recounted that in April of 1913, he, Bankhead, and John B. Burnham, president of the American Game Protective Association, had an audience with President Woodrow Wilson to advocate for an international treaty for migratory birds. Wilson, Wallace remembered, "gave me a most attentive hearing and manifested the keenest possible interest in the conservation of the migratory wild life in the Western Hemisphere" and requested Wallace summarize his views in a memorandum, which he did. The next day, the group met with Secretary of State William Jennings Bryan to repeat the message. Wallace credited this work with catalyzing negotiations for a migratory bird treaty between the United States and Great Britain, though the work only quickened with the 1916 Convention on the Protection of Migratory Birds between the United States, Canada, and Great Britain.[190]

Throughout the 1910s, Wallace worked for international treaties that would, in his mind and that of many supporters, settle the question of the constitutionality of US jurisdiction over migratory birds. The advocacy of Wallace and supporters, with action from a sympathetic Congress and executive branch, resulted in the 1918 Migratory Bird Treaty Act (MBTA).[191] The act and subsequent regulations were "more comprehensive" than the Weeks–McLean bill, setting prohibitions against any sale of migratory birds (thereby superseding the Lacey Act's provisions); naming for protection 537 species of bird; and setting uniform closed seasons (by region), bag limits, and regulations on shipment of birds.[192] Like the earlier Weeks–McLean bill, the act's regulations were overseen by the Bureau of Biological Survey and implemented by federal game wardens; the bureau appointed an advisory committee to inform regulations that included John Wallace.

The act's passage did little to calm opposition, once again erupting from midwestern states.[193] Wallace was keenly sensitive to attacks of anti-treaty sportsmen and, in 1919, began to float the possibility of creating a "friendly" test case that was sure to go to the Supreme Court and be decided in favor of the constitutionality of the MBTA. He sought advice from trusted and renowned advocates such as John B. Burnham and William T. Hornaday. Hornaday in particular wrote a lengthy response that was resoundingly in disfavor of the idea. In the first place, he argued, while he, Wallace, and others urged passage of the MBTA, "we never at any time intimated to Congress, or to the President, that there might be any doubt of question as to the constitutionality of the things we urged should be done!" Refusing to countenance any argument against the constitutionality of the act, Hornaday went on, "I am opposed to the starting by anyone, and least of all by a distinguished conservationist like yourself, of even a friendly suit to test the *alleged* questions which our enemies may claim exist regarding the constitutionality of our law."[194] After cautiously seeking other opinions, that test case never came to pass—Wallace, however, boasted about Alabama's record in prosecuting violators of the act, writing to the editor of *American Field* magazine that he was "sure Alabama holds record for conviction under this act."[195] True to his fashion, John Wallace pursued his principles with zeal.

After the passage of the MBTA, Wallace sought an extension to the treaty that would include South America. To that end, and as part of his work on the Bureau of Biological Survey's advisory committee, he corresponded with multiple US consulates in the Caribbean and in Central and South America to collect research on bird migration in the Southern Hemisphere.[196] Again, Senator John Bankhead Jr. supported his work.[197] Wallace's untimely death in 1922 interrupted this progress. He died after catching pneumonia doing what he loved—duck hunting. Alabama papers reported that he made a trip to Louisiana and returned January 8, after the federal closed season on waterfowl would have kicked in, only to succumb two weeks later.[198] Many mourned his death across the state, while his work moved forward under a new commissioner, I. T. Quinn. Quinn carried the flag of Wallace in efforts to support game laws in Mississippi. He worked on the national stage as well; he served on the MBTA Advisory Board from 1922 to 1931 and again in 1934.[199]

By 1922, the year of Wallace's death, almost all southern states (including border states) had some form of statewide body that regulated hunting and fishing, a development that Wallace partially credited to his own work in Alabama and then in surrounding states. Wallace had indeed achieved the feat of passing an unpopular measure with the help of national conservation advocates by virtue of his own ability to cast the legislation within the bounds of southern politics. He helmed a commission for fifteen years and, in that time, did not retreat in his rhetorical attack of Black and economically marginal hunters and celebration of how the Alabama laws curtailed Black mobility. At the same time, he cemented Alabama's role as a leading southern state in a growing national conservation movement, for which he found common ground in both its penchant for exclusion and its vision and dedication for wildlife protection. He presaged later arguments for clean water and protected habitat, all while hewing to and abetting a changing property structure wherein access to private property (through ownership or leasing) became a prime access to hunting grounds, a theme explored when we turn to Georgia. Consolidation of the state in the Progressive Era South, in its management of natural resources, in this case, was both central to and extended by Wallace's authorship of Alabama's 1907 game and fish laws.

3 Hunting Land, Hunting Labor: Charlie Young and the Growth of the Georgia Winter Hunting Colony

In 1964, Charlie Young (1883–1970) looked back at late nineteenth-century Thomasville, Georgia, and recalled a hometown where residents "just stood looking" as the neighboring communities of Moultrie and Cairo profited from producing cane syrup and turpentine. Thomasville, he recalled, "moved very slow . . . and you could hear white people talking" about the lack of growth in the town.[1] Things started to change in Thomasville, however, in 1893. Around that time, the Piney Woods hotel and Mitchell House hotel, both built in the 1880s to serve Thomasville's growing northern tourist population, "started paying of [and] this old town got a start."[2] To Young, northern tourists, including those who began to visit for seasonal hunting, drove the town's eventual prosperity in the postwar South: "The Yankies as they was called in those days started to come to this little town in fack they did great things for this town that will never die."[3]

As a boy, Young worked as a golf caddy for these tourists and later shaped a career as a wagon driver, dog handler, and landscaper for wealthy northern hunters who came seasonally to Thomasville and the Red Hills region, which stretched from Thomasville to Tallahassee, Florida. He was in a good position to judge the impact of the hunting colony on the fabric of the town. An apt observer, Young was right in his assessment—Thomasville, Georgia, and the surrounding region prospered as a destination for well-to-do northerners. Many areas in the South, in fact, encouraged a regional tourist industry that developed after the Civil War. By the late nineteenth century, coastal Georgia and South Carolina, mountainous Western North Carolina, and parts throughout Florida hosted hundreds of sportsmen and their families from the North and Midwest each season.[4] Northern hunters and their families returned annually in the winter months, first staying in Thomasville's hotels and boardinghouses but eventually purchasing or renting private hunting estates in the region.

Young, an African American hunter and dog trainer, knew this world of hunting plantations intimately and in this chapter serves as our guide. Young, in fact, set out to shape the historical record through his memories of the Red Hills. His "Reminiscences of Charlie Young for Bill Rogers," a forty-four-page handwritten and phonetically spelled account, had at some point after its authorship been quietly filed away at the Thomas County Historical Society (now the Thomasville History Center).[5] Young finished his piece in 1964, when William Warren Rogers (1929–2017) was a history professor at Florida State University and working on his first volume of Thomas County history.[6] Along with newspaper clippings, census data, and archival materials, local people aided Rogers's endeavor by offering valuable insight into the history of the community. Although Rogers did not conduct formal oral histories, locals informed his "official" history throughout its pages. Likely solicited by Elisabeth "Pansy" Poe, a descendant of the wealthy Hanna family who came to the Red Hills in the late nineteenth century, Charlie Young wrote to offer Rogers this kind of local information.[7] Poe commissioned Rogers's work as part of her support of the mission of the Thomas County Historical Society, where, in the 1960s, Young's second wife worked as a custodian. Rogers, however, did not draw from Charlie Young's work in his book—it is unclear whether he ever received it.[8] Yet Young had written with an audience of history readers in mind and now helps us to understand intimately the transformation of hunting in a modernizing South. If we take cues from Young's sense of historical change, we observe deepening relationships among transregional sportsmen and the ramifications of those relationships on land consolidation and access, hunting practice, and game and fish laws. His memories describe a culture built to serve the priorities of sportsmen at the turn of the twentieth century and the ways that a growing interest in southern hunting—even the creation of a sporting tourism—shaped discourse about hunting and conservation more broadly and framed the evolving parameters of hunting law.[9] Northern hunters came south at a time when southerners like John H. Wallace Jr. of Alabama began to craft significant regulations to protect game and nongame species as well as to limit access to hunting lands. These sportsmen proved to be allies to southern conservationists' cause and, in some cases, as Young's memories suggest, preceded in practice the spirit of the laws that would form across the South by the second decade of the twentieth century.

Charlie Young (center) guiding a hunting party that includes Charles Thompson (far right, with rifle), brother of Young's employer H. E. Thompson. Thomasville, Georgia, 1910. St. Paul Deaf Club–Charles Thompson Memorial Hall, St. Paul, Minnesota.

Charlie Young's story provides a clarifying depth of field by focusing on a corner of the Deep South in which an elite hunting culture flourished and fanned a growing conservationist ethos in the region. The essence of this story lay in social and political conflicts over land and race. Northerners sojourning south entered a world that hinged on a social order profoundly divided by race and class. They forged relationships with whites and Blacks of differing social classes, leveraging (and in some ways destabilizing) that social order. Elite northern and southern hunters employed local Black men and women, as well as some white men, to provide labor on their hunting estates, to cultivate regions of their estate for profit, to act as domestic servants, and to serve in the subordinate positions that their hunting culture required, while believing that their "progressive" attitudes would provide an uplifting model of labor relations to their southern counterparts.[10] Northern sportsmen built coalitions with elite southern whites for many reasons: to consolidate hunting lands, to influence hunting laws in their favor, and to bond with fellow hunters. They relied on alliances with elite southern sportsmen—and the prevailing social order that kept them in power—to fulfill their vision for a hunting colony in the Red Hills, a development that did not go unnoticed by white smallholders. These shifts, as we see in the Red Hills region, unfolded across the South, as hunting lands and fishing waters increasingly became accessible only by landownership and consolidation, leasing (often through membership in hunting or fishing clubs), or, by the 1930s, state-managed public lands. Land consolidation created the conditions, too, for experiments in wildlife habitat management; the Red Hills hosted a pioneering conservation movement for quail that showcased the evolution of game management science, a development that would in turn propel game and fish regulation in neighboring southern states.[11]

The "1893 Years": Origins of the Red Hills Hunting Colony

The Red Hills region arcs between southwest Georgia and northern Florida. Leon and Jefferson Counties (Florida) and Thomas and Grady Counties (Georgia) define the Red Hills' spatial boundaries; shaping its natural contours is a forty-mile stretch of rolling hills, lime sinks, longleaf pine stands and oak hammocks, wiregrass—flourishing in red clay eroded from the Appalachian Mountains at the end of the last Ice Age—and gently flowing streams.[12] Historically, Tallahassee, Florida, and Thomasville, Georgia, served as the centers of cultural life in the region, though Thomasville would maintain closer ties to the northern hunting colony that developed in the late nineteenth century.[13] Henceforth, wealthy outsiders set out to shape Thomasville's economic and social landscape. They patronized its small businesses, employed its citizens, engaged in local industrial enterprise, and developed the area as a premier destination for bird hunting and hound and horse trials. These families eventually funded Thomasville schools and area churches, hospitals, and the local historical society.

This demographic change was but one marker of dynamic shifts in the nineteenth-century Red Hills, a transformation that counters an early characterization of the region and its people as remaining stagnant in "unprogressive simplicity and strange isolation."[14] Across the course of a century, the area served as hunting lands for the Creek Nation, an outpost for white settlers, a booming "agricultural kingdom" based on cotton and enslaved labor, and, after the upheavals of the Civil War, a fashionable health, sport, and tourist resort for northern elites.[15] Along with these substantive historical changes came a remarkable shift in public perception of place—a landscape once considered unhealthy and uninhabitable by early white settlers came to be lauded as a place of healing. In the words of historian Albert G. Way, a "codified taxonomy of climate" developed by the 1870s, a guide to well-being that set some places apart and transformed them into destinations for those fighting respiratory illnesses, especially tuberculosis.[16] By 1873, shortly after Reconstruction ended in Georgia, locals in Thomasville advertised in newspapers across the state and even nationally, attempting to appeal to those seeking a travel cure. T. S. Hopkins, a local physician, tirelessly promoted Thomasville's "salubrious" climate and its superiority to Florida, one of the area's biggest competitors in attracting consumptive patients. According to Hopkins, Thomasville's rich pine forests, its abundance of fresh water, and warm winters made it the perfect place to convalesce.[17]

The trickle of northern visitors to Thomas County after the Civil War did not garner early notice, but as the number of visitors grew, townspeople learned to capitalize on this shift in perception, monitoring tourist expectations and accommodating them accordingly. By the early 1880s, Thomasville had two large resort hotels, the Mitchell House and the Piney Woods, and a number of smaller hotels and boardinghouses that served leisure and health seekers from the North. Though the Mitchell House burned and was rebuilt and the Piney Woods was eventually lost to fire, both hotels served Thomasville's tourist industry into the early 1900s.[18] But as other places across the South became tourist destinations—Asheville, North Carolina; Aiken, South Carolina; and Jekyll Island, Georgia—tourism to the Red Hills region would fade by the 1890s.[19] As rail travel increased to Florida and cities such as Ft. Lauderdale and Miami gained in popularity with elite travelers, the numbers of health sojourners to Thomasville waned. Although Thomasville eventually lost the revenue provided by the resort era, the "pleasant friendships" based on the common ground that northerners found with southerners on race, leisure, and sport proved especially important to the birth of the area's winter hunting colony.[20] These northerners had come to the town as part of the larger population of health and leisure tourists in the 1870s and 1880s. They now appreciated Thomasville for its beauty and climate, but, most importantly, the tourist era had nurtured relationships with local southerners that would provide the engine for subsequent land acquisition in the county. Purchasing homes in Thomasville's downtown and hiring wagons, horses, and guides from one of the town's many stables for hunting trips on land leased for shooting, northern hunters soon realized they could create their own personal hunting preserves. Land sale and consolidation began in the 1880s and continued well into the twentieth century; by the 1950s there were fifty hunting plantations stretching across the Red Hills region.[21] As late as 1976 these plantations were intact and together made up 350,000 acres.[22]

Coming to Thomas County and the Red Hills region from November until April (when the hunting season traditionally ended), sportsmen took advantage of the area's renowned shooting. Turkeys, doves, waterfowl, and deer (sometimes even the elusive wildcat) were all prime targets. But the preferred game were bobwhite quail. Quail are ground-dwelling birds that, in the fall and winter months (which coincide with quail hunting season), gather in coveys. The Red Hills region is an ideal environment for the bird, which thrives in the brushy edges of cultivated fields, abandoned fields, and longleaf grassland forests.[23] The pine forests that surrounded Thomasville and the tenant system of labor that broadcast farms across the countryside created perfect habitats for quail. One writer to *Forest and Stream* noted the abundance of the bobwhite in Thomas County and the zeal with which "everybody hunts them, both natives and Yankees."[24] He observed, "Sometimes one will see a dozen wagons full of men and dogs starting out every morning" to shoot quail.[25] The formal hunting party, with wagons, dogs, and drivers, was the province of wealthy hunters, and the quail plantations they built gave ample room with which to pursue the practice.

Quail hunting was not new to northern or southern hunters, though only during the Gilded Age did it become especially popular in the South (when many southerners still called them partridges). As Nicolas Proctor has argued, small game like quail was often overlooked in the antebellum South among elite hunters in favor of "trophy" animals like the deer and bear that served as symbols of mastery and manhood.[26] Early sporting periodicals, however, attest to the popularity of the bird, at least among northern sportsmen; writers gave much attention, for example, to the natural history, habitat, and behavior of quail. One northern writer considered it a "bird of value" because of its intelligence and the skill, firearms, and dogs required to bag the bird.[27] Hunters in mid-nineteenth-century Illinois, according to one historian, "agreed that quail was the most desirable game and the most difficult to kill on the wing."[28]

Northerners who sojourned south during the quail hunting season often drew fortunes from the new industries that dominated American enterprise in the late nineteenth century—oil, railroads, and steel. The connection between northern money and southern sport was so apparent across the South by the early twentieth century that one Savannah newspaper credited industrial wealth for a newfound conservation ethos in the South that limited access to game: "Many of the men who have been made immensely wealthy by the opportunities of the past few years have helped [wildlife protection] by either leasing or buying outright thousands of acres of land."[29] For these men, hunting was more than just a pastime; it was charged with an ethos of wealth and domination.[30] Historians have argued that hunting by prosperous sportsmen was directly tied to the age of empire in the late nineteenth century; in Britain, for example, hunting often preceded or went hand in hand with territorial domination; the mastery of another territory and its fauna was synonymous with the control of its people and institutions. In the United States, sportsmen "served empire in another way," as Daniel Justin Herman argues, by continuing to associate hunting and white American manhood and casting it in the light of late nineteenth-century ideas about scientific organization and racial hierarchy.[31] Theodore Roosevelt perhaps best personifies these themes; he idealized the western hunting adventure and later, traveling for the Smithsonian, the big game safari.[32] Other wealthy hunters followed his lead onto western lands and eventually to faraway places to pursue sport and wrote about their experiences.[33] These sportsmen, like those who built the winter hunting colony in the Red Hills region, had the means to reenact a social tableau that reaffirmed the power of wealth and racial hierarchy. Their capital bought them adventure and a chance to prove manliness and, by employing a cadre of subordinates as helpmates, the opportunity to perform paternal mastery of the hunt. These men traversed the country in plush, private Pullman cars (they might even own the railroad itself) in search of game and adventure. When they first came to southwest Georgia, they found not only abundant game but a place where farmers were struggling after decades of unstable crop prices and where there existed an abundant and cheap labor supply. The South was the perfect place for wealthy sportsmen to enjoy their own desires for a genteel but rugged life.

By the late nineteenth century, then, northern sportsmen had the capital to transform hunting into a participatory spectacle, replete with the best dogs, guns, wagons, and an entourage of other hunters, wagon drivers, and dog trainers, like Charlie Young. These men and their families also relied on local white elites to share sport, find real estate, and navigate the southern landscape. In Thomasville, they found an advocate and compatriot in Henry W. (or H.W.) Hopkins, a local judge and eventual town mayor and state senator. Hopkins provides a perfect example of the hunter-as-sportsman; one writer from a national hunting magazine declared emphatically that Hopkins was a sportsman whom "I wish all sportsmen could know."[34] It is no coincidence that he did much to attract northern hunters to Thomasville and helped to build the winter hunting colony. In promoting the region, he followed his father's lead; Dr. T. S. Hopkins's study of the benefits of pine resin for tuberculosis patients helped spark the area's early reputation as a sanatorium.[35] The younger Hopkins's passion, however, was shooting game and breeding dogs, and he possessed the means to invest time and money into these pursuits. An 1882 *Atlanta Weekly-Constitution* article illustrated this commitment. Hopkins was, at that time, constructing a large kennel in downtown Thomasville, what one local called the "dog hotel," to support the breeding and training of setters, pointers, and hounds. The "hotel" included room for 100 dogs, a kitchen, a trainer's house, and a few acres for an exercise ground. The reporter, calling Hopkins an "authority" on dogs and hunting, also noted that Hopkins had introduced the beagle breed to hunters in the area. His reputation for breeding and training the best dogs had been cemented in the early 1880s among northern hunters in Thomasville; one person told the reporter that "Hopkins's dogs work like clocks, and no yankee ever shoots over one without wanting to buy him."[36] Hopkins also kept up with the latest in the sporting press and actively engaged with other hunters through the pages of these national periodicals. He sent, for example, the wing, tail, head, and foot of a bird to the editors of *Forest and Stream* to get help identifying it (their response: "The bird is a king rail, or fresh water marsh hen").[37] Hopkins was a part of a national network of sportsmen because of journals like *Forest and Stream*, and he connected with northern hunters who came to Thomasville as tourists by hosting fox hunts and shooting parties in the Red Hills region and by loaning and selling his hunting dogs. Hopkins's enthusiasm for sport and sportsmen and his influence in the Red Hills would pave the way for a winter hunting colony.

Charlie Young began to work for northern hunters in his early teenage years as a supplement to cash wages in nearby cotton fields. He remembered traveling with his older brother "out in the country cotton picking time and what a time we had picking cotton we wood get 50¢ a hundred pounds a day and no we was doing well." Though he and his brother may have been fast pickers, Young noted that, despite the work, "you would get plenty to eat but no money and you did not cear mutch about it."[38] Things began to change for Young and for Thomasville, however, "in the 1893 years." His family moved to Thomasville in 1893 (when Young was ten years old), which would become his reference point for transformation in the small town. It is not surprising that, moving just next to the Atlantic Railroad station so that he could watch for the private railcars of visitors that rolled into Thomasville, he began to take notice of the town's many outsiders. So, in his telling, it was in 1893

Henry W. Hopkins (right) with A. H. Mason at Mason's quail hunting plantation, Susina, in the Red Hills region, ca. 1905, after a quail hunt. Thomasville History Center, Thomasville, Georgia.

that northerners really began to come to the town, using it as a gateway for the wider countryside, with its scenic drives and abundant bird populations.

Young's life, from an early age, was intertwined with the seasonal population that came to Thomasville. Even Metcalf, his beloved childhood community, was named after Dr. J. T. Metcalfe, a native New Yorker who was one of the first men from the North to buy property and settle seasonally in Thomas County. Dr. Metcalfe became one of the community's most avid promoters, already by 1880 at work heralding its unique landscape and potential as a winter colony.[39] Young also noted that "as a boy," he "spent all the time I could get out at the J Wiman Jones place."[40] Jones, of Englewood, New Jersey, was another early winter resident who purchased a plantation, Elsoma, and worked to build Thomasville as an attraction. In 1889 Jones purchased land to build a park, Glen Arven, which became the country club and golf course where Young would work as a caddy.[41] Jones also had "a very fine young step son," Charles M. Chapin, "and what a step son he was," according to Young. "I think he was the fines we ever had his life was to get as meny of his frends to Thomasville and that he did." Not only did Chapin, a good friend of H. W. Hopkins, recruit many of the people, such as the Hanna family, who would populate the town's winter colony, but by Young's account he also built the first dog kennel on an estate in the region: "Their was not eny wire to fence in felds and yards as to day so he had to use 6 foot ralings and it work fine for a long time untill wire come in stile and he had a fine kennel." Chapin's "very heart was dogs," according to Young.[42] Young would have known Chapin's hunting habits well; his uncle Jim Mitchell served as Chapin's dog trainer, which is why Young spent so much time at Elsoma and likely where he received his own training with dogs.[43] Young and his family, like other Black families in the Red Hills, found opportunity on the growing estates of the seasonal visitors.

"Thousands and Thousands of Acers of Land for the Northan Hunters": Land Consolidation in the Red Hills

The changing legal landscape that foreclosed the open range in the South supported the consolidation and enclosure of the Red Hills northern hunting colony. Northerners, Young remembered, were the first to build fences and post lands, the former not an easy feat as estates grew in size. And the acquisition of hundreds, sometimes thousands, of acres of land by sportsmen went against predominant patterns of landholding in the Deep South in the first three decades of the twentieth century. Census data reveal that the average farm size in acreage decreased between 1900 and 1920 in the Deep South. In Georgia, for example, the average farm size was 117.5 acres in 1900; 92.6 acres in 1910; and 76 acres in 1920.[44] In part, this was because the number of farms increased as did the acreage of improved agricultural land, highlighting the "slavish devotion" to cotton production that gripped the South, even in the midst of unstable prices.[45] The acquisition of land by northerners was less reflective of the experience of the average southern farmer and more in line with the land consolidation by emerging New South industries across the region—for example, the lumber industry as it moved from the Northeast to the South (wherein lumber companies acquired millions of acres collectively) and the "rationalized" cotton farming operations of the Mississippi Delta (both industries were often funded by northern investors).[46] Though northern sportsmen did exploit their landholdings by continuing crop production and harvesting timber, these lands were managed predominantly for leisure. Their example of accruing land for hunting and fishing soon made its way across the South as southern sportsmen formed hunting and fishing clubs for the purposes of buying and leasing land.

Northerners helped to shape a trend of buying land from Red Hills farmers in the late nineteenth century, a time of cyclical economic depression. Reports from visiting journalists often commented on the potential of Thomas County as a place not simply to hunt but to operate a farm. D. L. Palmer of Brookings County, South Dakota, informed readers of the *Brookings County Press* that Thomasville offered "many inducements to the northern farmer who would like to live in a warmer climate," including cheap fuel and fecund soil that yielded "nearly all kinds of fruits, all kinds of vegetables, cotton and tobacco as staples and never as failures."[47] Thomasville was often compared to the settlement of Fitzgerald, Georgia, eighty miles northeast, which was settled by a group of Union veterans in the late nineteenth century.[48] Editor John Triplett reported on the growth of the colony, noting that the land around Fitzgerald would soon "blossom like the rose" with newly settled ten- to fifty-acre farms. But, Triplett noted, that small acreage was not enough to forge a successful farming operation. He reported that D. L. Palmer and his brother planned a similar colonization scheme in Thomas County, concluding after a tour of the Georgia and Florida border that the county "offered as many, or more, advantages than any other place." The men, under the name "Palmer's Home Colonization Company," bought land and planned to advertise "extensively in the West and Northwest."[49]

Though nothing came of this farmers' colonization scheme in Thomas County, the attention such plans received is notable; it illustrates that land was available at such prices that men like the Palmer brothers could buy it in bundles.[50] By the early 1890s, another reporter from Wisconsin noted that while exploring the main streets of the town, he passed "the winter residences of many northern people—some from Chicago, but as yet mostly from New York." He pointed to the growing trend, however, to purchase land outside of the town proper: "Land is very cheap near town and ranges from $2 to $10 an acre according to improvements and location. . . . Already some New Yorkers have estates of several thousand acres, notably the places of John W. Masury, S. R. Van Duzer, and J. Wyman Jones, all of New York." The reporter attributed cheap land sales to the "thin farming population compared to the extent of territory."[51] It seems that it was less an issue of sparse population than a growing inability in the region to keep farmlands in local hands. Historian and journalist Clifton Paisley notes that by the early 1880s, there was a "growing distress" among southern landowners in the Red Hills region due to a scarcity of capital and inability to maintain ownership of farms. Many began to sell off their lands, in parcels and as entire farms, and for relatively cheap.[52] A reporter from the Green Bay Gazette who, like D. L. Palmer, was interested in Thomasville as a farming colony reported on the success of David McCartney, a farmer from Fort Howard, Wisconsin. By 1893, McCartney owned 7,000 acres of land in Thomas County, which were divided into separate plantations. Some of the lands were planted in cotton, but McCartney diversified his holdings by planting corn, fruit orchards, and sugar cane.[53] Palmer noted with delight that "the old Southern cracker" in Thomas County would "gladly divide his lands and sell them at a very low figure to induce energetic northern people to settle."[54] Although he was confident that "these old Rebels" would never make it "'too hot'" for northerners and would welcome them with characteristic southern hospitality, these "Southern crackers" likely cared less about who bought their lands than that they sold them at all; in a cash poor economy, which characterized the South after the Civil War, any buyer's money was green.[55]

Northerners seeking exclusive recreational estates bought the lands and homes of people who were once scions of the planter class. Sketching the genealogy of some of the purchases helps to illustrate this point. J. T. Metcalfe's first land purchases in 1883 were in the southeastern portion of Thomas County; he bought the old plantation lands of James L. Seward, a prominent state congressman.[56] Though he sold these lands to David McCartney of Wisconsin in 1886 (the celebrated farmer singled out by the press), Metcalfe once more purchased land in 1887, the 1,600-acre Cedar Grove plantation, from the Blackshears, one of the oldest and largest planter families in the area. Metcalfe's purchase included the original plantation home, which he renamed Susina, for his wife, Susan. He did not remain long at Susina; he sold the property in 1891 to A. H. Mason, the heir to a shoe-blacking business in Philadelphia, but Metcalfe had garnered enough influence in the area to become the namesake of a railroad stop and Charlie Young's home village, created in 1889, Metcalf (the town later dropped its final "e").[57]

Another early buyer was John W. Masury, a wealthy paint manufacturer from New York who had also built a hotel in Thomasville to cater to tourists. In 1887, he purchased a 1,500-acre property that he named Cleveland Park, where he often hosted picnics and parties for wealthy northern and southern whites.[58] The land had once belonged to another branch of the Blackshear family.⁵⁹ In 1889, S. R. Van Duzer, also from New York and a "millionaire," according to the local press, bought a 1,300-acre plantation, Greenwood, owned by the Jones family, another prominent planting family in Thomas County.⁶⁰

The Hanna family, wealthy oil refiners from Cleveland (who sold out to Standard Oil in 1876), their partners in business, and family friends came to dominate landholding in the Red Hills region, holding together 150,000 acres of land in forty-one estates by 1976.⁶¹ The early purchases in the 1890s were made by Salome Hanna, the sister of Howard Melville (H. M.) and Mark Hanna. She and her husband, J. Wyman Jones (who developed Glen Arven Country Club in Thomasville), bought a plantation in 1891 that they named Elsoma. The same year, Salome's son by her first marriage, Charles M. Chapin, purchased Melrose plantation from a branch of a prominent local family also named Jones. He later acquired Elsoma for himself. H. M. Hanna, who was a director for Standard Oil and jointly ran the M. A. Hanna Company (a coal, iron ore mining, and shipping conglomerate) with his brother Mark, purchased Pebble Hill plantation, an antebellum estate once owned by Thomas Jefferson Johnson, a state congressman who had introduced the bill to create Thomas County.⁶² In the 1880s and 1890s, lands in Thomas County and the Red Hills region were transferring from southern to northern ownership. Local families like the Joneses, Blackshears, and Johnsons—who had built their fortunes on cotton and enslaved labor—found themselves willing to sell to northern families, like the Hannas, who created their wealth in the booming industrial age of the late nineteenth century.

This lineage of former owners appealed to northerners, who found they could invest in the romance of the Old South, replete with racial deference. For the sportsmen, the antebellum homes were remnants of an old aristocracy that projected a gentility they wanted to claim. According to a former director of the Georgia Historic Sites Survey, the Classical Revival homes in Thomas County that became winter hunting estates "fit the dream ideal of the antebellum South better than those from any other part of Georgia."⁶³ Greenwood, the Van Duzer estate, later owned by the Whitney family, is perhaps the most famous of these. With its massive Ionic columns, two-story portico covering the entire front facade, and elaborately hand-carved pediment, it stands as a temple to the agrarian social order. Many of the homes on northern hunting estates—Susina (Metcalfe's home until he sold it to the Mason family), Pebble Hill (owned by H. M. Hanna), Elsoma, and Melrose—were antebellum in origin. Though they would install modern amenities, the northern owners largely left the facades of the homes unchanged (though a few of the homes, such as the original house at Pebble Hill, later burned).⁶⁴

They were now the resident gentlemen of these country estates, kings of sporting leisure instead of cotton.

Grandeur also characterized the homes that sportsmen built when no suitable antebellum structure existed. A visitor praised Masury's Cleveland Park, a sprawling Queen Anne–style mansion, as an "architectural poem" with "rich and costly" furniture, "made to order by the best houses in New York City."[65] The homes of J. H. Wade (Millpond) and John D. Archbold (Chinquapin) were both rambling Mediterranean "villas."[66] Lula Mae Hamilton, who worked for the Wade family as a governess in 1919, wrote to her mother about the impressive surrounds: "The house is sort of Spanish in architecture—white plaster with red tile roof—mostly one story. Just now the wisteria is coming to its prime and I never saw such a beautiful sight. The house is literally covered on all sides + the roof. It is huge of course. The glass covered court is filled with gardens + paths, a fountain in center with a stuffed crane looking at his reflection."[67] Charlie Young remembered Wade's home as "one of the finest manchons of all of the Places."[68] Along with the massive acreages these sportsmen assembled, their hunting "lodges" reflected the kind of elite accoutrements their fortunes provided.

The Red Hills region was not alone in its development of a northern hunting colony. The South Carolina Lowcountry, the Georgia coast, and the Currituck Sound in North Carolina, for example, became sites of winter retreats for hunters. The Lowcountry, in particular, saw a similar trend of wealthy northerners buying and leasing land and modernizing former rice plantations. Daniel J. Vivian, who has chronicled this phenomenon, argues that "rehabilitation coupled with elaboration and embellishment" created a new kind of plantation, a space that recalled the past while embracing modern recreational uses.[69] The "refashioning" of former plantations for use as hunting estates was concomitant with land accumulation—in the Red Hills and Lowcountry South Carolina, hundreds of thousands of acres came to be tied up in a private recreational culture. In the Lowcountry, by World War II, seventy-six hunting plantations stretched from the top end of the South Carolina coast in Georgetown County down to the state line, near the Savannah River.[70]

In the Red Hills, H. W. Hopkins brokered countless land deals for northern hunters. Hopkins combined an extensive knowledge of local land and people with a business savvy that resulted in the formation of the winter hunting colony. He initially connected with northern sportsmen over a shared love of hunting, but his local influence undoubtedly added to his credibility among the northerners.[71] He was a powerful man who had the ability both to secure land at good prices and to inform northerners of local and state laws that would affect their property and hunting customs. By 1879, Hopkins had established a real estate company that formalized his role as a local agent. Through him wealthy sportsmen acquired private hunting preserves and also leased shooting land well into the 1930s.

Shared hunting customs and business relationships cemented friendships between Hopkins and many northern sportsmen. These friendships attracted new sportsmen to the winter colony and marked the different plantations as an elite enclave. Hopkins would often join the northerners on their own hunting grounds or on fishing expeditions in Florida and might even visit them in their home states. He also had hunting camps in the Red Hills region where he and northerners would spend time hunting, eating and drinking, and telling tall tales. Stories from these expeditions passed down to Hopkins's descendants; his great-grandson Theo Titus III remembered them well. Titus recounted an anecdote that illustrates the conviviality of the hunting trips and the friendship between Hopkins and the northerners. At a hunting camp on Miccosukee Lake in northern Florida, the hunters had gathered and were treated to apple pies from Hopkins's favorite Thomasville bakery, Isaac's. As they sat, told stories, and ate their pies after the hunt, Hopkins "turned to Mr. [Charles] Chapin and said, 'Charlie, this is the damndest, toughest pie I have ever eaten.' Mr. Chapin looked at him and said, 'Judge if you would take the paper plate off of it, it wouldn't be so tough.'"[72] The story suggests that Hopkins was important in making Thomasville the nucleus of the colony (in that Isaac's and many other town businesses were patronized by sportsmen) as opposed to Tallahassee. But, certainly, "Judge," as he was known affectionately, successfully created lifelong friendships with northerners that served as the backbone of the winter colony.

Most of Hopkins's business began from social connections made in Thomasville and continued through word of mouth. In many cases, interested investors sought him out rather than vice versa. In 1901, for example, D. L. Shepard of St. Paul, Minnesota, wrote Hopkins about a potential buyer in "an old and esteemed friend Mr. Marvin Hughitt Paes of C. + N.W.R.R. [Chicago and Northwestern Railroad]." Shepard "told him about Thomasville and the Keifer place and he was impressed very favorably.... He is decidedly such a man as you would like to add to your Northern Colony."[73] If interested buyers secured an introduction to Hopkins and made a trip to the Red Hills region to survey available property, Hopkins put himself at their disposal. Charles S. Hebard of New Jersey, owner of Ty-Ty plantation near Thomasville, wrote Hopkins in 1903 thanking him for his careful attention to the interests of buyer J. H. Wade of New York. Wade, wrote Hebard, "seems pleased with [the property] and with the way you treated him—he is a very fine man and will be a great acquisition to the place."[74] The correspondence suggests that before a land sale took place, buyers such as Paes and Wade had to be satisfied with Thomasville and what it had to offer, but they also had to win the tacit approval of Hopkins.

Northerners were always ready to purchase contiguous lands or parcels that were advantageous for shooting and that increased their estate acreage. One example of the process is the accumulation of lands by J. H. Wade. In 1904, Wade wrote to Hopkins agreeing to purchase the "Girtman place," a farm next to his Millpond lands.[75] In 1907, he purchased another parcel of contiguous land from a Miss McCartney of Green Bay, Wisconsin.[76] Three years later, he acquired two parcels owned by the McIntyres (known as the Futch lands), a prominent local family.[77] In 1916, Wade again wrote to Hopkins wishing to enlarge his holdings: "I would like to buy the South ½ of lot 91 owned by Mrs. Lillie if she will sell it at $15 per acre. This would connect my Futch land with the Hammond place I recently bought. Please see what you can do."[78] Lula Mae Hamilton, the Wade family governess, informed her mother that Wade loved "to buy the land and then go through laying out roads where he sees fit." She also noted that not all small farmers were willing to sell. Although Wade had successfully bought land from a few African American landowning families and "let them live on" to farm shares, "there is one little place near here that two darkies own and won't give up—some beautiful woods too."[79] Hamilton's slur belies the empowered stance of the smallholders who refused to sell out to the wealthy sportsmen.

Prominent northerners also extended their grip over exclusive hunting grounds by leasing land from local farmers, Black and white. If northern hunters secured the lands, the local owners would also post signs to stop unauthorized shooting. The US Department of Agriculture encouraged farmers to take advantage of the newfound interest by sportsmen in land leases. In a department circular, T. S. Palmer of the Bureau of Biological Survey urged farmers to consider leasing. Using North Carolina as an example, Palmer observed that farmers had been leasing land to hunters since the late nineteenth century because it "secure[d] to the owner a substantial financial benefit." In Guilford County, where hunters leased some 150,000 acres, Palmer argued for the benefit of a system of private "preserves" that "do not in any way interfere with the cultivation of the land or the rights of individuals." The benefits were plain: continued cotton cultivation attracted birds, only lessee hunters were allowed on the land, and the proceeds paid to farmers offset property tax rates. All that was required of farmers was the posting of land. "In other words," he assured farmers, "by merely keeping trespassers off their lands and joining their neighbors in leasing the hunting privileges to certain individuals or associations, [farmers] are relieved entirely from their real-estate taxes or receive an equally large or even a larger amount of cash each year. Sometimes the lessees hunt very little or perhaps not at all during the hunting season, in which cases the owners may for a year or more enjoy immunity from hunting as well as from taxation."[80]

Such an overlay of use rights is what economists call "optimal ownership": on one piece of property, the farmer controlled crop production and land use; a hunting club purchased lease rights and thus had exclusive access to the game and fish therein; and a government agency controlled the regulation of the take.[81] Optimal ownership arrangements grew with increasing frequency across the South in which the culture of sport hunting and fishing held sway.

Much like his role in land sales, Hopkins acted as agent and mediator between northerners and southerners in lease arrangements. Charles Chapin wrote Hopkins, for instance, asking if he would "mind dropping a line to Baum near Metcalfe I can't remember his initials and ask him if I could have his dove fields for last weeks in January and would it be worthwhile."[82] Hopkins often drafted the lease agreements between northern hunters and local farmers. In 1908, for example, John Hawkins leased his land under the following agreement: "For the sum of thirty dollars I hereby sell to Chas Thompson the exclusive shooting privilege on my plantation in Jefferson Co Fla ajoining Wm Cargill's in Thomas Co Ga being 500 acres for the season commencing Nov 1st 1908 and ending (in Florida) Mch 1st 1909."[83]

Sometimes the contracts would cover an extended period of time. In an undated contract, Mrs. Mary Eason leased 268 acres to John F. Archbold (John D. Archbold's son) for the "exclusive right to the hunting and shooting of game on my land . . . for and during the next three open shooting seasons under the laws of Ga. with right [to Archbold] and his associates of ingress and egress necessary to the enjoyment thereof."[84] Charlie Young told of the work of another local broker, R. L. Stringer, who also served as an agent for wealthy sportsmen in the Red Hills. Stringer "leasted thousands and thousands of acers of land for the northan hunters and had a Big Pasture where he boded their horses those that didn't have places of their own."[85] After sportsmen began to buy large plantations, Stringer acted as an estate superintendent. Both Young and Stringer worked for L. S. Thompson of Sunny Hill plantation by the 1920s.

Leasing lands proved so common among northern hunters that certain lands became almost proprietary. In fact, squabbles ensued if one northern hunter upset an agreement between another hunter and local landowner. Such was the case when Sidney E. Hutchinson, owner of Foshalee plantation, surreptitiously acquired hunting privileges from several locals who had previously leased to C. A. Griscom and Edward Crozer. Not only that, but Griscom, Crozer, and Hopkins accused him of paying more than five cents an acre for land, which transgressed the gentlemen's agreement among northern hunters that none would pay more to avoid competition between them. Although Hutchinson denied the accusations, he was effectively ostracized from the collective. Crozer wrote Hopkins that "there never was an unpleasant question arose between any of the shooters before Hutchinson and I would be only too glad if some way could be brought to drive him out of it."[86]

With Hopkins and other locals as agents, consolidation of lands progressed across the Red Hills region. By 1950, land consolidation in northern Leon County, Florida, claimed 80 percent of the most productive agricultural lands.[87] Because the estates grew so large, only wealthy northern hunters could afford them when they went up for sale. In 1915, Hopkins conceded to northerner Edward Crozer that "property like yours is beyond the average villager for a home at anything like its value."[88]

By the second decade of the twentieth century, the practice of buying and leasing land to hunt extended throughout the plantation and coastal districts of the Deep South. Southern sportsmen in Jackson and Greenville, Mississippi; Tuskegee and Selma, Alabama; and Milledgeville and Savannah, Georgia, chartered hunting and fishing clubs, the purpose of which was to find camaraderie, support the enforcement of game laws, and to acquire hunting and fishing land through purchase or lease.[89] These clubs, part of a rising trend among sportsmen across the country by the late nineteenth century, were often made up of elite men from the local areas in which they were situated.[90] Some acquired, like their counterparts in the Red Hills, thousands of acres for hunting grounds, though the lands were managed and accessed collectively by members of the club. Clubs, now a common way in which hunters access land, were a hallmark of the transformation of hunting in the modernizing South.

"A Great Help to the Laboring Man": Land, Labor, and Cultural Transformation

Expansive estates set the backdrop for sportsmen's elite hunting culture, which included Black labor in forms agricultural and recreational, and transformed certain aspects of the hunt. In the Red Hills region, quail shooting acquired a specific pageantry, replete with thoroughbred dogs and horses, wagons, and a cast of servants. Sociologist Stuart A. Marks, who writes about hunting in North Carolina, has attributed this cultural transformation specifically to the Red Hills, arguing that "the purchase of Southern plantations by Northerners and their use as retreats . . . perpetuated the image of quail hunting as a recreation for the leisured and privileged classes."[91] Quail hunting, in its elite form, centered on the Georgia hunting wagon and formal hunting party. Developed in Thomasville, the wagon (used for hunting today) has high wheels to enable it to run smoothly through tall grass and brush in the open field. As H. W. Hopkins described the wagons to hunter D. L. Hebard, they "have to be of extra long bodies" to accommodate the "boxes on sides for guns" and "dog crates in rear" (that held from four to ten dogs and a water tank).[92] These wagons, pulled by mules, made the profession of wainwright a lucrative one in Thomasville; Hopkins informed Hebard that in 1930, when wagons were still in demand, they cost around $350. The wagon's accoutrements allowed for socializing attendant to formal hunts; Hopkins noted that "lunches, ice, liquid refreshments, etc." were kept in a dash compartment for the midday meal.[93] At that point, the driver(s) would unpack a princely lunch for the hunters, who would linger at the picnic for an hour or so before returning to the hunt or heading home. Hunters, who might ride atop the wagon or follow on horseback, were accompanied by the wagon drivers and dog handlers, who were also sometimes on horseback.

This type of hunting party differed markedly from traditional local Red Hills hunters who pursued game on foot with a single dog and a years-worn gun; northerners proffered their hunting rituals as displays of conspicuous consumption far out of reach for most. Black laborers were key to that image. The observations of Grady C. Cromartie, whom Clifton Paisley interviewed for his work on the Red Hills in 1970, illustrate the kind of spectacle that northern hunters created in rural Georgia and Florida. In 1908, Cromartie clerked at a store that served the farming community surrounding Lake Iamonia in Leon County, Florida—also a prime destination for northern hunters and their allies, including Judge Hopkins. When asked whether he remembered the northern hunter Edward Beadel, who owned a quail plantation on the north side of the lake, Cromartie remarked on Beadel's hunting wagons that were "almost always painted yellow," including the wagon wheels. Cromartie also remembered that Beadel's wagon driver, a Black man, "had to be dressed like they wanted him to be dressed," with "leather lines" and formal livery; the driver "had to go neat, don't you know." With conspicuously bright-colored wagons and uniformed drivers, Cromartie noted wryly that northern hunters "were kind of particular . . . about how everything looked."[94]

Showcases of wealth were present in other types of hunting rituals and in the daily interactions of northerners with locals. Northern hunters also hosted foxhunts on their lands, which were formal affairs that William Rogers notes "were replicas of similar events in the North and in England."[95] A staple of elite southern hunting culture, plantation-based foxhunts featured large packs of dogs, riders in formal habits, and a crowd of spectators. Often taking place on the plantations of J. Wyman Jones and Charles Chapin, these hunts were held each season.[96] The sportsmen had acquired so much acreage that it allowed riders to chase the baying hounds without leaving their own property. The plantation lands, perfect for quail shooting and large fox hunts, enabled northerners to act as aspiring gentry. Northerners also sought to display their status when visiting Thomasville. Lula Mae Hamilton remembered that when the women of the Wade household were taken to tea or to do their shopping in town, they used one of the seven buggies or four automobiles in the possession of J. H. Wade. The driver, "Hi," had to don a special suit and a silk top hat for public outings—what Hamilton called driving "*in state!*"[97]

Charlie Young was a member of local Black families who spent lifetimes working for northern families. In 1897, "the year of the Spanish and American War," Young remembered, he began to work permanently as a hunting field assistant for H. E. Thompson, a banker and sportsman from St. Paul, Minnesota. Fourteen years old, he got the job by being a keen listener; when, on the way to his caddy job at Glen Arven, Young heard Thompson yell to the caddies and say, "The first boy get hear I will give him a job," Young "got their first and he said to me you are the smalist boy of all but I will try you and he gave me the job."[98] Soon, Young was able to prove his ability, despite being the "smalist" of the caddies vying for work. On his first day, he served as an errand boy, working around the Thomasville home of Thompson, carrying wood and fetching laundry. "But the next day come," Young recalled, "and that was the day he went quail shooting and what a day it turn out to be." Young recounted the way he quickly gained Thompson's confidence during the shoot. Soon after the party descended into the field with their hounds, a brace (or pair) of dogs "had a point" and the men managed to flush a covey of quail into the open range. Although Thompson and his shooting partners were "champion" shots, they managed to kill only two birds of the fifteen. So, remembered Young, "hear is the time to try me. The first thing was boy did you see those birds down. Yes, ser I did. How meny. About 10 are 12 look like to me. Did they all lite together. No ser 2 birds lit over near that log to the right all right young man take me whair the 2 birds lit all right ser and their they was." Thompson was impressed by Young's ability to track the birds; he remarked to the shooting party, in Young's words, "this boy I started not to hyer on the account of being the smalest of all. I no now he is the best of the crowd."[99] Young's narrative highlights his skill in the field and how seasoned sportsmen recognized that skill while disconnecting any link between physical stature and ability to do the job. His own marksmanship in the field takes precedence in the narration of his rise to a successful career with northern hunters. In addition, Young would have known the countryside well; Black men who supported white hunters, northern or southern, were prized for their knowledge of environment and terrain.[100]

Before employment with Thompson, Charlie Young was already an avid hunter. His skill came through natural ability, though rural hunting customs of the Jim Crow South required that his free exercise be limited when in the field or woods. He recounted in his memoir that southern racial custom was a deterrence to his pursuit of game. He recalled, for example, that "you no in those days when a wite boy run across you hunting you was sopose to not shot eny more until hee leaves you." Not only was Young supposed to stop hunting, but he was also expected to "watch where the birds go and help [the white hunter] as long as he is their." In return for the Black hunter's help in marking birds, the white hunter would "give 2 are 3 birds are some shells are some money."[101] Young cushioned the dishonor shown by the white hunter by casting the interaction in reciprocal terms; he was compensated for his deference and so "everything went on all right." Young's memories complicate the observations of sociologist Arthur F. Raper, who included documentation of leisure activities in his 1936 study, *Preface to Peasantry*. Raper noted that Black and white hunters in rural Georgia "are constantly meeting by day and night in the open fields and in the woods and swamps."[102] In the course of the hunt, custom dictated that whoever's dog got to the game first took home the prize, no matter who made the killing shot. Historian Jack Temple Kirby named this "a sort of rural etiquette" that allowed for the possibility of an equitable outcome.[103] Still, Young's memories of rural custom suggest that white hunters' command of the woods and fields could curtail the ability and mobility of Black hunters.

White hunters' expectation of Young's deference as an aid continued from boyhood to a career of more than forty years working for northern sportsmen. Charlie Young would not have been an atypical laborer in the postwar sporting tourism economy, in which the South became a premier destination for its abundant game and for its supply of cheap labor. Historian Scott Giltner, who has focused on Gilded Age hunting, labor, and race, argues that, from their perspective, white sportsmen relied upon Black labor for a number of reasons. They used menial laborers to complete tasks they felt were unfit for sportsmen—scouting and recovering game, cleaning firearms, and preparing meals at night and while in the field. They relied on other skilled workers as well, and these men trained dogs and drove hunting wagons. But, according to Giltner, who draws from sporting periodicals of the late nineteenth and early twentieth centuries as well as private accounts of individual sportsmen, Black laborers also "carried out the other crucial function of being Black."[104] By the 1870s and 1880s, he suggests, white sportsmen, northern and southern, had begun to rely on Black laborers to enact what they deemed an appropriate racial hierarchy, particularly in a post–Civil War order in which African American emancipation challenged white supremacy. There was no little amount of nostalgia in using Black labor to hearken back to the Old South, a postbellum mythic creation populated with benign masters and loyal "servants." Loyalty, in this case, translated into assumptions by white sportsmen that "their Black laborers experienced as much excitement over the prospect of sporting service as did whites over having Black workers at their disposal."[105]

Although white sportsmen's motivations to employ Black labor may have had little to do with Black well-being, Charlie Young saw his work as materially advantageous and personally meaningful. He called northerners "a great help to the laboring man."[106] Though seasonal, the work sometimes paid higher wages than agricultural labor. Some payments, too, might be in kind, such as in game or firearms, the latter of which was harder to come by because of expense and social prohibitions.[107] Giltner also notes that benefits of hunting labor went beyond the pecuniary: "Laboring for white sportsmen ... sometimes provided opportunities to counterbalance the images of dominance and subordination that ... elites sought to perpetuate."[108] Black sporting laborers, who were often hunters and fishermen as well, could demonstrate their abilities in the field, sometimes bettering their white employers. When Charlie Young was able to prove his skill in the field, his specialized abilities counterbalanced, as Giltner suggests, images of white mastery and Black subordination.

Yet it is easy to overstate the advantages of hunting labor. It was an option available to very few Black men throughout the South. Although sporting tourism became broadly popular after the Civil War among both the elite and the middle class, the advantages it offered for work were available only to those African Americans who lived in popular sporting destinations. Also, although it might offer better wages, at bedrock the leisure economy based on hunting and fishing exploited Black labor. There were no set wages, for instance, and no guarantee of work from one year to the next. And, as Giltner notes, although Black hunters and fishermen might outperform white sportsmen, "the biracial sporting field did not produce racial equality. African Americans had a permanent role in Southern hunting and fishing, but only because of their subordination to whites while in the field."[109] This inequality was nowhere more clearly expressed than in the debates over hunting laws in the early twentieth century; just as John H. Wallace Jr. had been in Alabama, the State of Georgia was expressly concerned with limiting the mobility of African Americans in its development of hunting law.

In his account, Young never mentioned a set wage or how compensation changed over his career. This is unusual since he took care to document the wages of his earlier years as a caddy and cotton picker. This omission may be because Young's work did not take the form of a straightforward wage per task or wage per hour but was more of a package of wages and in-kind payment, as was common among sporting laborers. For instance, Young recounted a typical scenario in which workers were given leftover food after a noontime meal:

> . . . but the grandest thing about hunting with Mr HE Thompson was lunch time he all ways stop for lunch at 130 and you talk about a picnic that was it no 6 men could think about eating all they had for 2 shuters and the 2 helpers Mr Thompson wood have us broil a big stake . . . chicken and coffie . . . now you no that is a feast so we would take the Backseat of the hunting wagon and all ways carried a folding table big a plenty for six people they would eat and when they get finished they would tell us to come and get it.

Despite how large the party of hunters, Young remembered that "meny times the [pork] chops are the chicken [wouldn't] evan be turch and Mr Thompson would tell us not to let anything go back to the house so we had to eat it are carie it home." Young assured readers, "Beleave me nothing ever went back to the house."[110] The scene points to the rituals common to a quail hunting party (the grand picnic) and to the subordinate role that Young and, by extension, other sporting laborers played in these rituals (displaying deference and letting the hunters eat first). But it also points to the particular perquisites that such labor might offer—extra food to supplement the diet of Young and his family.

Equally important, Young's decision to remain in the employ of white northerners allowed him to pursue his love of hunting and to train and care for hunting dogs, an art first learned from his uncle. On the second page of his memoir, he made clear the relationship of his work with sportsmen and his love of dogs: "I allwways have ben a dog lover most espely Bird dogs and they carried me over meny parts of this country. . . . I gest I could say and tell the truth it has ben more bird of difrence kind of eny liveing man in the US today."[111] Traveling gave Young experience hunting for a variety of birds. That is why, perhaps, his memories of working with sportsmen include accounts of traveling north with his employers. He supported hunts and hunted himself from the reaches of Texas to North Dakota, where he observed the piled, sunbleached bones of buffalo, symbols of another kind of commercial hunt for fertilizer and hides and to exert western domination over Native peoples.[112] For a time, his life revolved around seasonal travel with northern employers. In the early 1920s, he lived and worked for L. S. Thompson in New Jersey in the summer months, overseeing a landscaping crew on Thompson's estate.[113]

Young was thus an integral part of the workforce of the "season," with its hunting parties, soirees, and elaborate picnic outings, which lasted from the fall until early spring. But "off-season," another labor force, tenant farmers, produced modest income for northern estate owners.[114] During the spring and summer months, northerners left much of the business on the plantation, including managing labor, in the hands of local southern whites. Management decisions on the hunting plantations sometimes fell under the purview of local men like Hopkins. Because he proved himself to be a trusted local contact, estate owners often looked to Hopkins to act as a sort of overseer of their plantations in the spring and summer months. His correspondence suggests that although northern estate owners sometimes overrode his decisions, they generally relied upon his advice in matters of agriculture and labor. The letters also illustrate the scope of his work as plantation manager and agent.

As early as 1894, just as land consolidation began in the Red Hills region, Hopkins performed managerial duties for absentee owners. J. J. Healy, an Episcopal minister from New England and owner of Sherwood plantation, wrote to Hopkins regarding his appointment as overseer. Healy expected that the judge would "[collect] rent . . . and exercise general supervision of the same as my interest may require."[115] "General supervision" referred to the implementation of Healy's directives for cultivation of land and management of tenants. Other plantation owners also gave Hopkins broad permission to act in their stead. A. H. Hough, owner of Spring Hill plantation, sent Hopkins a formal notice of employment to use for business purposes: "This is to certify that Hon. H. W. Hopkins has been appointed my Agent, with full power to act in any and all matters to the management of this plantation, and his orders are to have the same weight as if issued by me."[116]

Hopkins was happy to accept such powers because they added to his yearly salary (he asked for $150 per year) and because the role of manager solidified his friendships with and influence among wealthy northerners.[117] He wrote to C. B. Raymond, owner of Mayhaw plantation, "It will give me great pleasure to look after the property for you, and will take this matter up with you later. In the mean time, I will see that nothing goes wrong with the property."[118] Hopkins was also careful to assume deference in his role, and he assured northern owners that theirs would always be the final decision. He expressed this sentiment clearly to A. H. Hough: "My letters to you will be more in the nature of suggestions, and don't adopt any of them unless they meet with your entire approval . . . but want to remind you again of what I said to you in my room at the bungalow, just before supper Monday evening, as to the conditions upon which we are running the plantation. Business is business and friendship is friendship, and this must be a judicious mixture of both."[119] The letter also suggests the lucrative nature of Hopkins's friendship with the northern owners and reveals more than an opportunistic agenda on his part.

In turn, the northerners illustrated their regard for Hopkins with implicit trust in his ability to manage the plantations. They granted him broad powers as agent, and much of the time these powers related to plantation labor. J. J. Healy, for example, asked the judge to sell any cotton collected in rent rather than keep it.[120] Hopkins retained a good deal of power to influence those orders relative to local agricultural and employment practices. For example, Healy's request that Hopkins sell the cotton was based on Hopkins's "explanation" that this action was advantageous for Healy's income (although it is not clear why Hopkins thought so). Also, Healy left Hopkins with the charge to find good tenants and see that they paid their rent on time; how Hopkins did so did not concern the owner. Healy was not the only owner to leave all labor matters up to Hopkins. In 1904, J. H. Wade wrote to Hopkins inquiring about tenant rents: "Several tenants on my property have asked [to] . . . whom they shall account for their rent. As we know nothing about what arrangements you may have made with them will you kindly give me a list of the tenants on all my property and what arrangements you have made with each."[121] By allowing Hopkins to have full purview of tenant farming labor, northern estate owners showed their trust in his management abilities.

Managers also acted as arbiters of discipline in the owner's stead. Charles Hebard, a Pennsylvania native and owner of Ty-Ty plantation, wrote to Hopkins in 1904 to advise him in the case of a worker who stole a harness. The thief had been discovered, and Hopkins was in charge of deciding the punishment. Hebard asked Hopkins to "wait a little before beginning proceedings on my account" so that Hebard could be fully compensated for the damages.[122] A year later, Hebard again wrote to Hopkins concerning disciplinary strategy. Hopkins had apparently brought to his attention incidents of mishandling hunting dogs. Hebard responded, "I know all you say about dogs and coons is true. It does no harm to let them know that they can't let dogs run the way they did last year but I don't mean to be too hard on them."[123] In this case, Hebard's orders to not "be too hard on them" overrode Hopkins's initial impulse, whatever it was. But Hebard's validation of Hopkins's complaint about "dogs and coons"—even his use of racial slur—illustrates his sympathy with Hopkins.

Clearly, northerners were willing for traditional southern patterns of labor to continue. On one hand, owners hoped to make a profit on their lands; on the other, the spatial pattern of tenant farming, with its scattered field edges, provided a superb habitat for quail. Northern owners' benefits from tenantry meant that Thomasville and the surrounding region exhibited the same trend of the postwar South in that the land tenure system became more entrenched as the nineteenth century progressed. In the Red Hills region, the numbers of tenant farmers were racially skewed; in 1875, for example, there were 2,155 Black farmers in Thomas County who sharecropped, rented land, or worked for wages on a larger farm. When comparing those with the 562 white farmers in the land tenure system at the same time, racial distinctions are hard to ignore.[124] In 1900, the numbers continued to reflect racial disparity; of 1,498 farms operated by Black farmers, 1,133 of those were run on a cash or shares basis (as opposed to the 644 white tenants operating within 1,685 white-run farms).[125] Northern owners became landlords of primarily Black tenants and sharecropping families when they bought property in the area.

The rent lists that Hopkins created as manager reflect this reality. In 1910, Hopkins sent a memorandum to A. H. Mason, owner of Susina plantation, that included rents collected for the previous year as well as all accounts paid for Mason by Hopkins. Of the twenty-one tenant families on the plantation, two were white. The 1910 census identifies the rest of the families as "negro" or "mulatto."[126] Of these farmers, only Spence Hadley, a Black man, paid rent in cash. The rest of the families paid in shares, between 350 and 500 pounds of cotton.[127] Hopkins's role in managing tenant rents was important to northern owners in order that they make a profit from their lands. There are numerous examples in Judge Hopkins's letters about a concern on the part of northerners to increase rents. Healy issued a directive to "look for good tenants for the coming year and see if we may not somehow increase the income."[128] A. H. Hough told Hopkins that "while I had poor shooting this year—except on turkeys—I had the additional satisfaction of getting my rents up from 12 to 23 bales."[129] In another letter, he expressed dissatisfaction about tenant turnover on Spring Hill: "I am mighty sorry to hear we have lost 2 tenants just when we are prepared for more instead of fewer. I hope you can sign up some good ones this fall."[130] The northerners assumed that Hopkins could indeed "sign up" farm labor fairly easily, and he probably could—by the first decade of the twentieth century, he had earned a solid reputation among local Black workers who sought employment with the northerners. Ross Johnson wrote Hopkins with the hope of becoming a plantation manager at Susina, the Mason estate. Johnson assured Hopkins that he knew "Plantation work."[131] Although Johnson was not looking for a job as a farm laborer, it is possible that Hopkins received applications from those who were.

Beyond farming their land in cotton, which continued until World War II when quail conservation advocates pushed for diversified farming, northern estate owners also exploited their lands for additional commodities, especially timber. Northerners could draw premium prices for pine, particularly the longleaf variety, much valued for its use as lumber. Oscar Zeller, a local timber dealer, wrote Charles Hebard in 1903 with regard to the trees on Hebard's estate: "The timber on your property should be worth to any man with a mill at least $15,000.00 or more than the cost of the plantation." Though Hebard was selling stands of both short- and longleaf pine, the longleaf was much more valuable; Zeller noted that one 248-acre stand of longleaf would sell at $12 per acre.[132] Two years later, Hebard was again making timber deals and, as in other arenas of plantation management, was relying on Hopkins to act as a middleman. Desiring to conserve timber stands for future sale, Hebard asked that Hopkins trade only acreage that had been "turpentined." Hebard continued his directive that Hopkins "go ahead and make a trade but dont sell any part of the timber that you think I could ever want and *sell land too* if you sell only such as I will not need at all." Though Hebard was concerned about maintaining any "pretty hammock" of pine, his note to Hopkins confirms that, though sites of leisure, quail plantations were also exploited for natural resource extraction.[133] These examples of production on private estates mirrored a larger growth of the timber and naval stores industries across the South, a development that would put pressure on wildlife habitat and hunters' access to land.

Northern land consolidation and land use angered local white smallholders. Not all farmers in southern Thomas County and the Red Hills region looked to be bought out of their lands by wealthy northerners, and voices of dissent peppered local newspapers. Efforts in 1904 to form a new county from parts of Thomas and Decatur Counties, for example, provided the perfect opportunity to air grievances against the sportsmen. The "county movement" of that year was statewide; an earlier amendment to the Georgia Constitution ruling against the creation of new counties (in a state already encumbered by many) was challenged by then governor Joseph M. Terrell. With Terrell's support in 1904, the state legislature adopted a constitutional amendment allowing the admittance of 8 new counties (and established a cap at 145 counties entire). The amendment began a clamor by enterprising towns throughout the state to go their own way, one of which was Cairo, Georgia, located fourteen miles west of Thomasville.[134]

Cairo was an emerging market town and railroad stop that served as a trading center for farmers in western Thomas County and eastern Decatur County. It had been a Populist stronghold where party sympathizers still remained.[135] The initial push for a new county was cited largely as a matter of logistics; as the editor of the *Cairo Messenger* explained, a new county "would be a great convenience for the people in this neighborhood, as this is another instance where the people have to go from 15 to 25 miles to reach the county seat."[136] Traveling the fourteen miles to Thomasville or the twenty-two miles to Bainbridge (county seat of Decatur), the editor argued, was simply inconvenient and costly for farmers in and around Cairo who needed to move produce or conduct business at the county courthouse and in the cities' shops. Creating a new county, with Cairo as the county seat, would allow for new and convenient municipal buildings and, as the argument went, would spur Cairo's growth as a market town.

Yet a cadre of locals opposed the movement. Chief among these dissident voices were the editors of the *Thomasville Times-Enterprise and South Georgia Progress*, who used their paper to attack the movement and raise concerns over the possible dangers of breaking up two large counties. They argued that by doing so, the dominant source of revenue would be lost, thereby raising taxes in Thomas County. They questioned the necessity of a new county seat so close to larger towns and wondered aloud whether the new county movement was a power grab by would-be politicians.[137] In even more emotional terms, the anti-faction also raised the issue of race and politics. At a public debate held in Thomasville in 1905, for example, a resolution created by opponents to the new county argued that because Blacks made up a majority of the citizenry in Thomas County, a new county "would subordinate again their former associates and neighbors" to "this overwhelming mass of ignorance and idleness." Appealing to the new county supporters, the resolution entreated them to "have a human regard for the safety and well-being of their neighbors, who were their comrades in the long and bitter struggle [during Reconstruction] for white supremacy in Thomas County."[138] Piggybacking on fears of whites becoming a racial minority, the anti-county movement referenced the presidential election of 1896, when Thomas had been the only county to vote a majority for McKinley, the Republican candidate. When H. W. Hopkins came to the defense of the new county with arguments of popular sovereignty, editors in Thomasville, for example, accused him of "endeavoring to bring about a coalition of affairs by which Thomas county might become Black Republican." Though "Black Republican" was a common epithet in the one-party system of southern politics, attacking Hopkins, who everyone knew was an ally of the northern sportsmen—including the Hanna family, who had invited McKinley to Thomasville to meet with southern Republicans in 1896—was symbolic. Questioning Hopkins's appeal to republican principles, the editors complained of his "sophomoric . . . repetition of trite catch phrases—'vital principles of republics, essence of Democracy freedom and independence.'" They asked Hopkins, "Do you want to square your actions by a definition? Are you willing for white and black to vote? Did Webster know about the color line?"[139] Raising the specter of Black political autonomy and control and subtly connecting that to the influence of wealthy northerners on county politics, these opponents of the new county relied upon fearmongering to rail against the new county movement.

Supporters of the new county counterattacked, going beyond arguments for convenience to strategies that pitted the new county and its population of small farmers against the landed interests in Thomasville. The attacks went to the heart of Thomas County's reputation as a hunting destination: its seasonal northern population. Countering the claim that a new county would raise taxes in Thomas, Grady County supporters, as reported by the *Cairo Messenger*, wondered why they should "any longer help to pay taxes to keep up Thomasville and to work the Thomasville roads so their 'distinguished winter visitors' can air themselves luxuriously around in rubber tire carriages and four horse tallyho's?" The editor continued, "If Thomasville has let her winter birds roost, and set, on all the land around there, driving out home people from their little farms . . . who is responsible for it?" Proponents of the new county pit the "foreign and privileged millionaire class" who had "gobble[d] up . . . lands" against the "home people" who were shut out of the "rich soil . . . which surrounded" the town. In the rhetoric of heated argument, Grady County supporters cast themselves as the heirs of a Jeffersonian Republic of yeoman farmers and the "distinguished winter visitors" as land-hungry fat cats who earned their wealth from "favored trusts."[140]

Voices in Leon County echoed concerns about land consolidation of northern sportsmen. In the Tallahassee *Weekly True Democrat*, one writer compared the game preserves of the Red Hills region to the sporting domains of British gentry and noted that in both cases small farmers were forced out of the area. A 1914 editorial in the paper argued, "As much as the *True Democrat* appreciates the good judgment of wealthy men buying up large landed interest in Leon County for game preserves, it prevents the prosperity we are so anxious to see. Small farms are the true source of dependence, and the policy that prevents an increase of population is wrong and damaging."[141] Earlier, the editor had expressed a wish to see "the adoption of some plan whereby the large landed interests of Leon County could be converted into small, profitable farms."[142] By 1920, this vision had not been fulfilled, prompting the editor to lodge another complaint in the paper: "Leon County is suffering much because large landlords are not bringing their immense acreage into production of needed crops."[143]

Locals would have had natural resentment in the face of other changes wrought by northern presence. For one thing, the alluring prey for northern hunters—quail—meant that the bird both was the subject of early, countywide protective laws and commanded a premium at local markets (when selling game was still legal). When Charlie Young was a boy in the late 1880s, "quails was every Whair no one ceard about them," and locals could buy the birds at the market for fifteen cents. If a hunter wanted to sell the birds, Young remembered, "those was the days when you could set a trap eny whair you wanted to and some time catch the hole covey of 15 Birds no one thought enything about it." Trapping was outlawed in Thomas County by the state legislature in 1876; the observations of Young suggest that these laws, as was the fate for so many local game and fish laws, were ignored.[144] But, as land was increasingly privatized and posted and trespass laws were enforced by game wardens, the trapping and hunting on the part of local Blacks and whites were curtailed.

Northern hunting culture also changed the kind of ammunition that local stores carried. Even the traditional black powder shells that Charlie Young remembered were out of reach for many Black hunters. Shells, he noted, "cost in those days 40 C a box all Black Powder shells," which was "so hye" that Black hunters "could not go mutch." The black powder shells were generally inconvenient for bird shooting; the smoke produced by a shot meant "you would have to step down to se did you get a Bird." When the "Yankie started to come hear . . . he had what was call the Smokeless Shells no smoke at all."[145] But, the smokeless shell cost was too high for the average hunter, white or Black. Yet Young noted that in some ways Black hunting culture was not affected by white elite hunting priorities—especially for Black landowners, "the ones that had they own land," Black hunters "never ceard for bird hunting ... coons rabbit posom was their joy at night and it is about the same today they love hound dogs so do I."[146]

As Young suggests, landowners, Black or white, were generally insulated from the worst ramifications of elite hunting culture. But, the consolidation of lands in the Red Hills aligned with changes happening across the region that curtailed the open range and prioritized private property protection.[147] As early as 1885, several local citizens attempted to keep their lands free from shooting by posting an advertisement in the *Thomasville Times*, warning that "all hunters are hereby forbidden to hunt on the grounds of the undersigned with dogs or guns."[148] Notices of this sort, however, remained unheeded and poorly enforced, and until 1916, though there were laws related to trespass and posted lands, no fence laws existed in Thomas County.[149] When northern hunters built quail estates of their own, they established their own rules, effected by enforcement through fences and game wardens.[150]

Young commented on the closing of common hunting grounds. When he was a boy, he remembered, "if you wanted to hunt you could go and hunt eny whair you wanted to White are Black did not make eny difrence." Access to land lasted "untill all the of the local hunters was stop by a law that you would have a Pas from the oner to hunt eny whair." Young likely referred to the 1895 Georgia law that allowed the posting of land as a way to control hunting and fishing on private property. Though it did not explicitly require a pass, in 1903 Georgia extended the law, requiring that landowners file their name, notice of posted lands, and the land boundary in a "Register for Posting Lands" kept by the county ordinary. In Thomas County, the third, fourth, and fifth entries in the county register were posted by H. W. Hopkins on behalf of his own lands and northern owners J. H. Wade and Charles H. Thorne.[151]

Young recounted that signs on northerner-owned property and fences began to dot the rural landscape, notifying trespassers of their illegal status and warning them of the consequences if caught poaching. He recalled that "the first sign put up in this country was by ... Dr. Metcalfe."[152] Northerners also fenced their property. In 1904, just as he was beginning to purchase land in the area, J. H. Wade wrote to Hopkins that "I am going to fence my entire property at once. The two ten acres pieces on the Boulevard I would like to sell in order to avoid fencing around them. What can you get them for? I will fence around the Girtman place west of the road and run the present road around it also."[153] A. H. Mason, owner of Susina plantation, purchased 1,000 posts from a local man in 1910 in order to fence in his lands.[154]

None of these efforts, however, successfully kept out poachers. Charles Chapin asked Hopkins if he had "heard of any shooting or poaching on my T. C. Mitchell lands and if so is there anything you could do or I, to stop it." He ventured to Hopkins that "maybe something could be done to avoid finding birds shot up as I did last year."[155] C. A. Griscom, who owned land in Leon County, wrote to A. H. Mason that he was anxious to find a warden for his lands: "As far as I know we have no Game-warden yet and I consider the situation precarious. Mr. R. G. Johnson, who is my Agent and lives on Horseshoe Plantation, is trying now to find a man for reasonable wages who has the ability and the nerve. It is no easy position to fill. I will seek your advice if we succeed in securing a suitable man."[156] Griscom's letter suggests that northern hunters took poaching and trespassing very seriously, and his anxiousness reflects that locals continued to hunt as they did before, regardless of posts or fences. He also indicates that efforts to employ a warden were sometimes collective, or at least that northerners shared information when it came to the hiring process. Sometimes a group of plantation owners actually did share a warden, as was the case with the Iamonia Lake Club. The club, like its predecessor, the Cracker Gun Club, was a collective of wealthy northern hunters and a few of the southern elite, including Hopkins (the club's president), who shared shooting access to exclusive lands. The club's bylaws provided a clause to employ a game warden who would protect lands from trespassers.[157] In later years, the position of game warden became one appointed by Georgia's Department of Game and Fish, but Hopkins and the northerners continued to hold sway over appointments in the area. In 1933, C. D. Jordan, from nearby Monticello, Georgia, wrote to Hopkins seeking the position of game warden in Thomas County. He asked that Hopkins "write Mr. Lou [sic] Thompson and the other millionaire owners of estates down there and ask them to endorse me to Governor [Eugene] Talmadge."[158] Hopkins, who was well connected in the Department of Game and Fish, likely had no problem securing the appointment.[159]

Some customary privileges prevailed on the quail hunting plantations in Thomas County and the Red Hills region. Workers who were employed by northerners, such as Charlie Young, and tenants on the property had permission to hunt on the estates. Young remembered that "you could hunt eny whair you wanted to . . . all the felds was fenced in and all the owners ask you to do is to put up the fence when you open it . . . and the owner ask only of you not shoot his stock and that stod a long time."[160] This allowance, however, was considered a privilege extended to other elite sportsmen or their employees, not a right for southerners who had previously been accustomed to an open range.[161]

Indeed, sportsmen were building their estates just as game laws in Georgia became more stringent and, as some argued, reflective of the interests of elite hunters, including the desire to stop roving hunters from accessing estate lands. Critics of the laws pointed out that sportsmen had a good deal of influence on game policy. H. W. Hopkins, in fact, was an active voice in solidifying the state's transformation of game laws. Hopkins, who served in the state legislature throughout the early twentieth century, was active in the development of the Department of Game and Fish. He became such an important advocate for the department, in fact, that in 1915 the commissioner called him "one of the best friends of game protection in Georgia" and invited him to use the department's offices as headquarters for his senate term.[162]

Hopkins and two other congressmen had been part of efforts to create a regulatory department in Georgia during the Progressive Era. Hopkins introduced the bill in 1911 to create a Department of State Conservation. Though the measure was initially tabled and sent to a special committee, amended, and renamed, the Department of Game and Fish, which standardized game and fish laws throughout the state following similar laws in Alabama, was in place by August of that year.[163] The department had powers to appoint a state game and fish commissioner, to select wardens and deputy wardens, to create a licensing structure for in-season hunting, and to criminalize violations of game and fish laws. By 1911, those state laws went beyond the establishment of seasons, the outlawing of trapping, and bag limits (which, for quail, were twenty-five birds per diem), all restrictions that were in place by the 1890s. New laws in effect August 21, 1911, and given "teeth" by the creation of the Department of Game and Fish made licenses necessary. As in Alabama, to hunt in one's own county cost one dollar, in the entire state, three dollars, and for a nonresident, fifteen dollars. The law did allow that "a person may hunt and fish in the open season in his own militia district or on his own land without a license," and it was legal for tenants to hunt without a license on "leased and rented" land with the permission of the owner. New laws also made it illegal to transport game to another state or county unless accompanied by the game hunter, an amendment squarely aimed at criminalizing market hunting and subsequent sale of game.[164] These laws, shaped as they were by men such as Wallace and Hopkins, followed the statutes of sporting culture elsewhere in the United States.[165] New laws, ostensibly for the conservation of game, privileged hunting for leisure and made operation more difficult for those who hunted for sustenance or additional income. Hopkins, an avid sportsman and ally to northern hunters in Thomas County and the Red Hills region, supported state game laws that reflected the priorities of elite interests.

As in Alabama, the Georgia game laws did not go unchallenged. Farmers from across the state took notice of the state's nod to sportsmen. Some wrote to *The Jeffersonian*, the magazine of famed Populist Tom Watson, to air their grievances. Even before the Department of Game and Fish was in place, W. L. Dorris echoed similar themes, casting the interests of sportsmen and farmers as being at odds. While sportsmen, he argued, came during hunting season "to the different railroad towns" to shoot indiscriminately, even on posted lands, farmers and tenants who had spent the year raising the birds for meat and for the eradication of insects had to stand by "indignant." Dorris was against a state licensing program; he argued that "under a State license the State is their domain, and the farmers must stand by and see their birds shot down and their crops trod down, without recourse." Dorris's descriptions of sportsmen, with their "imported setters and pointers and brand new guns that glistened in the November sunshine like so many mirrors," emphatically stressed the moneyed aspect of sport hunting. He warned that Georgia would be without a truly protective game law as long as the "sporting fraternity" had influence over game policy and the "legislature enact[ed] laws to meet their hearty approval."[166] Dorris would foreshadow the later criticism of new game laws after 1911.

Another landowner, for example, called for the repeal of all extant game laws in 1916 and took particular issue with the illegality of trapping and marketing game. Citing a property owner's traditional right to kill and sell game on his own land, the writer lamented that only "evils" resulted from the law and that the farmer was "deprived of making money legitimately; those not sportsmen are deprived of the privilege of occasionally eating a little game." Ridiculing concerns about conservation as merely lip service, the writer wondered why "conservation" meant sacrifice by the farmers (when it was they who could raise, trap, and transport birds to other lands, for example) while no one stopped the "'sportsman' killing twenty-five birds" per day "during the open season for 'sport.'" The writer argued that "the law operates against the landowner and farmer, and prevents real conservation, and likewise against everybody other than the 'sportsman.'"[167] Three years earlier, when the laws were still new, Francis H. Harris of Brunswick, Georgia, a coastal destination popular with hunters and anglers, lambasted the state laws as protective only of sportsmen. Like the writer in 1916, Harris found the outlawing of killing and selling game found on one's own property to be an egregious violation; he reasoned that if farmers could raise and sell their own stock, they could likewise raise and sell wild game. After Harris's lengthy critique and call for farmers to cry out in protest, *The Jeffersonian*'s Watson agreed that "no man could be deprived of the legal right to protect his crops, at all times," from wild game and birds by trapping and shooting outside of hunting season. "Legislative enactments to the contrary," Watson concluded, "are pluperfect hog-wash."[168]

Not all farmers were critical of the new laws, however, and some wanted them to go even further with regard to the curtailing of Black mobility. Although the law allowed that people could hunt in their own militia district without license and that tenants could hunt and fish on land they farmed, with permission of the owner, some smallholders, such as Thomas County local R. R. Redfearn, supported the curtailing of even these rights. He wrote to Hopkins concerned about the need for shooting and fishing restrictions because of "triflen negroes" who fished anywhere they pleased.[169] Though Redfearn may not have known it, the State of Georgia was on his side. Charles Arnow, the commissioner of the Department of Game and Fish in 1917, wrote in his annual report that "many irresponsible persons" took advantage of the militia district exception and disregarded "other rights of neighbors" who might have posted their land. He singled out "large numbers of negroes" for these types of transgressions "who are glad of an excuse to prowl through the woods, with dog and gun, when they had far better devote their time and energies to pursuits more in line with their temperaments and necessities." Not considering that the "necessities" of Black farmers might include food supplied by hunting, Arnow considered the mobility of Black hunters—who were within their legal right to hunt without a license—dangerous. To keep Black farmers "in line" and at work, he recommended amending the game law to make hunting without a license legal only for property holders.[170] Sam Slate, the commissioner in 1918, echoed Arnow's recommendation in his report the next year.[171] Game laws enacted in the Progressive Era in Georgia, just as in Alabama, could work as a form of social control.

"The Place I Call Home": Life and Labor in the Red Hills Region

By the 1920s, northern sportsmen had changed their approach to land use, largely due to the decrease in quail population that became acute in the second decade of the twentieth century. Concerned about the lack of game, a group of hunters (including Charles Chapin, L. S. Thompson, owner of Sunny Hill plantation, and Arthur B. Lapsley, owner of Meridian plantation) approached the Bureau of Biological Survey, which appointed naturalist Herbert L. Stoddard to study the quail population and offer remedies to the bird's decline.[172] Stoddard published his results in *The Bobwhite Quail*, which became the preeminent guidebook for protection of the bird. Stoddard's management techniques criticized commercial agriculture, particularly cotton cultivation strategies. Large-scale agriculture depleted the soil, deteriorating the food supply for quail and leaving them with no cover for a habitat. Instead, less-intensive "patch-style" agriculture (small plots of cultivated land separated by brush or tree stands) was the best environment for the bird to thrive.[173] This directive was an incentive for northern hunters to maintain the sharecropping system, which employed patch-style farming, but to allow for less intensive agricultural production. The result of the move toward conservation was, as the *Tallahassee True Democrat* editor put it in 1914, fewer acres of land for smaller farms and cotton cultivation.

The game preserves affected local smallholders yet also put a ceiling on the upward movement of tenants and sharecroppers in the region. Not only did it become less likely for people to own land because of scarcity, but it was also less likely for tenant farmers to produce enough cotton or corn to make a substantial earning above their rent. The new land management strategies disrupted other tenant farming practices that had continued under northern purview. Stoddard, for instance, disparaged stock-raising practices on northerners' estates: "There are entirely too many scrub cattle on many Southern quail preserves: Fifteen to twenty head per negro tenant family are not uncommon in an area where one or two well-bred cows would give more milk and do vastly less harm to the place." He went on to argue that "the most destructive practice of all is to run the animals out over the [quail] nesting ground 'minded' only by some irresponsible pickaninny, for many nests are then certain to be trampled on."[174] Using racist language, Stoddard reminded the northern owner to manage his labor with more efficiency. The warnings proved effective, as northern owners began to supply their tenants purebred cattle so that the number of stock would be reduced.[175]

Albert Way argues that Stoddard, in his work on the quail preserves of the Red Hills region, is an important and often overlooked figure in the American conservation movement that took hold in the Progressive Era. Stoddard's ability to bring together the emerging professional and scientific priorities of land resource management and local environmental knowledge and practice—particularly controlled burning—set into place a model of "biocentric" management that persists today (several of the game plantations, including Tall Timbers, once home to Edward Beadel's yellow wagons, remain intact as preserves that are dedicated to research and conservation initiatives). But Way also affirms that the southern conservation movement headed by Stoddard and the northern estate owners was essentially conservative in nature. The quail plantations always remained in private hands, as opposed to state and federal land trusts, and the movement was founded as "less an oppositional reaction to the growth of industrial and corporate America than a concomitant to it." Ultimately, northern owners "did as they pleased under the property rights structure of the post–open range New South."[176] Although northern owners moved away from southern methods of crop cultivation, they maintained their close connection to men like Hopkins, who continued to promote their interests locally and statewide. Hopkins acted as agent for many northerners through the 1930s, including L. S. Thompson, John F. Archbold, and George F. Baker, of New York.[177] The main purpose of the winter colony, hunting, never changed, nor did Hopkins and the northern set stop identifying as sportsmen. The leisure economy had, beginning in the late nineteenth century, only continued the social divides that characterized the South: the continuation of the land tenure system, overwhelmingly populated by Black farmers, well into the twentieth century; the struggle by small farmers against the privatization of hunting grounds and consolidation of the area's most fertile lands; and the representation of elite interests in state law, in this case with regard to the creation of the Department of Game and Fish and the game laws enacted therein.

But the development of new considerations of habitat conservation forecast efforts to unfold in Mississippi by the 1930s, when changing attitudes toward wildlife protection underlay attempts to finally create meaningful regulation in the state. Charlie Young was an eyewitness to this new conservation push; he spent his later career working for L. S. Thompson, who led efforts to pursue scientific quail study. He remembered Herbert Stoddard as "the man that came hear in 1935 through the greatest quail lover of all and would do anything to make more birds Mr Stodards moto was to have 3 Birds whair we has only got 2." In Young's opinion, Stoddard "did all hunters a great favor."[178]

Young did not tell why or when he stopped working for his former employer H. E. Thompson as a young man, but on "the first day of March 1915" he began employment with the other Thompson, not related.[179] "So funy," Young recalled, "I do Beleave I had the 2 Best shots in the US and they both was Thompsons."[180] L. S. Thompson, for whom Young worked until 1936, was the son of an oil refiner who had joined the Standard Oil conglomerate early and became its treasurer. The younger Thompson inherited his father's fortune and spent much of his time hunting. He had come to Thomasville in 1905 through the proselytizing of Charles Chapin, who employed Young's uncle Jim Mitchell. Thompson quickly began to make land acquisitions in both Thomas County and Leon County, Florida, contiguous counties in the Red Hills region, buying from other northerners as well as locals, and eventually built an estate that covered 20,000 acres.[181] It was on this estate, Sunny Hill, that Young eventually worked into the early 1940s (he remained on the estate when Thompson died and it transferred to New Jersey governor Walter E. Edge).

Young and his family lived both on and off of Sunny Hill plantation, and there his duties continued to expand. According to the memories of his granddaughter Jule Anderson, he lived on the plantation in the late 1930s, when she was a child. She recalled staying at Sunny Hill for short periods in the summer while her parents visited New York City. Anderson remembered that during her visits, Charlie Young still cared for and trained the hunting dogs. "The kennel was just outside of our house," she recalled, "and he would go get the ticks off the dogs and bathe them." Young also got the dogs ready for hunts; "he would have the dogs ready to go into the hunting wagons." Young himself would don a uniform when he accompanied the hunters. "Even the men," Anderson noted, "had special caps and jackets they wore."[182] Young also continued to do landscaping work at Sunny Hill. His daughter, Virginia Anderson, Jule's mother, remembered that "he landscaped the whole place. He hauled the shrubbery from the Gulf of Mexico and it was a beautiful, beautiful place. Everybody liked to see it."[183] Along with his regular duties as dog handler and landscape gardener, Jule Anderson recalled that Young served as a kind of liaison between other workers on Sunny Hill and the owner: "I remember that people picked cotton and did other jobs on the plantation and they would come to our house to be paid. There was a screened-in front porch and I remember people coming in there to get paid."[184] She noted that her grandfather received the money to dispense to these workers, indicating that, in this case, they were not paid by the plantation superintendent as might normally be the case. Like his work for Thompson in New Jersey, where he served as more of a foreman, Charlie Young was separated from other workers in position and rank on Sunny Hill.

The size of his home and his material possessions also reflected this separation. Anderson remembered that "on the plantation, other houses that I saw, this is of Black people's houses, I thought his was one of the nicer houses."[185] The insurance records of Walter Edge, who bought Sunny Hill in 1938 after the death of L. S. Thompson and who continued to employ Young, reflect that

Young's house was among the larger on the estate. It, along with that of R. E. Stringer, the white superintendent, was listed ("Charlie Young's House") as being insured at $2,000. Of other employees' homes, only the "servants house" near the main estate was listed for as much; most other "employee's dwellings" were listed at $500 each.[186]

Young benefited by being a favorite of Thompson's before his death. Thompson not only trusted Young to take on many duties at Sunny Hill and at Thompson's northern estate but also took Young on many hunting trips to the King Ranch, a famous preserve in Texas, and other locales. Thompson also presented Young with gifts of game from his more adventurous hunting trips. Jule Anderson recalled that Thompson

> would go to Africa to shoot. I remember he had killed a buffalo, an African buffalo. And after going to the taxidermist and having it all stuffed he gave this particular trophy to my grandfather. So in the living room [at the home on Sunny Hill] over the mantelpiece was this huge head of an African buffalo sticking out, so I can remember this African buffalo that he ended up bringing to Thomasville. He actually had it on the front of the house on 411 Pine Street [near downtown Thomasville]. That was really funny, and of course the weather decayed it, so that African buffalo was gone.[187]

Gifts like this one were signals that Young was respected and well-liked by Thompson. The African buffalo seemed to have been a treasured trophy for Young, who, as Anderson mentioned, continued to hang it on his home in downtown Thomasville for all neighbors to see until it fell away from decay. Young certainly spoke of Thompson with admiration in his text and as more than just a "Great shot." He remembered his employer in elegiac prose: "Mr LS Thompson who Bones are Blacking in his grave to day gone but will never never be forgotten."[188]

Young wrote of his time working at Sunny Hill in positive terms, emphasizing his love of dogs: "What a great place it was at that time from 1915 to 1941," he wistfully noted, "a time I shall never never forget had some great dogs their old John John Binkins was one."[189] There was much about the work, such as caring for dogs and hunting, and even living on the estate for Young to remember with real pleasure. Jule Anderson recalled, for instance, large parties he threw on Sunny Hill. Young "invited people from in-town, from Thomasville." Anderson recalled especially the abundant watermelons that grew around the house: "People would take the watermelon and throw it down and crush it and . . . eat the center of the watermelon."[190] These parties

Charlie Young pictured with his first wife, Carrie, and granddaughter, Jule Anderson, ca. 1930s. In author's possession.

would likely happen in the summer, when the watermelons were ripe and when the northern families had returned to their homes, yet the gatherings and large gardens suggest that Young was free to use his own grounds as he pleased.

Still, living on Sunny Hill meant the loss of some autonomy, especially during the fall and winter hunting season when Thompson and his family would be in residence. Virginia Anderson, Young's daughter, recalled as a child moving off the plantation because "we didn't like the country. It was lonesome out there."[191] Perhaps Anderson was speaking for herself rather than for her mother and father; it might not have been loneliness that prompted Young to move but rather that his family owned several property lots downtown. Other plantation workers cited the search for autonomy as a motive for their families to buy homes in the growing Black neighborhoods around Thomasville. Jack Hadley, whose family worked on Pebble Hill plantation, noted that his family moved downtown in 1947 for similar reasons: "When I look back on that I think my dad [the Pebble Hill chauffeur] saw the handwriting on the wall. He knew that one day that life was going to come to an end and he wanted to make sure that his family was situated in their personal home and not living on the plantation and depending on the owners of the plantation to provide for his family after he left. That's my only conclusion, that my dad made that decision."[192] That some Black plantation workers, like Hadley's father and Charlie Young, could afford to buy a home speaks to the decency of their wages. Their choice to reside off of the plantation also suggests that whatever the benefits and furnishings provided by plantation owners, they were limited in the sense that support for families seldom continued after workers' retirement or death. Many workers preferred to live out of sight of the northerners, within their own communities.

Charlie Young ended his employment at Sunny Hill in 1941 and by 1946 is listed as living in Thomasville, the town that he designated as "the Place I call home."[193] Young resided in a house around the corner from one of the properties his parents had owned and operated as a boardinghouse. His daughter, Virginia, and her husband, Essic Anderson, and daughter, Jule, now occupied that familial home and continued renting rooms while Essic ran a café called the Paradise Grill (the café served Black soldiers who came to Thomasville for training and could not patronize other restaurants in the Jim Crow South).[194] Young was married to his second wife, Grace, and operated a lunchroom called the Oak Street Whip in 1946, although it seems that this establishment was closed by 1950.[195] In that same year, he again was listed as being a dog trainer, indicating that he may have continued to work for other plantation owners or even locals. By the time he wrote his "Reminiscences" in 1964, however, he had fully retired.

The context in which Young wrote down his memories influenced the choices he made about what to tell. Concerns of authorship—clearly writing for a white historian and his implied audience—shaped Young's narrative of race relations in Thomas County and his willingness to temper commentary on the oppression of Jim Crow in the Red Hills. Furthermore, Young's age at the time of writing might have given plantation work a brighter corona than it deserved; the limitations or hardships of the work—mercurial employers, petty humiliations, disruption of family life—disappear in Young's narrative.

But, even within the contexts in which he wrote, the meaning Young attributed to his life and work runs through the text with clarity. He reminded readers again at the end of his memoir of his true passion and pride: hunting and dogs. "When you can get a good pack of hounds runing a fox all to gather," he said, "now there is joy in the first degree."[196] Young's account illustrates the broader strokes of working in the sporting tourism economy and that working was contingent upon the growth of hunting estates, which wrought the land enclosure and consolidation of the Red Hills. His guidance provides an invaluable cue to historians of the present; he saw and commented on legal, social, political, and environmental changes that emerged in the early twentieth century, as transregional sportsmen cemented ties in the South around elite forms of hunting. This bond, and the world it created for local whites and Blacks, worked together with changes in property law to extend enclosure begun after the Civil War, the influence of the growing conservation movement, and an increasing presence of federal policy, to create new conditions for hunters and their game in the Deep South. The story now turns to Mississippi and a lover of flora and fauna, Fannye Cook, to chart the role of the federal government in setting up a regulatory regime for game and fish in that state.

4 Fannye A. Cook, the Federal Government, and the Maturation of Game and Fish Laws in the Deep South

At a statewide conservation convention held in 1931, Mississippi secretary of state Walker Wood brought a message to attending lawmakers: Mississippi's lack of meaningful game and fish regulation was an embarrassment to the state. He pleaded with attendees to support and lobby for a department of game and fish. His office, he argued, "continuously [got] official publications, magazines and annual reports from the Fish and Game departments of a great many states and from the Federal government. These reports show that the whole country is very much awake to conservation needs and that great things are being done by the various states to perpetuate their wildlife." He lamented, "In all survey reports it is observed that Mississippi is the only state from which information concerning game conditions is not available."[1]

The state lagged behind the rest of the country, even neighboring southern states, at a time when the federal government (and concerned citizens) increasingly turned attention to conservation policy. Echoing Wood, Mississippi congressman W. M. Whittington lamented the state's failure to embrace conservation work in a speech given to the Mississippi Association for the Conservation of Wild Life. A federal congressional report just completed by a special committee on wildlife conservation sought to survey "federal activities for the conservation of all forms of wild life, the first attempt to outline a comprehensive national program and to analyze the situation and propose remedies." Mississippi, being the "only state in the nation without a fish and game department," was losing out in efforts to coordinate federal and state partnerships in conservation policy. "I trust that the next Legislature," Whittington added, "will establish an adequate department."²

Indeed, by 1932, Mississippi would have a statewide commission dedicated to the regulation of game and fish. But the story departs from that of Alabama and Georgia. Mississippi's crusader for game and fish regulation was no less passionate or prepared than John H. Wallace Jr., but instead of coming from the ranks of committed sportsmen, the Magnolia State's premier conservationist was a scientist—and a woman. Though Fannye A. Cook (1889–1964) understood the role of sportsmen in game, fish, and bird preservation, her motivation for species protection was impelled by Mississippi's lack of action to value its wildlife for recreational, commercial, and aesthetic reasons. As someone committed to scientific education, Cook's vision for game, fish, and bird conservation would extend to regulatory enforcement as well as to a broad-reaching educational program and partnerships with Mississippi secondary schools, colleges, and universities.

Cook came of age in the Progressive Era, of which women were a shaping force and when the conservation movement matured and gained legislative ground in states across the nation. The 1930s maintained movement toward state consolidation that began during the Progressive Era; some politicians argued that centralized departments, such as that of a state game and fish commission, would result in a more efficient implementation of the state's many functions. Perhaps most significant, by the time Cook made it her mission to protect Mississippi wildlife, she and other advocates would do so with the backing of the federal government—not just federal agencies, like the Bureau of Biological Survey, that had been so important to conservationists across the South, or federal legislation like the Migratory Bird Treaty Act of 1918. With the advent of the New Deal and its expansive program for conservation of diverse kinds, Cook and the Mississippi Game and Fish Commission could rely on federal funds to enlarge and fulfill their objectives of enforcing stronger protection of wildlife and, as they saw it, to finally convince rural Mississippians of the value therein.³ Cook's career illuminates the growth of federal presence in game, bird, and fish protection and the maturation of game and fish laws, and what was called "conservation work" more broadly, by focusing on the evolution of Mississippi's laws and their flowering in the 1930s.

"A Little Island of Destruction for Wild Life": Fannye Cook and the Mississippi Association for the Conservation of Wild Life

Fannye A. Cook was born in Copiah County, Mississippi. Her father, Gilbert Morris Cook, was a farmer, and he and her mother, Martha Ellen Pierce, began family life in rural Copiah County. Fannye was the seventh born to the Cooks, who eventually had ten children and moved to the town of Crystal Springs in 1902.[4] Cook inherited a love of the natural world from her father, and as a child she collected specimens from the surrounding flora and fauna.[5] With encouragement from her family, and as a woman buoyed by the currents of the Progressive Era, Cook would pursue informal and formal education in the biological sciences and would bring her love of the natural world to children at home and abroad.

Cook began her professional life as an educator, and this early experience in rural schools and abroad shaped her later work in conservation advocacy and outreach. In 1911 she received a bachelor of arts degree from the Mississippi State College for Women (now university) in Columbus, Mississippi, yet even before she graduated, she spent a year teaching in a rural school in Holmes County. After obtaining her degree, she moved into the role of principal at a high school in Beauregard, Mississippi, where she also taught botany. She did not remain in Mississippi, however. In the summer of 1913, she ventured to take graduate courses in history and English at the University of Colorado and study the flora around Boulder and Denver. Stories from these travels give a sense of her self-possession and taste for adventure. The writer Eudora Welty, with whom Cook boarded in Jackson, Mississippi, during the 1930s, documented some of these tales. Welty related to a friend that "once in the West [Cook] was climbing a mountain and as she got level with the top she saw a rattlesnake looking right into her eyes. She just looked right back. She knew all about him."[6] Two years following her time out west, she undertook study of the plants of the Panama Canal Zone and stayed into 1916, teaching in Canal Zone schools.[7]

During World War I, Cook briefly served as manager and bookkeeper at Cook Motor Company, run by her brother W. D. in Forest, Mississippi, relieving two men who had been drafted into the war.[8] Not long after the Armistice, she sat for and passed the civil service exam to find work as a tax auditor with the Internal Revenue Service, where, she noted in a curriculum vitae, she "received five promotions in position and salary."[9] Her move to Washington, DC, gave Cook proximity to graduate study at area universities and within the Smithsonian collections. She reported that "evenings and holidays given to regular undergraduate courses in Botany and Zoology at George Washington University" in 1922 gave way to "evenings and holidays" in "graduate courses in natural sciences at George Washington University" in 1924. She also conducted research, with a focus on Mississippi plants and animals, at the Smithsonian Libraries and the Department of Agriculture.[10]

Fannye A. Cook pictured later in life with a white-tailed deer exhibit. She was featured in a 1953 issue of Mississippi Game and Fish *magazine. Mississippi Museum of Natural Science, Jackson.*

In 1924 and 1925, she traveled home to collect plant and animal (including fossil) specimens for the Smithsonian.[11] The National Museum of Natural History's Department of Botany has digitized some of Cook's collections; she gathered and dried, among other species, oakleaf hydrangea, Le Conte's thistle, lobelia, saltmarsh mallow, and pink evening primrose.[12] Her time in DC brought connections to leading natural scientists, including Paul Bartsch, who taught zoology at George Washington and curated the Division of Mollusks at the Smithsonian Institute. Bartsch became a teacher and mentor. Cook also formed a professional connection with ornithologist Alexander Wetmore, who at the time was a field assistant for the Bureau of Biological Survey and later became secretary of the Smithsonian.[13] She would correspond with these men throughout her career.

Fannye Cook's urge to craft a conservation code in Mississippi began in the mid-1920s while traveling between Mississippi and DC for specimen collection. In 1925, her brother W. D. Cook won a seat in the Mississippi House of Representatives to represent Scott County.[14] Letters from family indicate that by March 1926, Fannye had forwarded her brother a draft bill that would create a centralized wildlife protection agency but was "disappointed" in him "not being able to get the bill passed by the Senate that she was so much interested in."[15] She enlisted her family in Mississippi to help produce bulletins championing conservation in the state and to distribute them as her proxies.[16] In this initial effort to wield influence, Cook waded into political waters in an effort to organize popular sentiment and political will toward game and fish laws.

By the summer of 1926, Cook returned to Mississippi to begin a campaign on the ground. Driving herself across the state, she organized talks and exhibits on the bounty and plight of wildlife in Mississippi. R. W. Harned, a professor and entomologist at Mississippi A&M in Starkville (now Mississippi State University), noticed Cook's work and offered her office space at A&M, and from there she continued her advocacy.[17] Cook's message to Mississippi audiences was a clear one—in one interview, she argued that Mississippi was "a little island of destruction for wild life" and warned that game animals and birds were fleeing to neighboring states, "all of which have conservation commissions and preserves and refuges."[18] She appealed to economic interests by comparing Mississippi's lack of regulation of fur trapping to law in Arkansas, which, according to Cook, led to fur market profits of $1.5 million in 1925. Unless Mississippians acted soon, "musk rat, skunk, mink, squirrel, rabbit, mole and other valuable fur-bearing animals . . . will become extinct as has the otter, and the beaver, but for a few isolated pairs and groups."[19] The threat and reality of extinction was a part of Cook's appeal to action.

Cook knew the limits of working as a one-woman campaign, and in 1927 she organized the Mississippi Association for the Conservation of Wild Life (MACWL) to build popular support for conservation and move toward centralized game and fish regulation. Other conservation supporters, including R. W. Harned, joined in the cause. The MACWL directed its work toward advocacy for measures to protect plant and animal life: establishing preserves for fish, game birds and animals, and "wild plants"; "rescuing fish, birds, deer and other wild life from high water and other destructive forces; lecturing to children and the public in interest of wild life conservation; discouraging the pulling and breaking of wild flowers, shrubs and trees which are becoming rare and those which lend beauty to the roadside and landscape; encouraging setting aside of community parks and state and county preserves; insisting upon full enforcement of federal and state game laws; encouraging legislation favorable to the conservation development and proper utilization of wild life."[20] Cook, who named herself executive secretary of the MACWL, welded a commitment to public education to a penchant for organizing: she created the state's first formal lobbying group on behalf of natural resource regulation.

As founding executive secretary, Cook traversed the state to enroll new members.[21] In interviews with newspapers and in press releases, she stressed the aesthetic and economic value of game and fish preservation, often speaking directly to readers: "If you would have a better appreciation of the living things which make Mississippi beautiful and interesting, if you would help pass this appreciation along to others, if you would continue to enjoy and utilize Mississippi's natural resources, pool your interest with that of the rest of us—join the Mississippi Association for the Conservation of Wild Life."[22] Two years after the organization's founding, its leaders claimed to have built support among game wardens and sportsmen, key allies in the work of the MACWL, and no doubt thanks to Cook's organizing work.[23] Beginning in 1927, she "prepared" annual meetings that brought together scientists, game wardens, farmers, and those interested in conservation.[24] These featured key speakers from neighboring game and fish commissions, including I. T. Quinn, who had followed John H. Wallace as head of Alabama's game and fish commission, now called the Alabama Department of Conservation, and Stanley Arthur, director of the Louisiana Department of Conservation.[25]

By the late 1920s, Fannye Cook was prominent as a southern woman advocating vocally for game and fish regulation, yet she was not alone in the South or more distant regions. As the Progressive movement matured in the first two decades of the twentieth century, middle- and upper-class women had increasingly become involved with issues affecting the environment, urban and rural. Women were central to the regeneration of the Audubon Society in the early twentieth century, as noted in chapter 2, and in that organization found welcome from male leaders.[26] The General Federation of Women's Clubs, founded in 1890 to coordinate the booming club movement among white women at the national level, excluded Black women. Black women instead founded the National Association for Colored Women's Clubs and created a Forestry Committee that employed committee leaders to orate widely on the values of forest conservation.[27] In addition to lobbying for forest and bird protection, women of all racial and ethnic backgrounds pushed for reforms in public health, fought against urban pollution, and joined civic improvement societies that began to ameliorate the worst effects of urbanization in the country. Middle-class Black women, through their own women's clubs, documented public health concerns in Black neighborhoods (the Neighborhood Union in Atlanta is an important example), becoming early advocates for what today we would term environmental justice.[28] Women, then, shaped and built the many arms of conservation work, defined broadly, including in advocacy for wildlife.

But men and women often came to these causes with different motivations, or at the very least, different rhetorical strategies for advocacy. Middle-class women were influenced to protect and steward the realms to which late nineteenth- and early twentieth-century society traditionally assigned them—the home and the family and, by extension, the neighborhood and community. These concerns shaped the urgency they brought to fights for beautification, sanitation, and purification of food production. Women like Fannye Cook also argued for the aesthetic value of conservation, a value that men in the late nineteenth century often echoed. Historian Adam Rome, however, points to an early twentieth-century shift in gendered language deployed by conservation activists; by the second decade of the twentieth century, male leaders in the movement tended to shun arguments for the virtue of aesthetics (of birds and landscapes, for example), which they deemed sentimental and feminine, and put emphasis on the economic value of conservation.[29] By 1910, the American Forestry Association leadership even stopped supporting women's auxiliary work focused on forest conservation, arguing that "much harm has been done in the course of the forestry movement, and the same is true of all branches of conservation, by immature thought arising from insufficient knowledge." Women's clubs "sometimes undertake too much and gain only that little knowledge which is a dangerous thing, on the subjects they take up."[30] The growing professionalization of fields like forestry and, later, wildlife management, the doors of which were not fully opened to women, led to a dismissal of the value of women's extensive contributions—mostly volunteer—to conservation.

As historian Nancy C. Unger holds, and Rome concedes, "sweeping gender-based assertions rarely hold up under close scrutiny" in the early twentieth-century conservation movement.[31] Though we can unspool the ways gender shaped the possibilities and motivations for southern advocates of game and fish laws, hunters like John H. Wallace and Charlie Young stressed the beauty of the landscape and the artfulness of the hunt, and Fannye Cook would repeatedly include the economic value of game and bird conservation in her advocacy of regulation. In short, to a certain extent in the South and elsewhere, the "gender politics of the Progressive era were fluid."[32] By the 1920s, when Cook was moving seriously into her focus on game, fish, and bird advocacy in Mississippi, the role of women in conservation was subtly shifting. Newly franchised and well educated, some middle-class women like Cook moved out of volunteer labor and into professional conservation work.

"Deucedly Unpopular": Early Twentieth-Century Attempts to Centralize Game and Fish Law

Fannye Cook infused her fight for game, fish, and bird protection law with her own wish for better scientific study of the state's wildlife. From the very first meeting agenda, Cook made clear the MACWL's push for centralized game and fish legislation and for a biological survey of Mississippi funded by the state.[33] By the end of 1927, Cook was publicizing the organization's drive for a new bill to create a "Wild Life Conservation Commission." At the same time, Hugh Miller, a representative from Fannye Cook's own Copiah County, authored a "more comprehensive" omnibus bill that would "combine various commissions—forestry, minerals, animals, fish and birds—in one with a head for each different division." Yet perhaps fearing a dilution of focus on game, birds, and fish, the MACWL preferred a "separate commission" plan with two divisions, "one for enforcement to be under the direction of a state game warden and a survey division to make a survey of the state and advise suitable localities for the preservation and propagation of certain forms of wild life."[34] The bill did not pass that year, and the MACWL continued its advocacy.

Mississippi was not entirely without game laws, but the lack of a central enforcement agency betrayed a key weakness from the perspective of the MACWL. Efforts to pass game and fish regulation at the state level had been halting in the first decades of the twentieth century.

The lack of success of conservation advocates did not have to do with a lack of support from state politicians, even at the highest level; Mississippi political leaders of the Progressive Era and New Deal called for a more extensive conservation code (including Governors Edmund F. Noel, Theodore Bilbo, and Martin S. "Mike" Conner). Opposition, however, came from multiple motivations—the kinds of reaction we have seen in Georgia and Alabama by small farmers and rural people who would not accept changes that limited access to prey and from politicians wary of state centralization, not least because, they argued, any new state-level department could become a political plum of the governor. Given the factional politics of Mississippi in the first three decades of the twentieth century, politicians were loath to see power consolidated in the hands of the state executive. The fight over game and fish laws thus illustrates the "distinctive blend of New South progressivism and provincialism" that prevailed in Mississippi.[35]

Frank H. Miller, who directed the Louisiana Audubon Society in the early twentieth century, worked in Mississippi to advocate successfully for the passage of the Model Law in 1904.[36] In 1906, supporters of stronger regulation of game and fish introduced a bill in the legislature that garnered support but found itself "murdered" by the state senate, "mutilated to such an extent that the author would not recognize it."[37] Yet the bill set precedent for the next two decades of debate about increased regulation. First, it defined "game" broadly as "all kinds of animals and birds found in the state of nature," naming only certain species as requiring closed seasons or other protection. It vested county boards of supervisors with the power to enforce and modify laws (so long as they did not run counter to the law's spirit) and so retained a decentralized and localized implementation regimen. Familiar statutes were part of the code—the state declared ownership of fish and game, fish traps and seines were prohibited, nongame bird nests and eggs were protected (though those species were not named explicitly in this code), and open seasons were assigned for turkeys, quail, deer, bears, some birds ("swan, geese, brant, river and sea duck, rail [mud hen], coots [poule d'eau], chorooks [sandpipers], tatlers, plover, grosbec, cedar birds, and robins"), and wood duck. Wild game named in the act could not be sold or shipped out of state, and county supervisors had authority to appoint wardens, who were promised no specific salary or compensation.[38] The press did not report the "mutilation" in fine detail, but the senate removed the power of wardens to search for any violation of the law or to confiscate illegal hunting contraptions (like traps), game, or dogs without redress.[39] In the end, no part of the law had much impact even as passed.

In 1907, the National Association of Audubon Societies employed a special agent, ornithologist Henry H. Kopman, to canvass the state and advocate for new game and fish laws.[40] The annual Audubon report tabulated his presence as a guest lecturer "before hundreds of planters in Mississippi at farmers' institutes." He also began a Mississippi Audubon chapter, circulated educational materials on the value of birds in newspapers across the state, and prepared an exhibit for the Mississippi State Fair, a popular venue that would continue to be important for Fannye Cook over the next two decades.[41] Despite the optimistic annual report, Kopman faced popular resistance to his advocacy for new game laws. In 1906, the state legislature created a statewide nonresident license law that cost ten dollars. Two years later, the prospect of a resident hunting license was on the minds of advocates in the state, including Kopman, who edited a column for the *Mississippi Union Advocate and Southern Farm and Home*. Kopman appealed to readers' sense of economy, that a one-dollar local license would fund warden enforcement. Comparing Mississippi with its neighbor Alabama, he argued that Mississippi missed an opportunity for revenue. And, echoing protection advocates across the country, including fellow southerner John H. Wallace, Kopman appealed to race: "Not the least of the advantages that would be secured by the license law is that it would cut out a large number of trifling negroes roaming the country and killing whatever their fancy dictates instead of working at some more suitable and profitable employment."[42]

Kopman's supporters in Mississippi could get behind popular education on bird and game protection, but a warden and resident license system was overreach to many. Col. Tom Haynie, a leader in the Farmers' Union Advocate, expressed contempt for the proposed law, calling it an example of "too much law and not enough liberty" for farmers. He suggested Kopman "confine his efforts to the task of forming societies among the country children for the protection of useful birds and the elimination of dogs that are the most destructive enemies of birds," though he warned that "little 'societies' gotten up in towns for the amusement and possible instruction of the town folks . . . don't interest old 'Hayseed' at all." Meanwhile, Haynie spat, "we regard the birds that eat our crops and live on our lands as our individual property, and will protect and use them as such." Haynie warned Kopman to "keep your wardens in town to shoot bird dogs we will attend to business our own way."[43] An editor of the paper chimed in to support Haynie, invoking "old Mississippi," where a "man's house is yet his castle." A warden would unleash "darn foolishness" and only "collect fees from old Hayseed and . . . his boys, appoint spies or informers in each neighborhood, search for and break up boy's traps and incidentally pick bird shot out of his legs if the boys caught him at it."[44] Sounding much like the farmers who wrote to Tom Watson's paper to complain of Georgia's game laws, these men invoked independence and property rights to critique hunting regulation. As elsewhere, conservation cut across lines of class.

The NAAS and local supporters nonetheless continued efforts to support game and fish legislation. In 1909, the president of the Mississippi Audubon

Society, William Hemingway, reported that after a year of organizing, "the prejudices of the sportsmen have, to a great extent, been removed, and I feel we can now count upon them as allies in our efforts." Yet, he said, sportsmen remained "alarmed" at counties passing new game laws, especially those that put closed season on quail based on the "mistaken idea" that quail helped control the boll weevil. Hemingway seemed to shy away from outright support of closed seasons, calling instead for legislation that created a system of paid game wardens.[45] The next year, John H. Wallace corresponded with a farmer and game warden from Lexington, Mississippi, H. W. Watson, who, according to Wallace, was "taking active steps in Mississippi, looking to the enactment of a modern and model law" for game, fish, and bird preservation. Wallace connected Watson to William Dutcher, head of the national Audubon organization.[46] T. Gilbert Pearson, still directing the North Carolina Audubon Society, traveled to Mississippi to shape and support legislation for a game and fish commission; the bill was "a formidable looking document," Pearson remembered, and one that received the favor of Governor Edmund Noel (who supported other Progressive reforms, such as rural school consolidation) though failed to win needed support in the legislature.[47]

The Mississippi Audubon Society tried again in 1912 to push for legislation, and John Wallace plied the Mississippi press with arguments for its passage. Speaking directly to protests of the "plain people" in rural areas, Wallace noted the success of the Alabama game and fish bill (according to him) to win the support of farmers after they could see what value it provided.[48] He argued that the law favored the rural citizens and the small farmer—in an oft-rehearsed passage, he reasoned that "the money-king can step aboard his palace car and be spirited in a few hours to a veritable hunter's paradise . . . but not so with the farmer or ordinary citizen," whose game "must be found in close proximity to their residence." Game laws would protect the species that mattered most to Mississippians. The maligned "worthless class" would be staved off by "the hunter's license fee and written permission proposition," which made all lands in the case of Alabama "automatically posted." Though there was no statute in Alabama's law that limited access to guns, Wallace claimed that it decreased certain types of gun and ammunition sales, particularly single-barreled shotguns and black powder shells, "the kind that pothunters and negroes used." "Negroes," he continued, "formerly idled and pretended to hunt under this pretext, and committed every character of crime." Wallace assured Mississippi readers that "[Black men] have been completely disarmed . . . and must now pursue the avocation of an honest and industrious life." Wallace made the case again for the beneficial presence of birds for weeds and unwanted insects and tied Alabama's work to preserve its natural resources to its "splendid history" and "imperishable traditions." Wallace also laced his arguments for conservation with the racist assumptions that buttressed the Jim Crow South and its Lost Cause tradition.[49] He believed his own words and knew that white Mississippians, in an era that "tend[ed] toward racial demagoguery," would likely agree.[50]

Wallace's opinion may have held water with some in the Mississippi legislature but not all, especially politicians who saw a game commission as a pathway to aggregate political power. When the bill, sponsored by Pike County newspaper publisher Senator Joseph E. Norwood, who endorsed state ownership of game and fish, came to a vote in the Mississippi senate, it found support in only eight votes (and was thus "dead beyond resuscitation"). Papers reported that Senator Henry F. Broyles, from a district that bordered the northeast hill country (Monroe, Lee, and Itawamba Counties), challenged the wisdom of the bill's plan, calling out both Alabama and Louisiana for having "deplorable" conditions for game and fish laws.[51] He and other critics charged that the bill "would create more offices, and that there was a danger in the law being manipulated by a political machine."[52] Norwood countered that Louisiana's commission had been politicized by the governor but made no defense of Alabama, for which there was no other specific charge reported.[53] Mississippi's plan, which according to the paper would be a "far superior law" than those in adjacent states, seemed somewhat similar to Alabama's—it would create a state game and fish commissioner, a system of wardens and deputy wardens, and a licensing system (two dollars for county, five dollars for state, and twenty dollars for nonresidents). Different from Alabama, warden salaries would come from a county game and fish protection fund, not from a portion of conviction fines, and wardens would be salaried (not to exceed $2,400 per year). And, the governor could accept donations of land to use as game and fish refuges.[54] The particulars of the bill that cost its passage in the Mississippi senate were, in addition to Broyles's argument, the mandatory license and the closed seasons on squirrels and rabbits, which provoked "strong opposition."[55] No doubt senators were thinking of their constituents in rural Mississippi, who continued to hunt and consume small game and for whom game laws were "deucedly unpopular."[56]

Legislation failed in 1912, but in 1922 and 1926, policymakers advanced game and fish laws by strengthening enforcement, at least at the local level, and limning more carefully regulations around certain species, licensing, penalties, and game sales.[57] By 1926, the law required each county board of supervisors to appoint a warden.[58] Fish and animals were classed as game ("bear, beaver, deer, fox, opossums, raccoons, rabbits, and squirrels") or as fur-bearing animals, though sometimes animals fell in both categories ("beaver, fox, muskrat, opossum, otters, raccoons, rabbits, skunks, weasels, and minks)," and each—except for rabbits—had a shooting, fishing, or trapping closed season.[59] The shipment and sale of game in restaurants was regulated; in 1922, the law allowed for restaurateurs to purchase a license to prepare and plate game animals and fish, but by 1926, all sale was prohibited, once again except for rabbits, unless the patron brought his or her own kill to be prepared.[60] The 1918 federal Migratory Bird Treaty Act was incorporated into the code as the "law of the land" and thus shaped open and closed seasons for federally protected birds in Mississippi. Certain guns were outlawed (any shotgun bore with a gauge larger than ten or "with any rifle or any gun which cannot be shot from the shoulder"), as were reflectors or lights in nets or traps or any "contraption" that obstructed the passage of the fish; the latter qualifications were inherited from previous policy. Resident licenses were new, however, and county supervisors could charge individuals from one to three dollars. At its face, the 1920s code seemed to reflect the growing power of legislators with stake in game preservation, at the expense of restaurateurs, market hunters, and even farmers. Farmers did enjoy consideration in that the laws allowed them to kill nuisance animals (skunks and weasels, for example) at any time; in the list of "harmful" birds, including sparrows and great horned owls; and in the trespass laws baked into the code. Hunters, trappers, and fishers were required to obey "posted" notices on any property but could seek written permission from the landowner.[61]

Yet, without serious commitment to enforcement, the laws did not deter the behavior that alarmed advocates like Fannye Cook. In the early 1930s, thanks to her advocacy and that of the MACWL, there emerged a new moment for a centralized game and fish commission. That moment was also buttressed by gubernatorial support and the concern for a more efficient state government, in fact a national trend. In 1930, the Mississippi legislature commissioned an audit of its state government by the Brookings Institution, paying particular attention to the state's expenditures and revenue.[62] The report's authors did not mince words about what they saw as the state's byzantine and burdened governmental structure, and recommendations ran from diversifying taxation resources to county consolidation.[63] The report argued that the decentralized character of Mississippi's government underlay its problems;

authors referred to "how strongly rooted the county has been in the political habits of the people" and that most Mississippians "are probably disposed to view the county as a permanent, inherent and indestructible feature of government."[64] Though Mississippi was predominantly rural and seemingly better off with stronger county authority, a "lack of urban development, in the presence of such other factors as the increasing sphere and complexity of administration, the growing financial burden of government, and the modern rapidity of transportation and communication" argued for centralization. This general restructuring included game and fish laws. In the recommendation, the authors suggested, "There should be created a Department of Conservation headed by a Commissioner appointed by the Governor with the consent of the Senate." The department would be assisted by a conservation council and be merged with the State Geological Survey, Forestry Commission, and Sea Food Commission. Most of all, the authors recommended that the power of enforcement and implementation move from counties to the state commission.[65]

The explicit critique of county rule and the recommendation to centralize was not embraced by all Mississippi legislators; in fact, when Governor Mike Conner called for a constitutional convention in 1933 (a move he had supported since serving as Speaker of the House in the 1920s), his critics accused him of doing so in order to enact certain recommendations of the Brookings Institution, which they saw as a ploy to reduce the number of state departments and appoint Conner cronies at the head of those that remained. The results of such a move, his critics argued, would be "that the Bill of Rights will be destroyed, Jeffersonian principles ravished, and the people robbed of their privileges and powers by constitutional convention."[66] Conner took to the papers to defend himself, reminding readers that the legislature commissioned the Brookings report before he was in office and that, while he agreed with some of the findings of the report, those findings were simply "advisory." But, it was clear that Conner embraced some of the report's conclusions. After the report's publication, he called for a "state commission on conservation" in his inaugural address, seemingly drawing directly from the Brookings Institution's recommendations and lending weight to efforts of supporters.[67] He might have viewed such a move as advantageous in a number of ways, as a consolidated department of conservation could not only protect natural resources but also exploit them. His embrace also illustrates that the bureaucratization of conservation was a part of state consolidation in a moment when fiscal conservatives like Conner worked toward a more efficient government.[68]

"Not Bad": The Mississippi Game and Fish Commission Act of 1932

In 1932, Cook and the MACWL saw their cause rewarded in the Mississippi legislature. That year, the body passed a law establishing a centralized game and fish commission that empowered game wardens to enforce regulation, explored in detail below. Cook and the MACWL had done important work building allies and advocates across the state, but key legislators were important to the bill's passage. Underlining the significance of Fannye Cook's story, those lawmakers proved to be women. The passage of the Nineteenth Amendment in 1920 shifted women's status as political actors. Decades of organizing, fundraising, lobbying, and activism informed the actions of women after they secured the vote. In the South, that meant political campaigning and office holding for some white women. In Mississippi, the cause of suffrage had been led by several key women, including Nellie Nugent Somerville, who successfully ran for office in the state legislature in 1923.[69] Her daughter, Lucy Somerville Howorth, was a graduate of the University of Mississippi School of Law and had settled in Cleveland, Mississippi, with her husband, Joseph M. Howorth. Howorth and two other women—Madge Quin Fugler and Mildred Spurrier Top—made successful bids for the state's lower house in 1932.[70] As Howorth remembered in an interview with historian Constance Myers, the Speaker of the House, Thomas L. Bailey, said to her, "I'm going to make the three women, each of you a chairman and I will give you first choice."[71] Howorth chose to chair the Public Lands Committee, despite Bailey's argument that the committee had had an empty agenda in recent years. Bailey also appointed her to act as secretary of the Conservation Committee, which was a brand-new body of the chamber.[72] Though Howorth suggested some disdain for the title, she explained that the secretary position on any Mississippi legislative committee could wield more power than the role suggested:

> Then, they had for the first time a Conservation Committee . . . and I was secretary of that committee. That's the last time that I was secretary of anything, but the secretary of a legislative committee, if the chairman is kind of slow motion, the secretary can make up the agenda of a committee meeting, which means that you put the bills that the secretary is interested in on the agenda and the ones that the secretary wants to kill stay in the pocket. Also, when the chairman, this is a Mississippi rule, is not present and a bill has been approved by a committee, it is moved onto the calendar and the secretary can floor manage it, so that it is a position of power.

Howorth recalled with pride her role in creating game and fish regulation: "I was secretary of that committee when it established the Game and Fish Commission and all of the conservation programs that developed tremendously in the state." She credited Fannye Cook "for the development of the interest in wildlife conservation."[73]

On the Public Lands Committee, Howorth stewarded a new era in parks and public lands. She tied the committee's work to the beginning of the New Deal and renewed federal interest in parks programs: "My committee, you see, had this forestry bill and the federal government was coming in with the Roosevelt administration with all its development of public parks and public lands and public forests." The Public Lands Committee helped to foster "all of these laws giving the federal government authority to acquire lands... and greatly extended the authority of the forestry commission and the whole system of public parks was initiated."[74] Federal and state activity in establishing public lands extended the work of the new game and fish commission, as well, and Fannye Cook's vision for wildlife refuges.[75]

After the commission was established, newspapers across the state heralded its arrival. The news made it onto local radio programs, with one broadcaster crediting the MACWL as doing "splendid and effective work, and it was through its influence that the legislation creating the new state game and fish commission and the state-wide game law was enacted."[76] Cook and the MACWL shaped the final bill, as did conservation supporters in nearby states and farther afield. The first printed booklet of the new body of game and fish statutes named the MACWL and the "Isaac [sic] Walton League" as cooperating associations. The Izaak Walton League, still in existence and named in honor of the *Compleat Angler* (1653) author, began in Illinois in 1922 as a group of hunters and fishers concerned about destruction of fish and game habitat.[77]

The bill reflected national developments in conservation law and local concerns about access to game and fish. It was unsurprisingly more comprehensive than the first of such bills in the neighboring states of Alabama and Georgia; several decades of trial and implementation informed Mississippi's new law. At the law's heart resided a new enforcement body, a state game and fish commission made up of three members chosen by the governor who served for six-year terms. The commission elected a salaried game and fish commissioner to serve as its "executive head and secretary."[78] The body met quarterly and had the power to make and enforce game and fish policy and to commission scientific study of game and nongame wildlife. It made decisions on closed seasons, designated public and private wildlife refuges and fish hatcheries, took control of the propagation and stocking of game animals and fish, and conducted and circulated research on Mississippi's plant and animal life.[79] It regulated through permits dog trainers and field trials and collection for propagation and scientific study, and it controlled the harvest of nongame fish. The commissioner appointed wardens, with "all necessary powers" of enforcement, not at the county level but "in different sections of the State where their services are most needed."[80] In keeping with the game and fish laws since the earlier part of the decade, violation of the code constituted a misdemeanor with fines and jail time as possible penalties. The law required wardens to pass an examination before appointment, and it gave a salary (capped at $2,000 per year) and travel reimbursement. By the 1930s, state game and fish departments across the South had matured as more stable state bureaucracies.

The new Mississippi Game and Fish Commission forwarded a licensing structure that funded the newly created state game and fish fund, to be used at the commission's discretion, and that served to control who had access to game and fish. License tiers looked similar to other states—residents could buy a county or statewide hunting license for $1 or $3, respectively; nonresident hunters could buy a county license for $10 or a statewide license for $25; and residents could buy a trapping license for fur-bearing animals at $3. Clearly aimed to deter out-of-state market trappers, nonresidents were required to buy a trapping license for $200, less than the $500 required by the 1926 law.[81] The commission required fishing licenses only for commercial fishermen.

The basic structure looks familiar, but Mississippi's licensing requirements also included provisions that reflected how Jim Crow laws had calcified in the region by the 1930s: all residents were required to pay the poll tax before applying for a hunting license.[82] Though race does not appear in the text of the bill, using the poll tax as a barrier to certain rights was clearly aimed at Black hunters. I. T. Quinn, the director of Alabama's Department of Conservation, read a draft of the bill and sent comments to Fannye Cook, who, in the margins next to the poll tax qualification, wrote "bad (Quinn)." Rather than a protest on behalf of Black hunters, Quinn may have imagined that such a provision would be unpopular with poor whites who would also be restricted from hunting.[83] The poll tax provision had not been included in earlier forms of the license requirement and was absent from the game and fish laws by 1938, though laws retained a 1932 provision that allowed any official to refuse a license "to any person physically or mentally unfit to carry a firearm," giving broad discretionary power.[84]

Fannye Cook's marginalia, in which she included remarks from Quinn, show that she harbored questions about certain portions of the bill and, in a few cases, did not think penalties or regulations went far enough in protecting wildlife. She argued that the section on granting permits to researchers and propagators that would allow the permit holder to "buy, sell, possess, and transport" was giving "too much latitude."[85] She desired that the term "warden" be changed to "conservation officer." By the provision on sale of game in restaurants, which was similar to previous codes in that it allowed preparation of game brought in by the animal's killer, she wrote, "Stop serving in restaurants at all." She added an additional note from Alabama's I. T. Quinn—"Get permission to hunt on another's land."[86] John Wallace's commitment to protecting private property continued to be supported by his successor. These suggestions, objections, and edits seemed to have gone unheeded, however, for the draft, besides the soft pencil markings of Cook, was almost identical to the final bill.

Yet compared with its neighboring states, Mississippi's new game and fish laws looked rather thin. By the mid-1930s, Alabama's Department of Conservation displayed a more muscular bureaucracy; now advised by a seven-member Conservation Commission, the department was composed of five divisions: Fish Culture and Reclamation, Law Enforcement, Research and Statistics, Conservation and Planning, and Seafoods.[87] The department oversaw a state game farm for propagation and a state fish hatchery, continuing its partnership with federal fish restocking programs from the days of John Wallace.[88] The Law Enforcement Division was staffed with thirty-three district wardens and managed by a chief warden. In Georgia, the legislature created the Department of Natural Resources in 1937, which subsumed conservation work. The new bureau included four divisions: Wild Life; Forestry; Mines, Mining, and Geology; and State Parks, Historic Sites, and Monuments.[89] The Division of Wild Life was the former Department of Game and Fish, and by the time of its name change in 1937, it employed ninety "game protectors" to implement the law. Both Georgia and Alabama stressed the importance of organizing "Fish and Game Clubs" to assist in educating the public in game and fish conservation.[90]

Fannye Cook was patient with the Mississippi's creation, though she recognized its limitations. She wrote a few years later that "in inaugurating the work we chose the Commission plan, which has long been recognized as a regular channel through which to do state work. The plan is not bad. The problem is usually one of getting people on the Commission and along the working line who are both interested and *prepared* to do conservation work."[91] Cook, of course, was more than eager to take a role within the newly created department, but just what that might be was not clear. She wrote to her trusted mentor from DC, zoologist Paul Bartsch, for advice. She admitted to Bartsch that, after the Mississippi Game and Fish Commission Act was passed, she was promised a job with the commission but was not sure what title to claim—the commissioners were unpaid, and the director of the commission would be too tangled in enforcement. She suggested "Director of Research and Education" with a note that the work would be in line with her interests. Bartsch agreed that the title suited her but added, "If you were a man, any of the statutory positions would answer, but women are difficult problems to place (of course you won't like that, but the fact remains and we have to face it)."[92] As Cook's biographer notes, the title "Director" no doubt would have been used if she were a man. During her early years at the commission, however, she would be formally titled "Research Secretary."[93]

Cook and the MACWL claimed the achievement of the new legislation. They also applauded the state's move into a federal partnership that supported conservation initiatives. In a brief on the "origins and purpose" of the MACWL, Cook itemized the many "accomplishments through cooperation" since the organization's founding: "a. A State Commission has been established; b. A system of private and state owned reserves is being established; c. A program of research in improved wild life conservation has been provided by the state; . . . f. A legislative act has been passed authorizing the federal government to operate fish hatcheries in Mississippi; g. A legislative act has been passed authorizing the federal government to establish migratory bird refuges in Mississippi."[94] The creation of a department of game and fish and the continued advocacy work of the MACWL coincided with an energetic national policy focus on conservation, and Fannye Cook was there in Mississippi to claim federal funds for state work.

Cooperative Conservation Work: Mississippi and the New Deal

At its creation, the Mississippi Game and Fish Commission began to engage in what it called "cooperative" conservation work with federal agencies. Some federal cooperation was already in place—the Department of Agriculture's Extension Service had been in operation in the state since the 1910s, encouraging some of the educational aspects of conservation work (like the message about the agricultural benefit of birds). The Bureau of Biological Survey was and would be a key advisor in managing pisciculture in the state. And federal game wardens charged with enforcing the Migratory Bird Treaty Act worked with the commission and state game wardens in prosecuting violators of the law.

What would come, however, far exceeded any previous role of the federal government in state conservation efforts. The New Deal, a series of relief and reform programs authored by President Franklin D. Roosevelt and his advisors in response to the Great Depression, prioritized conservation measures and funded conservation work in southern states. New Deal funding shaped the possibilities and priorities of the new Mississippi Game and Fish Commission and conservation work elsewhere in the South. The South occupied the imagination of President Roosevelt and New Deal planners as one of the most affected places of the Great Depression. Economic suffering in the South worsened after World War I, when cotton prices bottomed after years of high market demand. The South, as a farming region, lay in the grip of a prolonged agricultural depression by the time Roosevelt was elected in 1932, though a few observers saw no difference in the new suffering from the old. Eudora Welty, who would herself benefit from New Deal programs as a publicity worker and photographer for the Works Progress Administration, remembered in a 1989 interview that, in Mississippi, poverty "really didn't have too much to do with the Depression. It was ongoing. Mississippi was long since poor, long since devastated."[95] In 1920, the state was 86.6 percent rural, and 70 percent of the farming population, which made up two-thirds of the state's overall population, were tenant farmers.[96] The contraction of farm prices and of what small industry there was, combined with environmental disasters—floods in 1927, 1932, and 1936, a regional drought in 1930–31, and damage wrought by boll weevils (which caused bird protection advocates to argue more loudly for the benefit of insectivorous birds)—exacerbated the poverty and devastation that Welty described.[97] Though the New Deal programs did not solve the region's economic problems, the $450 million in federal funds pumped into Mississippi's economy between 1933 and 1939 were beneficial, if not a solution, for some.[98] State-level and local control of programs meant they were implemented in alignment with the region's racial hierarchy, leading to historian Jack Temple Kirby's conclusion that the New Deal brought both "succor and suffering" in the South.[99]

Mississippi, along with the rest of the South, was poised to be a beneficiary of the federal spending of the New Deal. The 1930s ushered in a new moment for Democrats, who were elected to a majority in both houses of Congress by 1932.[100] Leading that dominant wave were southern Democrats who, by virtue of representing a one-party region that offered little opposition to incumbents, held deep institutional knowledge and, often, committee seniority.[101] Southern Democrats were important supporters of Roosevelt's early New Deal experimentation, which included a variety of economic relief programs that they welcomed.[102] Historian Gavin Wright credits New Deal spending with causing a "watershed if not instantaneous revolution" in terms of the South's modern infrastructure.[103] In rural electrification, road building and public works construction, public health initiatives, land reclamation, and wages to impoverished southerners, the New Deal set the table for the increase in federal spending brought by World War II and the Cold War. Some of the programs with the most far-reaching potential, those that might have strengthened the most marginalized tenant farmers and other working poor, were hamstrung by the unwillingness of southern Democrats to implement any program that upset the South's racial caste system. Laws that protected labor organizations (Wagner Act), created a social safety net (Social Security Act), and guaranteed a right to a minimum wage (Fair Labor Standards Act) did not include agricultural and domestic workers, attendant to objections by southern congressmen.[104] Senator John H. Bankhead Jr., Wallace's supporter in passage of the Migratory Bird Treaty Act and one of the supporters of the Agricultural Adjustment Act (which attempted to stabilize crop prices through a variety of measures), was keenly aware of the plight of tenants in the South. But, as historian Kari Frederickson notes, legislation he drafted to extend tenant support by providing low-interest credit to purchase land—the Bankhead–Jones Farm Tenant Act of 1937—assumed the "worthy poor" among tenants as implicitly white. Bankhead and other southern legislators were insensitive to the suffering of "black tenants and sharecroppers" who were, to them, "a fixture of the South's impoverished rural landscape."[105]

The exclusivity of New Deal monies, too, would define how the Mississippi Game and Fish Commission used its funds. Federal funding from New Deal programs began soon after the commission began its work. President Roosevelt, at the behest of the Department of Agriculture, initiated a program for the protection and restoration of wildlife through land reclamation in 1934. The "President's Committee on Wildlife Restoration" allowed the Department of Agriculture to use federal funds to purchase "suboptimal" agricultural lands for the creation of wildlife refuges. Part of the motivation for the program, reported papers, was to reduce the "surplus of agricultural products" and stabilize crop prices.[106] According to Jay N. Darling, then head of the Bureau of Biological Survey, adding wildlife protection to the use of emergency relief funds made economic sense; more recreational hunters meant more dollars spent in local economies:

> As we saw it, emergency funds were being spent to take land out of agriculture and to give to employment. We consider wildlife restoration

one of the most productive uses to which much of this land could be put and the development of such areas an excellent means of getting lasting benefits from the expenditure of money for employment. The economic and recreational values of wildlife are enormous. An abundant supply of wildlife will mean the expenditure of hundreds of millions of dollars more annually by those who go out of doors. That, gentlemen, means more and better business in the country.[107]

The program came after several years of the Mississippi commission working to secure additional lands for migratory fowl on the coast, for which commissioners had petitioned the Bureau of Biological Survey for support. With the Committee on Wildlife Restoration, the bureau had funds for at least some of the commission's hoped-for acquisitions. Of the nineteen areas recommended by the commission, the bureau funded two—the Winston-Neshoba reclamation area, at 200,000 acres, and the Washington County Waterfowl Refuge, at 22,000 acres.[108]

The same year, 1934, the commission supported federal measures to increase protection of migratory wildfowl and wildlife habitat. The Migratory Bird Hunting and Conservation Stamp Act, popularly known as the Duck Stamp Act, required hunters over the age of sixteen to purchase a separate stamp for hunting migratory fowl and affix it to state licenses. Game commissions and sportsmen's organizations across the country supported the bill.[109] Proceeds from sales could be used to restore nesting and resting sites along migratory flyways. The same month (March), the president signed into law the Joseph T. Robinson National Forest Refuge Act to promote the creation of fish and game sanctuaries within national forests, with the consent of states.[110] The Mississippi commission leaped at the opportunity presented by the Robinson Act, requesting sanctuaries in all six units of Desoto National Forest, in the southeastern part of the state.[111]

The funding for habitat creation and restoration expanded protected lands and began to address the original goals of Fannye Cook and the MACWL. She also employed New Deal support to create private sanctuaries for quail on individual farms, as we shall see. The commission, upon its creation, had begun to designate private land as game refuges—from 1933 to 1934, the commission registered seventeen such refuges, totaling approximately 53,000 acres.[112] The refuges were a mix of "subsistence property," or individual farms, and educational institutions, particularly the state's colleges: designated refuges existed at Mississippi State College for Women, on land owned by the University of Mississippi, and at what was then called Alcorn A&M College, now Alcorn State University, the state's first Black land-grant institution. Cook visited the refuges and made recommendations to state game and fish commissioners on how and whether animals and fish should be restocked, what warden power was needed at each site, and whether or not there was adequate local support for the refuge. Sometimes, hunting or fishing would be consigned only to property owners or users or would simply be outlawed, providing at least temporary sanctuary for wildlife. At Ellisville School, for example, a refuge that Cook described as "a sandy formation supporting a cut-over upland flora invaded by hardwood growth along stream valleys," she recommended posting the land in multiple places so no public fishing could take place in a pond and stream on the property, which had been the site of a lumber mill. But, she recommended that local students be allowed to fish there one day a week.[113]

By the 1930s, hunters and fishers, however, were more hard-pressed in terms of access to large acreage for hunting. By this time, the trends we have seen in places like the Red Hills region, where elite sportsmen purchased or leased large acreages of land, had continued to expand in southern states, and certainly in the Deep South. The Mississippi Game and Fish Commission asked all hunting and fishing clubs to register with the commission, and Cook created detailed tables of those clubs and how much acreage each club owned or leased. By the mid-1930s, Cook recorded that private clubs owned upward of 123,000 acres across the state—a small percentage of the state's overall land mass but a marked turn toward private preserves for recreational hunters.[114] Hunters and fishers who could not afford club membership would rely on public lands opened during the 1930s in Mississippi.[115]

New Deal programming also provided funding for man- and womanpower in which to conduct statewide conservation work. One cannot overstate the role of New Deal programs in funding environmental labor of all kinds—soil conservation, land reclamation, parks creation and expansion (and the trails, shelters, and fire towers within), and forestry. The Mississippi Game and Fish Commission also sought funding for labor related to another key initiative proposed early in the MACWL's agenda—a state survey of flora and fauna.

The legendary ecologist Aldo Leopold visited the state in 1928 to conduct a game survey funded by the Sporting Arms and Ammunition Institute's Game Restoration Committee.[116] The purpose of the institute's state surveys (which eventually included Illinois, Indiana, Iowa, Michigan, Minnesota, Mississippi, Missouri, Ohio, and Wisconsin) was, in the words of Leopold, "to appraise the chance for the practice of game management as a means to game restoration." The funder's aims, he noted, were obvious; game restoration meant "the continuance" of the arms industry and game depletion meant "its shrinkage and ultimate liquidation."[117] Herbert Stoddard, whom Charlie Young remembered for his work with the bobwhite quail in the Red Hills, aided the surveys as observer, data collector, and field companion and organized a series of Sporting Arms and Ammunition Institute–sponsored fellowships that grew out of Leopold's studies.[118] Leopold completed the fieldwork and authorship of surveys just before the publication of his influential *Game Management*, an essential text of the new field of wildlife management.[119]

Leopold spent months surveying sections of the state, making field notes, and corresponding with locals interested in his work, including Fannye Cook.[120] He visited her at her family home in Crystal Springs (by then she was living in Jackson to attend to MACWL work), and they visited local sites together. A letter to Leopold after their visit suggests what they saw and something about the drift of their conversation. She updated him with the scientific name of a partridgeberry plant they had seen, *Mitchella repens*, reminding him that the plant "is used a great deal in the eastern United States for Christmas decorations." She told Leopold that she and her father had gone to J. W. McGinnis, a "champion hawk killer" who was killing hawks to benefit from a countywide bounty of thirty-five cents per hawk.[121] Like the economic ornithologists of the early twentieth century, Cook hoped to study hawk stomach contents to show them to not be the predators that farmers so despised. But, she told Leopold, the hunter refused to offer specimens. And she worried about talking too much during their meeting. "You see," she said, "I had been shut in with the flu several weeks and had lots of time to worry about my work. I am not always so nervous." Calling the prospect of his finished survey an "inspiration," Cook shared her own vision for the MACWL statewide biological survey. She sent a "leaflet" that she "prepared several years ago and it probably expresses fairly well but of course in general terms what we shall hope to accomplish *eventually*."[122] Leopold's connection with Cook and the Mississippi Association for the Conservation of Wild Life was mutually beneficial, with Cook and others sharing local knowledge and Leopold sharing methodology.

Cook was one of eleven "cooperators" whom Leopold wished to review the report draft. He also sent the manuscript to Stoddard, who was then finishing his own quail study in the Red Hills region, as well as to Stoddard's patron L. S. Thompson, the "Great shot" of Sunny Hill estate who employed Charlie Young.[123] Cook read the draft of his final report and offered a friendly amendment—she was concerned she had given him the wrong impression when he reported that Copiah County offered bounties on cotton rats. "So far as I know," she offered, "no bounty has been given or discussed."[124] Cook was impressed with what Leopold had accomplished in Mississippi. "It seems almost impossible," she marveled, "that you should compile so splendid a report in so short a period of time." She thanked Leopold for "leav[ing] the situation well enough in mind to be of great assistance to us here in working out our game problems."[125] Aldo Leopold's report was a start in a years-long endeavor that the newly established Mississippi Game and Fish Commission would carry on.

Before the mid-1930s, the commission's work to survey state wildlife was limited. Much like John H. Wallace in Alabama two decades prior, without funds to devote to the project, commissioners relied on game wardens and hunters, fishers, and trappers to report their observations from the field. The "census," as the 1935 biennial report called it, documented "dates and locality notes" that were checked each season.[126] In the 1930s, the Bureau of Biological Survey also conducted smaller-scale and species-specific surveys, for example related to refuges for migratory birds.[127]

Fannye Cook dreamed of something much more encompassing and species-inclusive, including extending to flora of the state. As it became clearer that federal funding was possible for conservation work, in 1935 she applied to the newest jobs program, the Works Progress Administration, for support.[128] The WPA is better known today for its work in collecting the narratives of formerly enslaved men and women; for its arts and theater programs; and for its large infrastructure projects. It was a wide-reaching agency, employing men and women in various kinds of labor. In Mississippi, that work included building or reconstructing roads, bridges, and viaducts; planting tung trees on the coast to prevent erosion; and eradicating mosquitoes and expanding sewers. The broad-based work of the WPA, in the words of one study, "reshap[ed] and transform[ed] the natural environment in Mississippi."[129] For Cook and the Mississippi Game and Fish Commission, WPA funding allowed for multi-aspect research and educational initiatives that lasted from 1935 into the early 1940s. It vastly expanded the work of the commission, moving it beyond the creation and implementation of game and fish policy to a unit of scientific study of the state of Mississippi. The WPA illustrates the impact of federal funding on state game and fish departments of the Deep South that, by the 1930s, no longer had to justify their existence and work.

Cook's application to the WPA in 1936 was "one of the first in Mississippi."[130] The project envisioned in the application perfectly braided Cook's scientific interests and earlier work as an educator. She proposed five divisions of the project, A–E, that allowed for broad-ranging scientific study and collection and natural resources education in formal and informal settings. Cook crafted the work as collaborative—with state universities, women's clubs, 4-H and the Extension Service, sportsmen's organizations, and rural people more broadly.

Division A proposed the survey itself, "to determine the occurrence, distribution, and relative abundance, and economic importance of species growing wild in Mississippi, and making known to the citizens of the state and to science such information as is assembled with respect to various species found." Activities would include "collecting, identifying, and preserving plant and animal material" and preparing it for use in schools and museums (part of the proposal in Division E). She imagined college- and school-age students as primary beneficiaries of the work done, both in providing some of the labor but also in receiving collections. Cook imagined a whole host of beneficent outcomes lay in the work of Division A—identifying location of vulnerable or rare plants and animals for protection; locating native flowers that could be transplanted to public parks and road shoulders for beautification and for nesting and feeding sources for birds; and finding "aquatic plants" that could be translated to ponds and streams where little cover existed for fish. The survey would be administered from the state director's office (by Cook herself) and follow "recognized methods of doing biological surveys."[131]

Divisions B, C, and D aimed at rural populations and meant to raise awareness about the life cycles and needs of birds and spread the good word of conservation. Those working in Division B would demonstrate the construction and placement of bird shelters, baths, and feeders; C planned for district supervisors to "design nature booklets and posters to be used by County Directors in demonstrating the use of nature subjects and nature materials in booklets and posters." Although not clearly worded, Cook assured reviewers that "the value of nature booklets and poster work in influencing conservation has long been in states where conservation work has been progressed." Cook tied the need for posters, booklets, and birdhouses to a fundamental disconnection between rural Mississippians and their surroundings. "Mississippians," she told reviewers, "are by temperament and by circumstances rural. They derive their living from the soil and spend much of their time in the fields, and the forests, on the streams, the lakes, and the bayous." Though rural folk were surrounded by "as important and varied a fauna and flora as can be found anywhere . . . very few have any appreciation of the importance of these in their relation to each other and to man in his pursuit of agriculture, forestry, and recreation." Generally, she argued, Mississippians lacked aesthetic and economic appreciation for the value of wild birds and flowers, hence the "wanton" destruction of animals and flowers at the hands of many, especially little boys.[132] Division D continued outreach by empowering county directors to oversee "conservation lectures" in "schools, clubs, camps, and picture theaters," work that Cook herself had been doing tirelessly since the late 1920s.

Finally, Division E promoted a type of informal education not widely present in Mississippi, the natural history museum. Perhaps inspired by her own time in Washington, DC, at the Smithsonian, Cook felt certain that a new system of museums could forward the work of the commission of conservation more generally. She envisioned a free natural history museum in each county, the collections of which would be generated by local people who could more easily access and take more interest in the contents therein. Eventually, she imagined a Mississippi natural history museum in Jackson, based on collections from county museums across the state. "Although museums are no less important than libraries in any system of public education," Cook held, "Mississippi has never enjoyed the benefit of museum service." The museum system would inspire teachers and "encourage the collecting instinct in children" and would influence sentiment in favor of a statewide museum.[133]

The project was approved, and some elements continued into the 1940s. It began in March 1936 in Hinds County and then expanded to all six WPA districts in the state in June of that year. The structure did not, however, mesh well with the need for training largely unskilled employees who were new to biological survey work. So, the programs were centralized under a project supervisor at the state level, who by 1939 was Vivian Cook, Fannye's sister. Vivian reported in a narrative summary of the year's work that the project operated in thirty-four of Mississippi's eighty-two counties.[134] The establishment of a network of museums in collaboration with state junior and senior colleges had been especially successful, resulting in eighteen museums in colleges, three in high schools, and one in a state park. Education and outreach activities were robust; Cook reported headcounts of people served through a variety of educational programs, and the numbers are impressive: 190,549 "individuals instructed" at schools and camps; 6,396 "conservation lectures"; and 524,139 "persons attending [picture] shows and lectures" (the Mississippi Game and Fish Commission produced movies about conservation work that traveled the state). The birdhouse and poster program initiatives were likewise productive, creating 39,507 houses and 52,832 posters and booklets.

In the eyes of project supervisors, the wide net of the survey work—collecting, preserving, reporting, and interpreting—and its large staff brought a new awareness to conservation work. Vivian Cook wrote in her

Women and men work as illustrators and taxidermists for a natural history museum founded by Cook's WPA program in Columbus, Mississippi, ca. 1930s. Pictured (clockwise from left) are Marietta Ward, Blanche Cole, Sophie Kilpatrick, William Jones, Warner Williams, Lessie Johnson, and Loa De Loach Cotton. Mississippi Museum of Natural Science, Jackson.

1940 report that "the rapid change in public opinion toward the conservation and proper use of wildlife resources which has been brought about by this project will eventually make Mississippi a safe refuge for all forms of beneficial wildlife, and will insure favorable conditions for the continuation of a long time conservation program."[135] The impact reported by Cook was also a justification for continued funding of the program: "The enthusiasm with which the project program has been received by the public and the readiness with which it has been adopted and carried forward by the educators, farmers, sportsman, and others whom it touches, indicates to us the need for the program."[136]

The Cooks—Fannye and Vivian—and their state and local partners fulfilled the vision of Fannye Cook's initial application. That vision, too, extended to the inclusion of rural Mississippians, both as workers in the survey and museum network and as collaborators in game preservation. Over the course of the late 1930s, the survey employed 200 people completing survey work and preserving plant and animal specimens, creating taxidermy, painting museum murals, and educating or lecturing. These workers were almost, to a person, white, consistent with racial disparities in the hiring practices throughout New Deal programs. Though nationally, the WPA employed Black men and women at all skill levels (and some government agencies, such as the Housing Authority, required equal hiring), local management of federal monies in the South recreated hiring hierarchies that existed already, with Black men and women often hired for menial work.[137] Such was the case in the biological survey project; personnel rosters show very few Black employees. In an undated list of workers, only three Black men and women are listed—Will Cockrell, Bessie Gates, and Henrene Outley—as janitors for the projects in Hinds County (Jackson).[138]

White Mississippians, then, did a majority of the substantive work on the project. It was into these communities that Cook and other planners wished to reach and bring a conservation ethos where they assumed it to be undeveloped. The result within the survey work was a blending of different forms of knowledge—though the workers were trained, for the time, in up-to-date methods of surveying and instructed in biology, they often translated their observations through local understanding of place and its flora and fauna. Survey workers were assigned "units" in the county in which they worked and used forms provided by Fannye Cook to document characteristic animals and plants of the unit, as well as to note specific species of birds, for example, their numbers, and where they nested. But workers also supplied narrative reports from fieldwork, and these yield rich texture on the observations. One worker, perhaps J. R. Mullican from the Wesson Unit (the narrative report author was unidentified but report forms were submitted by Mullican), provided narration of several days' work in the field in language that reads as a prose poem: "Opossum tracks were seen along a place that had been washed over but which was dry sand <> We could not determine when the tracks were made <> We ran a coachwhip into a stump hole <> It was about four feet in length <> When once a snake goes into a hole it is difficult to extract it even by catching its tail <> They invariably allow their bodies to be pulled apart rather than come on out <>" Mullican, if he was indeed the author, used local names for certain species ("trout" for bass, as many southerners called them) and clearly relied on local farmers and hunters to inform his reports ("reports are from farmers in this locality that there will be an increase in both quail and squirrel this fall").[139] The biological survey, though it did capture data relative to the distribution of certain species and also identified rare species in certain counties, was never comprehensive. By 1939, Vivian Cook reported that the project operated on a "skeleton crew" and that more funds were needed to complete the survey work, to verify and catalog data and specimens, and to transfer specimens of plants and animals to the many small museums now operating across the state.[140]

Yet the impact on the survey workers was exactly what Fannye Cook had hoped, at least as reported by local supervisors of survey workers. Observers of WPA workers on the biological survey extolled the intangible value brought by project work. R. L. Caylor, head of the science department of what was then Delta State Teachers' College (now Delta State University), wrote to the WPA appraisal supervisor on the achievement of the biological survey project. He especially stressed the impact of the work on those hired to complete surveys and museum work: "To those people who have been employed on a W.P.A. Plant and Animal Survey there is no way of expressing in words the value and importance of this project. Of course, they have received remuneration for their services, but they have received more than that. They have received a broader outlook on life because of their contacts with people other than those in their own communities. . . . They have learned the value of the natural resources of Mississippi and in the past this group has been the greatest offender."[141] Clytee R. Evans, a biology professor at what is now Mississippi University for Women, wrote loftily about the impact on workers, crediting it with achieving civic growth for the women employed: "In the face of these fine women I have seen a return of pride in accomplishment, a realization of valuable work well done, a light of comprehension of interesting facts of nature, a growth of joy in living, and a feeling of economic security: all of which make for good citizenship."[142]

The biological survey project included another avenue by which Cook and the Mississippi Game and Fish Commission hoped to enjoin rural Mississippians in wildlife protection—creating quail preserves and fishponds on private properties. The "Quail Project" arm of the WPA biological survey was not proposed in Cook's initial application for federal funds. Yet it became a key strategy to enlist a group that Cook saw as harboring destructive tendencies toward wildlife, particularly birds—boys. The quail project began in 1937 and was designed for boys enrolled in 4-H clubs and who qualified as students enrolled in Smith–Hughes vocational agricultural training.[143] The Smith–Hughes Act had passed in 1917, following the Smith–Lever Act of 1914 that established state extension programs (which organized 4-H clubs). Smith–Hughes provided federal funding for all types of vocational education but focused primarily on agriculture. In the South, that funding was (unequally) funneled to segregated public schools and supplied salaries for teachers.[144] Under the provisions of the quail project, then, Black and white boys would have been eligible to participate. But Black schools were apparently not invited by Cook to participate. At the top of a list of state secondary schools with the names and addresses of "agricultural teachers," Black and white, by county, a handwritten note reads, "Mail letter + 2 copies of the 'Quail Project' to each teacher in the white schools."[145]

The project was directed by a conservation instructor in each participating county who was part of the larger program of educational work of the WPA. The instructor worked with local teachers to identify boys whose family owned or leased at least sixty acres of land; with "direction, advice, and material" from the WPA staff and vocational teachers, the boy would "improve the natural conditions on the farm . . . so the farm will be inviting to quail and will protect quail from its enemies." The boy was expected to make studies of the quail on the farm, including submitting "maps, survey, and reports as called for."[146] The lofty plans of the quail project seem to have borne fruit; Vivian Cook reported in 1939 that 2,204 "preserves" were established.[147]

The work of the WPA survey extended and complemented the educational work continued by Cook as research secretary to push conservation education. To that end, for example, on behalf of the state's game and fish commission and women's clubs in Mississippi, Cook helped to organize "Conservation Week" in Mississippi schools. In this, she had support from national advocates of conservation; the National Association of Audubon Societies, ever present in southern efforts, was involved, notably. Fannye Cook had long maintained a connection to the organization, and by the time of establishment of the game and fish commission, she served on its board of advisors. T. Gilbert Pearson, so central in leading the NAAS's efforts in the South, made a visit to Mississippi in 1935 for Conservation Week activities. Even after his retirement from the NAAS the year before, he remained active in his support to southern conservationists. He came especially to further Cook's efforts in conservation education, visiting universities and colleges and local organizations in the state. Cook wrote after his visit, "You made many, thousands, of friends, personal friends, and gave them such an appreciation of nature and wildlife as they have not had before."[148]

Unlike what Cook had done with the quail project, she and planners of Conservation Week coordinated with Black schools in Mississippi to host a number of activities. Greg Case, game warden in Jefferson County, reported to Cook that "several negro schools put on good programs during the week under the direction of the Jeanes Teacher of the county."[149] Case referred to teachers employed by the Jeanes Fund, which financed teachers in Black southern rural schools.[150] Conservation "Week" turned into a "Camp" at the "First Annual State 4-H Conservation Camp for Negro Boys" in 1940, organized by the extension office in Mississippi. Programs read like a compendium of New Deal conservation projects: "Land Use and Soil Erosion in Relation to Conservation," "Farm Security in Relation to Conservation," and "Forestry in Relation to Conservation." Cook was on hand to lead the boys on a nature hike for "Tree Study and Wildlife," and the boys also heard about the regulation work of the Mississippi Game and Fish Commission. Still, Black conservation work, which had been ongoing in parallel with the work of Cook and other white advocates, was organized along segregated lines.[151]

The Mississippi Game and Fish Commission continued its regulatory work, of course, during the years of the WPA plant and animal survey. It received another flush of support after the passage of the Federal Aid in Wildlife Restoration Act, also known as the Pittman–Robertson Act, in 1937. The act put a tax on firearms and ammunition, giving a portion of money gained from the sales back to conservation organizations to fund research, habitat restoration, and hunter education efforts.[152] By 1939, the commission received $21,000 from Pittman–Robertson funds.[153] Commissioners met regularly to issue rulings related to closed seasons, species protection, fishing regulations, and more. But the research and educational work spearheaded by Fannye Cook gained wide recognition. Mary Gamble, who sat on the state parks commission, wrote Cook in 1936 to report that she had effused to a newly appointed game commissioner "how valuable . . . you were not only to his Commission, but to the State."[154] Lee Yeager, who hailed from Mississippi but was a forester in Illinois, wrote to Cook to tell her of his conversation with Bureau of Biological Survey staff and how they "mentioned you and the work you are doing and have done in Mississippi." One of the men "was so enthusiastic about your achievements that I feel like renewing our acquaintance herewith."[155] Cook herself was proud of her cooperative work, particularly the WPA biological survey. She would draw upon words of others to express the accomplishments of the project—in a paper to the Mississippi Academy of Sciences, she quoted Si Corley, onetime director of conservation in the state, on the impact of the work: "The rapid change in public opinion toward the conservation and proper use of wildlife research which has been brought about by this project will eventually make Mississippi a safe refuge for all forms of beneficial wildlife, and will insure favorable consideration of a long time conservation program."[156]

Fannye Cook was honored in 2022 as "Mississippi's Pioneering Conservationist" in her hometown of Crystal Springs, Copiah County, Mississippi. Photo by author.

Cook went on to fulfill her vision of establishing a state museum in Jackson. In 1939, the State Wildlife Museum opened its doors and remained part of the Mississippi Game and Fish Commission. Cook directed the museum until her retirement in 1958. The last state in the Deep South to establish a game and fish commission, Mississippi did so at the urging and "agitation" (in Cook's words) of a scientist who deplored the lack of research on the state's flora and fauna. Cook's training and professional work as an educator, her local knowledge and skill in coordinating and finding compromise among different groups invested in game and bird preservation, and her harnessing of federal funds made the 1930s a vital decade for game and fish regulation in Mississippi and, indeed, in the Deep South.

Game and fish commissions were never detached from state building in the modernizing South.[157] They drew their power from the transformation of property rights in the late nineteenth century; from a protectionist sentiment on behalf of sportsmen, bird advocates, and scientists; and from the consolidation of state functions in the early twentieth century. Though they evolved to become more effective protectors of wildlife, the laws implemented by early twentieth-century commissions, like those crafted by John H. Wallace, had antidemocratic motivations and revealed a vision for the natural world that was exclusive according to race and property ownership. Game and fish commissions were distinctly shaped by southern politics and priorities but also meshed easily with a national conservation movement that found its bogeymen in the nonwhite hunter, trapper, and game seller. Though the last region in the nation to enact conservation code, the South quickly caught up, and by the 1930s, its approach to game and fish proceeded in line with national trends in the emerging field of wildlife management. Southern conservation, like the rest of the region, was modernized by federal funding and partnership, a relationship begun two decades before. The Deep South, with closed seasons and closed lands, was a landscape transformed for hunters, fishers, and prey alike.

Afterword:
The Outdoors Are for Everybody

Durrell Smith unites the hunting past and present in his work as an artist, dog trainer, upland hunting guide, and nonprofit president. His passions caught spark in 2017, a few years after he began to hunt and train hunting dogs. Waiting in a Publix checkout line, he paged through an issue of *Garden and Gun* magazine and landed on an article by Irwin Greenstein about Neal Carter Jr. and the Georgia–Florida Shooting Dog Handlers Club.[1] "I'll never forget it," Smith said to me recently. "That was the first exposure to that side of the culture for me."[2] A Black hunting and field trial club, the Georgia–Florida Shooting Dog Handlers Club provided the link for Smith to connect his own burgeoning interest with a rich tradition of African American hunting, dog handling, and guiding.

Neal Carter Jr. and others founded the club in the early 1980s; he and many of the original members worked for hunting plantations in the Red Hills region of southern Georgia and northern Florida. Like Charlie Young, they built careers, and passions, from the continuation of Gilded Age–era land consolidation and conservation that focused on quail shooting. Durrell Smith was not intimately connected to this past; from South Atlanta, he'd grown up in an increasingly sprawling metropolitan area. Yet even in that urban space, rural-rooted cultures found purchase. He learned to ride horses from Black men who set up a corral on the side of a gas station near Greenbriar Mall in southwest Atlanta. Since he had begun working with dogs at an early age, training pit bulls, when he learned of Carter and his group he saw an opportunity and contacted Carter at his home near Sinkola plantation. After an initial meeting, Carter began to mentor Smith in bird-dog training and upland hunting.[3] That began a years-long initiation, with Smith waking at 2:00 a.m. on weekends to drive down to the Red Hills to train with Carter and others. He documented knowledge as it was passed from the older men, drawing from a deep cultural archive to create his own in field notes, movement, stories, and artwork.

Like most southerners of the twenty-first century, Smith is an urbanite.[4] In the hundred years or so since Fannye Cook commenced her work, broad demographic, economic, social, and political shifts have made this so. New Deal infrastructure projects allowed for defense industries to move to the South during World War II, bringing more federal dollars and inaugurating a new era in southern demographic change. After decades of the Great Migration, when Black southerners left the South by the thousands, employment in defense industries pulled rural people out of the countryside and into urban centers, southern and northern. This flow was further fueled by mechanization in agriculture. When Charlie Young wrote his reminiscences in 1964, he noted the emptiness of the countryside around Thomas County, Georgia. "I go out in the country to day," he said, "and look for the People I use to no and they are all gone houses torn down are Burn down." Mechanization meant fewer labor demands, and Young observed that "one man can do what 10 did in mule time."[5] In Mississippi, rural population density went from thirty-seven people per square mile in 1940 to twenty-six people per square mile by 1970, while at the same time average farm size increased from 65.8 acres in 1940 to 300 acres in 1978.[6] After 1960, rural people increasingly became "country commuters," maintaining small farms but working five-day weeks in local industry.[7] The corporatization of southern agriculture, grazing, and natural resource exploitation, begun earlier in the century, continued with the cotton, timber, oil and gas, and later soybean industries with land consolidation in the millions of acres across the South.[8]

Rehearsing these patterns in broad strokes signals what would come for hunters and fishers in the late twentieth century.[9] The rural exodus had some beneficial impact on wildlife populations; whitetail deer, for example, stabilized by the mid-twentieth century and are now exploding in population.[10] But, southerners without access to rural land had to find other means by which to pursue cherished pursuits of hunting and fishing. They came to rely on membership in private hunting and fishing clubs, on leasing acreage, or on hunting and fishing in state and national forests, parks, and wildlife management areas. By virtue of partnership between state and federal governments, public lands became available for regulated hunting and fishing, and these lands would remain important for hunters and fishers. Game commissions throughout the twentieth century came to recognize the importance

A contemporary reminder for hunters to seek landowner permission in Western North Carolina. Photo by author.

of reacquiring access to privately held lands for citizen hunters and fishers. Those involved in Alabama's game commission in the mid-1950s thought the body had to address a "long felt need" for access to land by leasing acreage from private landowners for restocking and state-managed public hunts.[11] Today, the website of Georgia's Department of Natural Resources (DNR) includes guidance for those seeking to hunt on private land, and that advice points to the thriving marketplace of hunting land leases, which includes individual and corporate landowners.[12] Tina Johannsen, the assistant chief of game management at Georgia DNR, recently told me that 75 percent of Georgia hunters now pursue their passion on private land. Less than 10 percent of hunters rely solely on public land.[13]

Durrell Smith prefers to use publicly accessible land. Before his introduction to the Georgia–Florida Shooting Dog Handlers Club, he learned to hunt within Georgia's wildlife management areas (WMAs). "I only hunted public land," he recalled, "and I figured out how to do it." Though WMAs may have a reputation for depleted game or over-competition, Smith reasoned that if biologists from Georgia DNR confirmed that game existed on public lands via tracking and surveys, then game was there; it was just a matter of becoming skilled enough to find it: "You have to learn the areas where you'll be most successful, like any hunter." He studied maps, learned game habitat, and talked to locals. Gas station conversations offered clues for Smith's public land hunts. "You'd be surprised in 2024 how the sound of a bobwhite quail calling really resonates with people in the morning," he noted. "They get excited." Now, as a guide, Smith leads hunts on WMAs. Sharing the possibilities of public land with southern hunters has become part of his broader mission. "Access is key," he reminded me, "and if you don't have money to lease land, what do you do?"[14] Over a century removed from a southern landed commons, the WMA stands in as an open, if underutilized, resource.

Tina Johanssen, for her part, helps to lead a game and fish commission that has long since transformed from its predecessor of the early twentieth century. Laws in the Deep South were drafted initially with the sportsman and landowner in mind, and later coupled with the maturing sciences of field ecology and wildlife biology that stressed habitat protection as well as the well-being of individual species. As the twentieth century unfolded, state game and fish commissions reflected that shift in the expansion and compartmentalization of conservation activities. By then, commissions were divided into departments with specific foci that cooperated when necessity required. Alabama, for example, had by the 1960s reorganized into divisions of administration, forestry, game and fish, state parks, water safety, and seafoods. Those departments were further subdivided; the Game and Fish Department, for example, had sections dedicated to law enforcement, fisheries, and wildlife research funded by the Pittman–Robertson Act. It also had a Cooperative Wildlife Research Unit, which partnered commission staff with Auburn University and the US Fish and Wildlife Survey to "conduct research . . . and train students as wildlife managers and research workers."[15] Game and fish commissions illustrated what came to be the "North American Model of Wildlife Conservation": a regime that stresses public access to and recreational and commercial use of wildlife and natural resources, guided by scientific management.[16] The legacy of the 1930s in cooperative planning, federal funding, and scientifically focused planning is apparent.

Those legacies have their own challenges. Johannsen noted the critical importance of Pittman–Robertson funding, which supports the tenets of the North American Model of Wildlife Conservation by providing public funding for wildlife restoration work from an excise tax on firearms and ammunition. But, she acknowledged its limitations—its focus primarily on game species, for example, at the expense of broader conservation efforts. The model requires game and fish commissions to pour energy into the "three Rs"— retention, recruitment, and reactivation of hunters, fishers, and trappers—in

Durrell Smith in 2021 with bird dogs Vegas and Jughead. Photo by Sam Raetz, in author's possession.

order to benefit from license sales. And, it has led commissions to spend capital to build more shooting ranges.[17] Johannsen noted that the limitations of the Pittman–Robertson Act and the North American Model of Wildlife Conservation are part of a national conversation among wildlife management professionals seeking to provide robust resources for wildlife protection. She also highlighted Georgia DNR's "proactive" programming to move beyond a "hook-and-bullet" focus; for example, an urban wildlife programming arm provides education and outreach that attends to wildlife management needs of "sprawling suburban and exurban areas."[18]

Other resonances from the early period of commission building remain; the legacy of the hunting landscape rendered as a place for white middle- and upper-class southerners left an imprint, even if the lines from past to present are murkier to trace. Game and fish commissions of the Progressive Era evolved as part of the burgeoning Jim Crow state, reflected in the rhetoric of their creators and even in policy itself. Though the racist rhetoric abated, at least in official publications, as the twentieth century unfolded, the state continued to use commissions to enforce its political priorities. Alabama's game wardens, then called conservation agents, for example, were used in "riot control" at the height of the modern civil rights movement, including in the Birmingham campaign of 1963.[19]

Black and Brown people never stopped hunting, yet hard demographic data are missing that would tell us with accuracy who pursued sport a century ago or who does so today. License purchases require disclosure of age and, optionally, of ability but not of race, ethnicity, or gender. Johannsen noted that the contracting company that completes annual hunter surveys in Georgia does garner gender data, and hunting on public lands, at least, has remained 95 percent male as far back as 2014, when the surveys began. In important respects, modern game and fish commissions acknowledge the lack of women and people of color in the sporting field; the Alabama Department of Conservation and Natural Resources, for example, has partnered with Durrell Smith to mentor hunts for sportsmen of color and offers similar experiences for women.[20]

The relatively few numbers of Black southern hunters catalyzed Smith and his wife, Ashley, a lawyer, to create the Minority Outdoor Alliance. In the summer of 2020, after the murder of George Floyd, the Smiths, with their young children in mind, decided to found an organization that would aim at inclusivity in the outdoors. By that time, Durrell was a podcaster with thousands of listeners. He'd received a sponsorship from Beretta USA and won the 2021 Breaking Barriers Award from Orvis. The couple had important mentors in the conservation and hunting world—the National Wild Turkey Federation and Pheasants Forever, for example. "From there," Smith remembers, "it was about defining who we want to be in this space. It wasn't just enough to say, 'The outdoors are for everyone.' Okay, great. But what does that actually mean?" Durrell began a learn-to-hunt program to focus on upland hunting that now operates in thirteen states. Ashley spearheaded the Minority Outdoor Alliance Festival, now in its third year, which brings together diverse outdoor enthusiasts for bird dog exhibitions, fly casting demonstrations, archery, and more. And they both wanted to focus on job creation; to that end, they recently hosted a career networking fair, which brought 150 students from historically Black colleges and universities to meet with representatives from state DNRs, Ducks Unlimited, the Wildlife Society, and other conservation organizations. The Smiths have found avid interest in their work and have begun to mentor scores of Black men and women in outdoor sports.

Like Charlie Young before him, Smith has a keen sense of history and a commitment to sharing the past. In his guided hunts and in his demonstrations at the annual festival, he shares the stories of Neal Carter Jr. and the Georgia–Florida Shooting Dog Handlers Club and those of the long-standing relationship of Black Americans to the natural world. "It always goes back to the point of African Americans using the outdoors and hunting as a way to sustain a lifestyle, and that being done before emancipation and after emancipation. Especially when there were no options outside of a plantation, you go and be a hunting guide."[21] He sees a direct thread from the late nineteenth-century guides like Young to the "famous scouts" of the golden age of field trials in the mid-twentieth century to Carter and the creation of an all-Black field trial. Smith's work reminds us that hunting has long been shaped by issues of power and access and that hunters (and fishers) can become their own authorities of that past—and present. The many modes of public history, such as those practiced by Smith—oral history, storytelling, teaching long-tested field techniques—bring us to an open season to reimagine the field.

Acknowledgments

This project is rooted in my dissertation work, which was set in the Red Hills region of southern Georgia and northern Florida. I came to it by virtue of fellow graduate student and friend Lee Willis, who was pursuing his PhD in history from Florida State University while I was completing coursework for an MA in public history. Lee asked me to join him in an oral history project for the Thomas County Historical Society in Georgia, now the Thomasville History Center (THC), about the history of quail hunting plantations that emerged after the Civil War. Thanks to Lee and THC director Anne Harrison, I was introduced to a world that I had no idea existed. Little did I know how the history of hunting would come to occupy me for more than a decade.

As I returned to Thomasville and Tallahassee during my doctoral work, I was aided by a number of people whose passions about the past inspired me as a public historian. Anne and Ephraim Rotter, THC's curator, welcomed me for entire summers. They provided me with an office, access to archives, and lunchtime chats that included a seemingly endless supply of coffee and biscotti. They also introduced me to locals who aided in my research: Jack Hadley, director of the Hadley Black History Museum; Betty Jinright, who made it her mission that I see as many of the hunting plantations as possible; Brent Runyon, preservationist extraordinaire; and Jule Anderson, a granddaughter of Charlie Young and someone who became incredibly important to my understanding of Young's life. Jule talked to me for hours, gave me insight into the world of Black hunting guides, and introduced me to other pressing issues that continued to affect Black Thomas Countians, including heirs' property. I am inexpressibly grateful for these people and others who shared their lives with me; they are why this book exists.

As I developed chapters of the dissertation that would become parts of this book, I was supported by an intellectual community at the University of California, Santa Barbara. John Majewski, my advisor, gave patient and insightful feedback on chapter drafts and lent his deep expertise in southern history that ultimately made my work more substantial. Members of my dissertation committee, Ann Plane and Randy Bergstrom, sent invaluable feedback on methodology, narrative, and prose. Fellow graduate students Paul Baltimore, Megan Bowman, Sarah Griffith, Mira Foster, Paul Hirsch, Roger Eardley-Pryor, and Lily Tamai Welty read versions along the way and gave helpful feedback, encouragement, and critical support. Working under Lindsey Reed at the *Public Historian* introduced me to her extraordinary editorial eye, one that I try (and fail) to emulate.

After graduate school, historian Robert Weyeneth introduced me to Daniel J. Vivian, a scholar of northern hunting plantations in South Carolina. With Dan, I developed parts of the dissertation for an edited collection on sporting plantations in the Lowcountry and Red Hills region. Dan was an adept editor and an exemplary professional at an important time in my own early career; his continued collegiality has been invaluable.

Colleagues past and present have been instrumental in the research and writing of this book. Jennifer Dickey, Catherine Lewis, and Richard Harker were cheerleaders as I finished the dissertation. Ann McCleary, Keri Adams, and Stephanie Chalifoux all gave patient feedback on book ideas in the early stages of conceptualization and have continued to be important sources of encouragement. Friend and author Abby Greenbaum has dedicated long phone conversations to explore ideas in narrative structure.

History faculty at the University of Alabama have been unanimously supportive as I worked toward completion of the book while building a public history program. Lesley Gordon and Lawrence Cappello read drafts of and gave helpful direction on the book proposal. Jenny Shaw carefully read and commented on chapter 1, helping me to address inconsistencies and incomplete analysis (Jenny has also been a sage guide in my journey toward tenure). Kari Frederickson has given generously of her time, substantial expertise, and editing acumen to drafts of almost every chapter. Sharony Green and John Beeler offered unflagging confidence in my progress. Holly Grout, Andrew Huebner, Heather Kopelson, Di Luo, Juanjo Ponce-Vasquez, and Sarah Steinbock-Pratt all lent wisdom and encouragement as I worked through manuscript edits. Lawrence, Lucy Kaufman, and Matthew Lockwood gave abundantly of their humor, friendship, and empathy as we navigated pre-tenure academic life. The history department office staff, Kayla Key, Ellen Pledger, Morta Riggs, and Marla Scott, have made any work I do in the department possible. Finally, if succeeding in a faculty job can be compared to the tenacity of the Crimson Tide football team (and why not?), then Joshua Rothman, as department chair, has alternately been head coach, offensive *and* defensive coordinator, trainer, and recruitment lead. Many thanks go to Josh for the unfailing support, and Roll Tide.

As the manuscript took form, a group of scholars and editors helped it become a better book. The University of Alabama has a noteworthy publisher-in-residence program, and its lead, George Thompson, gave early and critical feedback that supplied confidence in the stories herein. Dr. David Durham and Prof. Albert Lopez of the University of Alabama School of Law offered guidance on the history of Alabama's legal system and the broader context of United States property law, respectively. Historian Peter Hoffer generously offered valuable feedback and guidance on framing of the closing of the commons and game and fish law. Drew Swanson, a historian whom I deeply admire, invited me to join a panel at the American Historical Association, where I held company with Drew, Mikko Saikku, and Mark Hersey, all giants of southern environmental history. Matthew Lockhart has exchanged ideas with me and asked probing questions that have deepened my engagement with research on the history of southern hunting. An anonymous reader of the manuscript gave thoughtful and encouraging commentary that shaped its final form. Albert Way has, from the beginning of my career, been a mentor and model of collegiality, and I cannot express how grateful I am for his effort, time, and care in helping this work to be the best version of itself.

Special thanks go to Brandon Proia, Mark Simpson-Vos, Mary Carley Caviness, Lindsay Starr, and Andrew Winters of the University of North Carolina Press. Mark and Brandon showed early interest in the book project, and Andrew stepped in to see it to its fulfillment. I am continually impressed with Andrew's patience and grace and his commitment to meaningful historical scholarship. Mary patiently answered my many questions about the final stages of manuscript formatting. Lindsay and her team designed a cover both personally meaningful and topically relevant.

(It goes without saying that none of these fine colleagues and friends are responsible for the shortcomings herein.)

I am (and we all are) indebted to the work of committed archivists and researchers. We are fortunate in this state to have the Alabama Department of Archives and History. Steve Murray, Scotty Kirkland, Meredith McDonough, Amelia Chase, Courtney Pinkard, Kayla Scott Gurner, and Roland McDonald have assisted this research and my broader public history work at UA in important ways. Friend and historian Micah Reuber clued me in to the story of Fannye A. Cook, who became the subject of chapter 4. William Thompson and Laura Heller, archivists at the Mississippi Department of Archives and History, helped me navigate the records of Ms. Cook, which were in the process of being transferred from the Mississippi Museum of Natural Science. Aaron Holbrook and Nick Winstead of the MMNS shared technical reports and images, respectively, from the MMNS collections, and former MMNS director Libby Hartfield offered guidance on the images. Adam Clemons of the University of Mississippi Libraries helped me to recover the thesis of Charles Wiley Prewitt Jr., and Amberley Sheffield generously scanned it for my use. Historian Dante Whitaker, then a graduate student at New York University, employed his considerable research skills to plumb the Audubon Society records at the New York Public Library to send me those that pertained to the Deep South. Hannah French, Abigail Gomez, Amelia Pugh, and Ellie Skinkle, all skilled UA history majors, served as research assistants in the fall of 2022 and 2023.

I'll long remain grateful to Durrell Smith and Tina Johanssen for lending their voices to the afterword. Their willingness to share their stories allowed me to connect past and present, a priority for public historians. Many thanks go to my cousin Elizabeth Ellis Babb for allowing me to draw from the stories of her father, Shad, as a way to introduce the book.

I've been fortunate to build a community of friends and compatriots in Tuscaloosa and beyond who have been instrumental to the emotional work of completing a book. Sara-Maria Sorentino and Elif Kalaycioglu are cherished pals who were front-row boosters as I winged my way to the finish line. I am beyond lucky to count Megan Gallagher, Misha Hadar, Jared and Heeyoung Margulies, Gina Stamm, and Seth Stewart, all brilliant scholars themselves, as good friends. Kirstie Tepper and Teresa Bramlette Reeves graciously allowed me to join them in work that blended public history and public art and saw this project unfold at every step. Artist Jamey Grimes, a partner in public history work, showed patience as the book distracted me from our initiatives in Tuscaloosa. Hilary Green's work has been a model of committed, engaged scholarship, and I am fortunate our paths crossed at UA. As I completed this book, Robin Morris, Jennifer Dickey, Kathy Knapp, and James F. Brooks commiserated with and cheered me at our annual meetings of the Atlanta Bowl of Holla(ndaise) breakfast club.

My family patiently bore the development of the dissertation and book and have been especially understanding when it called me away from family holiday time and summer visits. My mother and stepfather, Kendall and Charles Clotfelter, and my father and stepmother, Edward and Harriett Brock, have been wonderfully supportive. My father has read various versions of the work and always offered insightful commentary. He lent his memories to the book's introduction. My grandmother Helen Hayes Cobb Runninger passed away before the book's completion but was my rock throughout graduate school and into my career. My sister, Emily Sweitzer, always smarter than me and with her own interests in history, has uplifted me with good humor and good advice.

I had a surprise meet-cute with James F. Brooks at a public history conference in Baltimore in 2016. Little did I know then that we would join together to forge a life built upon shared passions and that he would offer me gifts that I previously had no way of imagining. Our world includes an emotional Redbone Coonhound (a redundant observation, indeed) and a charismatic calico, and I treasure what we've created in our time together. Thanks to James for the depthless ocean of inspiration and support.

Notes

Abbreviations
ADAH   Alabama Department of Archives and History, Montgomery
DC/AC   Alabama Department of Conservation, Administrative Correspondence
HC   Hopkins Collection
MDAH   Mississippi Department of Archives and History, Jackson
MDWFP   Mississippi Department of Wildlife, Fisheries, and Parks, Jackson
THC   Thomasville History Center, Thomasville, GA

Introduction

1. "Sure Grow Market Growing Like Its Cotton," *Anniston (AL) Star*, April 6, 1997, 39.
2. Edward Brock Jr., email message to author, June 17, 2023.
3. A shotgun plug is a plastic or wooden dowel that limits the capacity of the gun's barrel, reducing the number of bullets a hunter can fire.
4. John H. Wallace Jr. to T. T. Ashford, August 18, 1908, DC/AC, box SG20172, folder A 1908 August–September, ADAH.
5. Ownby's *Subduing Satan*, Kelly's *Hunter Elite*, Giltner's *Hunting and Fishing in the New South*, and Vinson's "Conservation and the South, 1890–1920" consider gender, class, race, and policy development, respectively, in the pursuit of hunting. Giltner's last chapter on the intersection of hunting laws, land, and race in South Carolina is an important building block for this work. Hahn's classic article, "Hunting, Fishing, and Foraging," inspired debate about the closing of the commons and political activism, yet it has not been tested against the constructs of nature, race, and class via hunting policy. Historians have more recently published works on sporting tourism in the South. Way's *Conserving Southern Longleaf*, though not squarely focused on hunting, examines the impact of northern sportsmen on the preservation of longleaf pine and quail habitats, so central to seasonal hunting in parts of the South. My and Vivian's coedited collection, *Leisure, Plantations, and the Making of a New South*, examines the social, architectural, and environmental history of sporting plantations in two distinct subregions of the South. More recently, Vivian's monograph, *A New Plantation World*, has offered an in-depth study of Lowcountry hunting estates. William D. Bryan argues that hunting laws were an extension of the new ideas about environmental "permanence" among New South advocates of conservation; see Bryan, *Price of Permanence*. I'm also indebted to Bryan's argument that the South must be considered, where typically it has not been, as squarely part of the national conservation movement. A soon-to-be published study on the history of hunting in South Carolina offers a comprehensive look at hunting from the colonial era to the present day; see Lockhart and Tuten, *Southern History of Hunting*. Foster's forthcoming volume, *So Great Was the Slaughter*, provides valuable insight into the state of Arkansas's journey to statewide fish and game laws and battle with market hunters. Other important works on the history of hunting—Reiger's *American Sportsmen* and Jacoby's *Crimes against Nature*, for example—focus on northeastern and western regions of the country. I also draw from recent critical

explorations of the conservation movement, including D. Taylor, *Rise of the American Conservation Movement*. For more on the transformation of the commons in the West, see Warren, *Hunter's Game*; and Jacoby, *Crimes against Nature*.

6. For an important study of how the public and private reorganization and management of Mississippi's forests perpetuated environmental and racial domination, see Hyman, "Cut and the Color Line."

7. See, for example, Hahn, "Hunting, Fishing, and Foraging"; Kirby, *Rural Worlds Lost*, 28–29; Sawers, "Property Law as Labor Control"; and Mauldin, *Unredeemed Land*, 116–26.

8. See Hahn, "Hunting, Fishing, and Foraging"; and Sawers, "Property Law as Labor Control."

9. Manning, "Emancipation as State Building from the Inside Out," 60.

10. Sarah Haley has provided a brilliant framework for the gendered foundations of the Jim Crow carceral regime, one in which dehumanization of Black women was central to the formation of stable gender categories of whiteness. See *No Mercy Here*.

11. For work on poaching as a folk crime, see Forsyth, Gramling, and Wooddell, "Game of Poaching."

12. For scholarship of continued rural resistance to game laws in mid-twentieth-century Texas, see Baker, *Bulldozer Revolutions*.

13. Historian William D. Bryan comes to a similar conclusion about the limits of hunting and fishing laws on Black mobility; see *Price of Permanence*, 167–68.

14. In this decision, I also risk the danger of devaluing fish in favor of more "charismatic species"; see Wadewitz, "Are Fish Wildlife?" Other scholars have focused on southern fisheries, including M. Taylor, "North Carolina Fisheries in the Old and New South"; Cecelski, "Hidden World of Mullet Camps"; Blount, "Coastal Refugees"; and Stephens, *Mississippi Gulf Coast Seafood Industry*.

Chapter 1

1. Thomas C. Hunter to Governor Bibb, November 1, 1818, in Carter, *Territorial Papers*, 452 (emphasis in original).
2. Knight, "Document and Literature Review," 49; Kelley, "Clear Boundaries."
3. Ethridge, *Creek Country*, 9.
4. Braund, *Deerskins and Duffels*, 71.
5. Braund, *Deerskins and Duffels*, 72.
6. Wolfe, "Settler Colonialism."
7. Ethridge, *Creek Country*, 137–39.
8. Saunt, *Unworthy Republic*, 22.
9. Quoted in Kelley, "Clear Boundaries," 99.
10. S. Mitchell, "Progress of the Human Mind," 359.
11. *Cherokee Phoenix*, April 21, 1830, Western Carolina University Digital Collections, www.wcu.edu/library/DigitalCollections/CherokeePhoenix/Vol3/n001/cherokee-phoenix-page-2-column-4a-5b.html.
12. See Miles, *Ties That Bind*.
13. Braund, *Deerskins and Duffels*, 139.
14. Saunt, *Unworthy Republic*, 93.

15. C. C. Clay to J. R. Poinsett, April 17, 1837, box SG6241, folder 7, Governor C. C. Clay Administrative Records, ADAH, https://archives.alabama.gov/timeline/1800/cwar17.html. For more on the extension laws in Alabama, see Haveman, *Rivers of Sand*, 85.

16. Anonymous, reprinted in *Daily Selma Reporter*, October 10, 1835.

17. Saunt, *Unworthy Republic*, 37–38.

18. Rothman, *Ledger and the Chain*, 104.

19. Rothman, *Ledger and the Chain*, 105.

20. Silkenat, *Scars on the Land*, 33.

21. Anderson, *Creatures of Empire*, 114; Silver, *New Face on the Countryside*, 173. For an overview of the relationship between common land, open access, and public land, see Blackmar, "Appropriating the 'the Commons,'" 49–79.

22. Ethridge, *Creek Country*, 163; Stewart, "From King Cane to King Cotton," 67.

23. Richard W. Judd notes that by the 1830s, for example, Massachusetts required stock owners to adhere to "stricter fencing laws." Judd, *Common Lands*, 46. See the entirety of chap. 2 for a nuanced portrait of the transition of the commons in New England.

24. Blevins, *Cattle in the Cotton Fields*, 50.

25. This was true in the colonial South as well. The Virginia House of Burgesses, for example, passed a law in 1648 that permitted hunting on "land not planted or seated up though taken." Quoted in Proctor, *Bathed in Blood*, 6.

26. See Thompson, *Whigs and Hunters*.

27. Georgia, Chatham County, Superior Court Minutes, 1782–1900, v. 5–7 1799–1808, 525, digital image, FamilySearch.org. See also Proctor, *Bathed in Blood*, 13.

28. Gosse, *Letters from Alabama*, 207.

29. Proctor, *Bathed in Blood*, 61.

30. Proctor, *Bathed in Blood*, 84, 85–87.

31. Harry W., "Deer-hunting in Mississippi," *Spirit of the Times*, February 17, 1844.

32. Proctor, *Bathed in Blood*, 61–62.

33. Proctor, *Bathed in Blood*, 16.

34. Dunlap, *Saving America's Wildlife*, 11–13.

35. For more on hunting as a "democratic pursuit" important to southern male culture, see Ownby, *Subduing Satan*, chap. 1.

36. Elliott, *Carolina Sports*, 285–86.

37. Elliott, *Carolina Sports*, 288.

38. Palmer, "A Review of the Game Legislation in Alabama," reprinted in Wallace, *First Biennial Report*, 72.

39. *Tuskegee Republican*, May 20, 1852.

40. Marbury and Crawford, *Digest of the Laws of the State of Georgia* (1802), 432.

41. An Act Respecting Slaves, in *Digest of the Laws of the State of Alabama* (1823), 627; *Revised Code of the Laws of Mississippi* (1823), 871–72.

42. *Digest of the Laws of the State of Alabama* (1823), 630–31; *Revised Code of the Laws of Mississippi* (1823), 379.

43. *Revised Code of the Laws of Mississippi* (1823), 372.

44. Cobb, *Compilation of the General and Public Statutes of the State of Georgia* (1859), 594.

45. Giltner, "Slave Hunting and Fishing," 27.
46. Giltner, "Slave Hunting and Fishing," 27.
47. Giltner, "Slave Hunting and Fishing," 25.
48. Giltner, "Slave Hunting and Fishing"; Stewart, *"What Nature Suffers to Groe,"* 136; Silkenat, *Scars on the Land*; Brown, *African-Atlantic Cultures*. Stewart suggests that sustenance procured by hunting and fishing made up as much as half of the diet of enslaved people on the Georgia coast.
49. Silkenat, *Scars on the Land*, 39.
50. Giltner, "Slave Hunting and Fishing," 33.
51. Georgia Baker, *Federal Writers' Project: Slave Narrative Project, Vol. 4, Georgia*, 41.
52. Jim Allen, *Federal Writers' Project: Slave Narrative Project, Vol. 9, Mississippi*, 6.
53. John Cameron, *Federal Writers' Project: Slave Narrative Project, Vol. 9, Mississippi*, 19.
54. Rachel Adams, *Federal Writers' Project: Slave Narrative Project, Vol. 4, Georgia*, 3.
55. Silkenat, *Scars on the Land*, 38.
56. MacIntyre, *Wiregrass Stories*, 43.
57. Brown, *African-Atlantic Cultures*, 162.
58. Brown, *African-Atlantic Cultures*, 161–62.
59. Brown, *African-Atlantic Cultures*, 163–65.
60. Proctor, *Bathed in Blood*, 145. See chap. 7 in the book for a fuller treatment of the ways that enslaved men imbued hunting with meaning.
61. Giltner, "Slave Hunting and Fishing," 33.
62. For the shift in southern landowners from "laborlords" to "landlords," see G. Wright, *Old South, New South*, chap. 2.
63. O'Donovan, *Becoming Free*, 208.
64. Browning and Silver, *Environmental History of the Civil War*, 196.
65. Mauldin, *Unreedemed Land*, 69.
66. See Du Bois, *Black Reconstruction*, 172–73.
67. Flynn, *White Land, Black Labor*, 115–16.
68. *Testimony Taken by the Joint Select Committee . . . Alabama*, 152.
69. *Testimony Taken by the Joint Select Committee . . . Mississippi*, 488, 483.
70. *Testimony Taken by the Joint Select Committee . . . Mississippi*, 200.
71. *Testimony Taken by the Joint Select Committee . . . Alabama*, 120.
72. *Testimony Taken by the Joint Select Committee . . . Alabama*, 574.
73. *Testimony Taken by the Joint Select Committee . . . Alabama*, 143.
74. Ransom and Sutch, "One Kind of Freedom."
75. Alston and Kauffman, "Up, down, and off the Agricultural Ladder."
76. Social Explorer, "Farm Ownership Status (White Farmers)"; Social Explorer, "Farm Ownership Status (Colored Farmers)."
77. Alston and Kauffman, "Agricultural Ladder," 274.
78. "Idolatry or Christianity, Peonism or Free Yeomanry, Chinese or White Man, Which?," *Banner of the South*, May 7, 1870.
79. Hahn, "Hunting, Fishing, and Foraging," 42.
80. Hahn, "Hunting, Fishing, and Foraging."
81. Kantor and Kousser, "Common Sense or Commonwealth?"

82. King, "Closing of the Southern Range"; Sawers, "Property Law as Labor Control."

83. For more on the persistence of stock herding on the open range in Alabama after the Civil War, which primarily continued in the uplands and in the southern piney woods (and in counties that King identifies as open range), see Blevins, *Cattle in the Cotton Fields*, 45–46.

84. King, "Closing of the Southern Range," 54.

85. Stock-law counties include Crenshaw Dale, Henry, Pike, Coosa, Lawrence, Monroe, Randolph, Butler Limestone, Tallapoosa, Marengo, Wilcox, Sumter, Elmore, Autauga, Tuscaloosa, Chambers, Calhoun, Barbour, Madison, Talladega, Macon, Bullock, Hale, Perry, Lowndes, Green, Lee, Russell, Dallas, Montgomery. Open-range counties include Geneva, Washington, Covington, Coffee, Marion, Jackson, Fayette, Walker, Clarke, Winston, Clay, Lamar, Marshall, Cullman, DeKalb, Franklin, Morgan, Choctaw, Conecuh, Cleburne, Bibb, Cherokee, Escambia, Lauderdale, Colbert, St. Clair, Shelby, Blount, Etowah, Chilton, Jefferson, Baldwin, Mobile. King, "Closing of the Southern Range," 67.

86. These laws included those that forbade camp hunting; those that created hunting seasons for certain species; and those that outlawed certain forms of fishing (e.g., muddying and dynamiting streams). Stock-law counties with a game law by 1880 include Autauga, Coosa, Dallas, Greene, Hale, Lawrence, Lowndes, Marengo, Monroe, Montgomery, Pickens, Pike, Randolph, Sumter, Talladega, Wilcox. Open-range counties that adopted a game law by the same time are Baldwin, Bibb, Blount, Chilton, Choctaw, Clay, Dekalb, Escambia, Jefferson, Marion, Marshall, Mobile, Washington, and Winston. Clarke County, an open-range county, passed a game law in 1877 that was repealed in 1880. This data was derived from the compiled acts of the Alabama legislature for the years 1865–1900; the acts have been digitized by the Alabama Department of Archives and History and are available via Internet Archive, https://archive.org/search?query=creator%3A%22Alabama.+Legislature%22.

87. An Act for the Preservation of Game, Animals, and Birds in the Counties of Mobile, Monroe, Marengo, Baldwin, Dallas, Lowndes, Hale, Montgomery, Clarke, Greene, Wilcox, Pike, Talladega, Pickens, Bibb, Autauga, Chilton, Clay, Jefferson, *Acts of the General Assembly of Alabama, Passed at the Session of 1878–1879*, 200–201. The act set seasons for deer and certain fowl, including quail and ducks, and made it unlawful to hunt at night or sell or ship animals included in the act. Marengo, Dallas, Lowndes, Hale, Montgomery, Clarke, Greene, Wilcox, Talladega, Pickens, Autauga, and Monroe Counties all had Black majorities. Data on demographic makeup of counties from US Census, "Total Population: White, Colored, Chinese, Indian," 1880, based on data from the US Population Census, 1880, prepared by Social Explorer, www.socialexplorer.com/2e495a7942/view.

88. An Act to Repeal "An Act for the Preservation of Game, Animals, and Birds in the Counties of Mobile, Monroe, Marengo, Baldwin, Dallas, Lowndes, Hale, Montgomery, Clarke, Greene, Wilcox, Pike, Talladega, Pickens, Bibb, Autauga, Chilton, Clay, Jefferson," approved February 14, 1879, so far as relates to the counties of Jefferson, Pike, Chilton, Clay, and Clarke, *Acts of the General Assembly of Alabama, Passed at the Session of 1880–81*, 145; To Repeal an Act for the Preservation of Game, Animals, and Birds in the Counties of Mobile, Monroe, Marengo, Baldwin, Dallas, Lowndes, Hale,

Montgomery, Clarke, Greene, Wilcox, Pike, Talladega, Pickens, Bibb, Autauga, Chilton, Clay, Jefferson approved February 14, 1879, so far as relates to that portion of the county of Bibb west of the Cahaba River, *Acts of the General Assembly of Alabama, Passed at the Session of 1884–85*, 324.

89. Fair Play, "Stock Law," *Southern Cultivator* 31, no. 2 (February 1873): 51, accessed December 1, 2023, HathiTrust, https://hdl.handle.net/2027/njp.32101050722840.

90. Geo. C. Dixon, "More about a Stock Law," *Southern Cultivator* 29, no. 1 (January 1871): 7–8, accessed December 1, 2023, HathiTrust, https://hdl.handle.net/2027/njp.32101050722477.

91. A Sufferer, "Loss of Stock," *Southern Cultivator* 27, no. 5 (May 1869): 148 (emphasis in original), accessed December 2, 2023, HathiTrust, https://hdl.handle.net/2027/uiug.30112039908980.

92. "Advice to Land Owners," *Southern Cultivator* 27, no. 5 (May 1869): 148 (emphasis in original), accessed December 2, 2023, HathiTrust, https://hdl.handle.net/2027/uiug.30112039908980.

93. For Mississippi laws, see J. A. P. Campbell, *Revised Code of the Statute Laws of the State of Mississippi*, 284–86, 291–92; for Alabama laws, see Keyes, Wood, and Roquemore, *Code of Alabama 1876*, 931–32; for Georgia laws, see Clark, Cobb, and Irwin, *Code of the State of Georgia*, 802.

94. Sawers, "Property Law as Labor Control," 360–61.

95. Sawers, "Property Law as Labor Control," 362.

96. Clark, Cobb, and Irwin, *Code of the State of Georgia*, 802; Hopkins, Anderson, and Lamar, *Code of the State of Georgia*, 76.

97. Thompson et al., *Annotated Code of the General Statute Laws of the State of Mississippi*, 377–78.

98. Kantor, *Politics and Property Rights*, 123.

99. *Marion (AL) Standard*, August 9, 1881.

100. Barrow, *Passion for Birds*, 59.

101. Barrow, *Passion for Birds*, 60.

102. "Governor Message," *Edgefield (SC) Advertiser*, January 28, 1873, 1.

103. *Revised Statutes of South Carolina* (1894), 406–7.

104. "The Granges Will Protect the Bird," *Rural Carolinian* 5 (1874): 144, HathiTrust, accessed January 8, 2023, https://hdl.handle.net/2027/hvd.32044048695977; An Act to Protect the Ring-Necked Pheasant (*fasianus forquatus*) and Mexican Quail, Sometimes Called California Quail, *Acts of the General Assembly of Alabama, Passed by the Session of 1892–1893* (1893), 819.

105. Evenden, "Laborers of a Nature."

106. "A Game Law," *Marengo (IL) News*, May 11, 1876.

107. Ex. Confed, "Fences, &c.," *Southern Cultivator* 28, no. 7 (July 1870): 203, HathiTrust, https://hdl.handle.net/2027/chi.096359219.

108. "Advice to Land Owners," *Southern Cultivator* 27, no. 5 (May 1869): 148, HathiTrust, https://hdl.handle.net/2027/uiug.30112039908980.

109. *Biennial Report of the Attorney General of the State of Alabama* (1884), 147.

110. *Biennial Report of the Attorney General of the State of Alabama* (1884), 774.

111. *Biennial Report of the Attorney General of Alabama* (1894), 15.

112. *Biennial Report of the Attorney General of Alabama* (1894), 17.

113. *Biennial Report of the Attorney General of Alabama* (1894), 17.

Chapter 2

1. Historian Karl Jacoby notes that by the 1880s, the Adirondacks were the center of "the most advanced experiment in conservation in the United States." Jacoby, *Crimes against Nature*, 17.

2. For in-depth reading on the conservation movement's reproduction of social hierarchies, see D. Taylor, *Rise of the American Conservation Movement*.

3. Hornaday, *Our Vanishing Wildlife*, 110. For a critical look at Hornaday's work, see Dehler, *Most Defiant Devil*.

4. Pearson, *Adventures in Bird Protection*, 144.

5. Pearson, *Adventures in Bird Protection*, 144.

6. Pearson, *Adventures in Bird Protection*, 144.

7. Barrow, *Passion for Birds*, 133. See also Dunlap, *Saving America's Wildlife*, chap. 3.

8. "Bonnet," 1890, Metropolitan Museum of Art, December 5, 2024, www.metmuseum.org/art/collection/search/84639?searchField=All&sortBy=Relevance&ao=on&ft=37.144.2&offset=0&rpp=20&pos=1.

9. See Price, *Flight Maps*, chap. 2.

10. Barrow, *Passion for Birds*, 52–54, 71.

11. "Legislation for the Protection of Birds," *The Auk* 19 (1902): 59–60.

12. Barrow, *Passion for Birds*, 117.

13. Barrow, *Passion for Birds*, 128.

14. Barrow, *Passion for Birds*, 128.

15. Barrow, *Passion for Birds*, 127.

16. Barrow, *Passion for Birds*, 134. Mine is a summarized account of the redevelopment of Audubon activity.

17. Barrow, *Passion for Birds*, 130.

18. Allen, "Present Wholesale Destruction of Bird-Life."

19. William Dutcher, "Report of the A.O.U. Committee on the Protection of North American Birds, and of the National Committee on Audubon Societies," *The Auk* (1903): 102, HathiTrust, https://hdl.handle.net/2027/hvd.32044107225351.

20. "State Reports," *Bird Lore* 1, no. 7 (1905): 78, HathiTrust, https://hdl.handle.net/2027/chi.39181823.

21. For notes on the Lacey Act and preceding legislation, see Palmer, *Federal Game Protection*; and Cart, "Lacey Act."

22. G. O. Shields, "The League Did It," *Recreation* 13, no. 1 (July 1900): 76, HathiTrust, https://hdl.handle.net/2027/hvd.32044106226483.

23. Reiger, *American Sportsmen*, 96.

24. Vinson, "Conservation and the South," 218.

25. Barrow, *Passion for Birds*, 133.

26. For a brief biography of Pearson, see Oliver H. Orr Jr., "Pearson, Thomas Gilbert," NCPedia, accessed November 26, 2024, www.ncpedia.org/biography/pearson-thomas-gilbert.

27. Pearson, *Stories of Bird Life*.

28. Pearson, *Adventures in Bird Protection*, 66.
29. Pearson, *Adventures in Bird Protection*, 73.
30. Pearson, *Adventures in Bird Protection*, 76.
31. Vinson, "Conservation and the South," 250.
32. Pearson, *Adventures in Bird Protection*, 88.
33. Moran et al., "Late Holocene Evolution of Currituck Sound," 828.
34. On the rise of urban game markets and the increasing shipment of game from the Midwest and South, see Smalley with Reeves, *Market in Birds*, 82–87.
35. Pearson, *Adventures in Bird Protection*, 116.
36. Vinson, "Conservation and the South," 254–55.
37. Vinson, "Conservation and the South," 255.
38. Pearson, *Adventures in Bird Protection*, 155.
39. For more on Aiken as a destination for northern tourists, see Youngs, "Lifestyle Enclaves," esp. chap. 2. For more on hunting tourism in Aiken and South Carolina, see Giltner, *Hunting and Fishing in the New South*; Brock and Vivian, *Leisure, Plantations, and the Making of a New South*; and Vivian, *New Plantation World*.
40. Pearson, *Adventures in Bird Protection*, 156–57.
41. Vinson, "Conservation and the South," 265–66; Giltner, *Hunting and Fishing in the New South*, 165. See chap. 6 for thorough coverage of South Carolina's efforts to establish hunting and fishing law. As with Wallace and Alabama, race-baiting was at the heart of the movement for game law in South Carolina.
42. "Audubon Society," *Miami News*, April 15, 1904, 8.
43. For a fuller telling of Bradley's life and death, see McIver, *Death in the Everglades*.
44. Vinson, "Conservation and the South," 245.
45. "Protection for Birds the Work of This Growing State Society," *Tampa Tribune*, May 13, 1906, 12.
46. Vinson, "Conservation and the South," 245–46.
47. Vinson, "Conservation and the South," 246.
48. Vinson, "Conservation and the South," 232, 234.
49. Pearson, *Adventures in Bird Protection*, 240.
50. Pearson, *Adventures in Bird Protection*, 240; "Game Preserves in Gulf," *Times-Democrat* (New Orleans), October 4, 1904.
51. Pearson, *Adventures in Bird Protection*, 200–201; Vinson, "Conservation and the South," 237–38.
52. Vinson, "Conservation and the South," 237–38.
53. In the late nineteenth century, Georgia passed a spate of countywide laws regulating hunting and fishing, as documented in Hahn, "Hunting, Fishing, and Foraging," 49.
54. Vinson, "Conservation and the South," 265–66.
55. "The Law and the S.P.C.A.," *Augusta Herald*, April 23, 1905.
56. "Audubon Bill Passes House," *Atlanta Constitution*, July 28, 1903.
57. *Acts and Resolutions of the General Assembly of the State of Georgia 1903*, vol. 1100–103.
58. Vinson, "Conservation and the South," 265–66.
59. Owen, *Alabama Official and Statistical Register 1907*, 28–29.
60. Wallace, *Senator from Alabama*, 176.

61. Hild, *Greenbackers*, 208.

62. Rogers et al., *Alabama*, 354.

63. *Journal of the House of Representatives of the State of Alabama*, 1898, 105, ADAH.

64. *Journal of the House of Representatives of the State of Alabama*, 1898, 409, ADAH.

65. William D. Jelks, "Editorial Correspondence," *Times and News* (Eufala, AL), December 1, 1898.

66. Jelks, "Editorial Correspondence."

67. T. S. Palmer, "A Review of Game Legislation in Alabama," in Wallace, *First Biennial Report*, 68.

68. Stewart and Purson, *Stewart's Purdon's Digest*, 1763–77.

69. Jelks, "Editorial Correspondence."

70. Palmer, "Review of Game Legislation in Alabama," 69.

71. Rogers et al., *Alabama*, 343.

72. Rogers et al., *Alabama*, 344.

73. *Courtland (AL) Enterprise*, November 10, 1899.

74. "Representative Wallace Says He Will Again Vote for Convention," *Weekly Advertiser* (Montgomery, AL), April 14, 1899.

75. Rogers et al., *Alabama*, 344; "Morgan Wins the Victory," *Alexander City (AL) Outlook*, April 20, 1900.

76. Rogers et al., *Alabama*, 344.

77. Riser, "Disfranchisement."

78. See *Official Proceedings of the Constitutional Convention of the State of Alabama*.

79. See Link, *Paradox of Southern Progressivism*, 131–59; Ziegler, *Schools in the Landscape*, 115.

80. *Official Proceedings of the Constitutional Convention of the State of Alabama*, 1921.

81. *Official Proceedings of the Constitutional Convention of the State of Alabama*, 1921.

82. *Official Proceedings of the Constitutional Convention of the State of Alabama*, 1922.

83. *Official Proceedings of the Constitutional Convention of the State of Alabama*, 1923; King, "Closing of the Southern Range," 54.

84. *Official Proceedings of the Constitutional Convention of the State of Alabama*, 1922.

85. Riser, "Disfranchisement," 238.

86. Mayfield, *Constitutions of 1875 and 1901*, 64.

87. Palmer, "Review of Game Legislation in Alabama," 68.

88. *Morning Mercury* (Huntsville, AL), June 10, 1906.

89. "To Protect Game," *Wilcox Progressive Era* (Camden, AL), July 5, 1906.

90. "Game Protection," *Morning Mercury*, December 29, 1906.

91. "Wallace Works for Game Laws," *Birmingham News*, September 3, 1906; "Game Protection Movement Grows," *Birmingham News*, October 18, 1906.

92. Wallace, *First Biennial Report*, 21.

93. Wallace, *First Biennial Report*, 21.

94. "Governor Jelks' Final Message Goes to Alabama Legislature," *Birmingham News*, January 9, 1907.

95. William Dutcher to John H. Wallace, November 24, 1906, National Audubon Society Records, Series A2: Correspondence of the Presidents and Other Officers of NAS, box A16, folder Alabama–Missouri, 1–13, New York Public Library.

96. Dutcher to Wallace, November 24, 1906, 3–4.

97. *1907 Game and Fish Laws of Alabama* (Montgomery: Brown Printing Co., 1907), 607, box SG01376, ADAH.

98. Dutcher to Wallace, November 24, 1906, 2.

99. Dutcher to Wallace, November 24, 1906, 6.

100. Dutcher to Wallace, November 24, 1906, 4.

101. Dutcher to Wallace, November 24, 1906, 1.

102. Dutcher to Wallace, November 24, 1906, 1.

103. John H. Wallace to Mrs. C. H. McClendon, June 30, 1920, DC/AC, box SG20189, folder M 1920 May–June, ADAH.

104. Dutcher to Wallace, November 24, 1906, 8.

105. Dutcher to Wallace, November 24, 1906, 9.

106. See Warren, *Hunter's Game*, chap. 1.

107. Henry Gannett, "Map of the Foreign-Born Population of the United States, 1900," The Gilder Lehrman Institute for of American History, accessed November 26, 2024, https://gilderlehrman.org/history-resources/spotlight-primary-source/map-foreign-born-population-united-states-1900; Brownell, "Birmingham, Alabama," 27.

108. "Proceedings of the Day in the Alabama Legislature," *Morning Mercury* (Huntsville, AL), February 21, 1907.

109. See Wallace, *First Biennial Report*, 29.

110. Wallace, *First Biennial Report*, 7.

111. Wallace, *First Biennial Report*, 7.

112. "Mr. Wallace Talks of New Game and Fish Law," *Daily Mountain Eagle* (Jasper, AL), March 13, 1907, 7.

113. John H. Wallace Jr., *Conservation of the Game, Birds, and Fish of Alabama: The Duties of the Game Warden Defined*, Alabama Department of Game and Fish, Bulletin No. 3, October 1, 1911, 10, box SG013084, State Publication, ADAH.

114. John H. Wallace to George W. Strell, January 13, 1910, DC/AC, box SG20172, folder S 1910 January–March, ADAH. Wallace did not report the demographics of license sales in his biennial reports.

115. Tober, *Who Owns the Wildlife?*, 148–49.

116. Geer v. Connecticut, 161 US 519 (1896).

117. *Geer*, 161 US 519.

118. Wallace, *First Biennial Report*, 6.

119. Reprinted in *Leighton (AL) News*, July 17, 1908.

120. Quoted in Vinson, "Conservation and in the South," 267.

121. John H. Wallace Jr. to Oscar S. Straus, June 30, 1908, DC/AC, box SG20177, folder S 1908 June–August, ADAH.

122. Wallace, *First Biennial Report*, 8.

123. J. M. Boshart to John H. Wallace, December 9, 1907, DC/AC, box SG20171, folder B 1907–1908 January 2–August 1908, ADAH. The quotation is a transcription of the original.

124. R. H. Bussey to John H. Wallace, March 20, 1907, DC/AC, box SG20171, folder B 1907–1908 January 2–August 1908, ADAH.

125. F. H. Walter to John H. Wallace, March 9, 1909, DC/AC, box SG20175, folder W 1909 March–May, ADAH.

126. Wallace to Walter, March 1909, DC/AC, box SG20175, folder W 1909 March–May, ADAH.

127. J. H. Cranford to John H. Wallace, December 10, 1907, DC/AC, box SG20171, folder C 1907, ADAH.

128. W. J. Reynolds to John H. Wallace, April 5, 1909, DC/AC, box SG20175, folder R 1909 March–May, ADAH.

129. Wallace to Reynolds, April 8, 1909, DC/AC, box SG20175, folder R 1909 March–May, ADAH.

130. Before 1915, the probate judge was the ex officio county judge in Alabama unless excepted by county law; after 1915, the probate judge was reinstated as the ex officio county judge in all counties that had a population under 50,000 people. See Barger, "History of the Probate Court," 14.

131. Emmett Crook to John H. Wallace Jr., December 9, 1907, DC/AC, box SG20171, folder C 1907, ADAH.

132. John L. Hughston to John H. Wallace, July 8, 1908, DC/AC, box SG20177, folder HIJ 1908 June–August, ADAH.

133. Wallace to Hughston, July 10, 1908, DC/AC, box SG20177, folder HIJ 1908 June–August, ADAH.

134. E. B. Tuck to John H. Wallace, n.d., DC/AC, box SG20175, folder TUV 1909 March–May, ADAH.

135. Wallace to Tuck, April 9, 1909, DC/AC, box SG20175, folder TUV 1909 March–May, ADAH.

136. A. H. Chrietzberg to John H. Wallace, March 21, 1907, DC/AC, box SG20171, folder C 1907, ADAH.

137. Jacoby, *Crimes against Nature*, 38.

138. E. P. Bean to John H. Wallace, August 31, 1908, DC/AC, box SG20172, folder B 1908 August–September, ADAH.

139. J. B. Stickney to John H. Wallace, January 26, 1910, DC/AC, box SG20172, folder S 1910 January–March, ADAH.

140. W. L. Graham to John H. Wallace, March 6, 1912, DC/AC, box SG20172, folder G September 1911–January 1913, ADAH.

141. W. D. Cuthbert to John H. Wallace, February 22, 1910, DC/AC, box SG20172, folder C 1910 January–March, ADAH.

142. Quinn, "Third Quadrennial Report," 91.

143. Judd, *Common Lands*, 215.

144. Cuthbert to Wallace, February 22, 1910.

145. A. W. Stewart to John H. Wallace, February 28, 1910, DC/AC, box SG20172, folder S 1910 January–March, ADAH.

146. D. B. Shotts to John H. Wallace, June 13, 1910, DC/AC, box SG20172, folder S 1910 June–August, ADAH.

147. Wallace to Shotts, June 15, 1910, DC/AC, box SG20172, folder S 1910 June–August, ADAH.

148. Total numbers were aggregated from Alabama attorney general biennial reports. See Garber, *Biennial Report of the Attorney General* (1908), 22; Garber, *Biennial Report of the Attorney General* (1910), 36; Brickell, *Biennial Report of the Attorney General* (1912), 526; Brickell, *Biennial Report of the Attorney General* (1914), 455; Brickell, *Biennial Report of the Attorney General* (1916), 576; Martin, *Biennial Report of the Attorney General* (1918), 123; and Smith, *Biennial Report of the Attorney General* (1920), 793.

149. C. L. Cleveland to John H. Wallace Jr., August 15, 1908, DC/AC, box SG20172, folder C 1908 August–September, ADAH.

150. Ancestry.com, 1910 United States Census, Kingdom, Bibb County, Alabama, digital image s.v. "John Hyde."

151. "Supreme Court Upholds Hunting Law," *Selma Times-Journal*, April 22, 1908, 2.

152. "Supreme Court Upholds Hunting Law," 2.

153. Majority ruling reprinted in Wallace, *First Biennial Report*, 13.

154. L. P. Hutchinson to John H. Wallace, January 26, 1909 [1910], DC/AC, box SG20172, folder H 1910 January–March, ADAH.

155. Wallace to Hutchinson, January 31, 1910, DC/AC, box SG20172, folder H 1910 January–March, ADAH.

156. Mary Ellin Curtin, "Convict-Lease System," Encyclopedia of Alabama, last updated March 27, 2023, https://encyclopediaofalabama.org/article/convict-lease-system/.

157. John H. Wallace to My Dear Sir, February 11, 1912, DC/AC, box SG20172, folder B September 1911–1912, ADAH.

158. John H. Wallace Jr. to A. C. Gorey, February 19, 1912, DC/AC, box SG20172, folder G September 1911–January 1913, ADAH.

159. John H. Wallace Jr. to S. H. Striplin, June 24, 1909, DC/AC, box SG20177, folder S 1908 June–August, ADAH.

160. John H. Wallace Jr. to William Dutcher, July 13, 1908, DC/AC, box SG20177, folder D 1908 June–August, ADAH.

161. John H. Wallace Jr. to T. G. Pearson, August 10, 1908, DC/AC, box SG20172, folder PQ 1908 August–September, ADAH.

162. F. I. Stone to John H. Wallace Jr., April 13, 1909, DC/AC, box SG20175, folder S 1909 March–May, ADAH.

163. *Acts and Resolutions of the General Assembly of the State of Georgia 1903*, 44–45.

164. Wallace to Stone, April 9, 1909, DC/AC, box SG20175, folder S 1909 March–May, ADAH.

165. Hoke Smith, "Here Is the Measure Passed for Protection of Game," *Atlanta Constitution*, September 4, 1911.

166. "Game Law Defined by Appeals Court," *Atlanta Constitution*, November 28, 1912.

167. T. Gilbert Pearson, "The New Georgia Law," *Bird Lore* 13–14 (1911–12): 273, HathiTrust, https://hdl.handle.net/2027/mdp.39015068346660.

168. Vinson, "Conservation and the South," 270.

169. "Wallace for Governor," *Alabama Times* (Montgomery), April 22, 1913, 3.

170. "Wallace for Governor," 3.

171. "Wallace for Governor," 3.

172. Wallace, *Fourth Biennial Report*, 76.

173. Quoted in "Wallace for Governor," 3.

174. *Bulletin of the American Game Protective Association* 2, no. 2 (December 1, 1913). HathiTrust. https://hdl.handle.net/2027/coo.31924056346509.

175. W. P. Patterson, "To Our Friends—Thanks," *Forest and Stream*, April 4, 1914, transcribed in *The Railroad and the Eastern Shores of Virginia*, University of Virginia, https://eshore.iath.virginia.edu/node/4817.

176. *Bulletin of the American Game Protective Association* 2, no. 4 (April 1, 1914): 2, HathiTrust, https://hdl.handle.net/2027/coo.31924056346509.

177. Barrow, *Passion for Birds*, 59–61, 169–71.

178. "To Kill Migratory Birds," *Nebraska State Journal*, May 21, 1905, 16.

179. Smalley with Reeves, *Market in Birds*, 192–93.

180. Smalley with Reeves, *Market in Birds*, 192.

181. Shiras, *Necessity for and Constitutionality of the Act of Congress*, 19.

182. Shiras, *Necessity for and Constitutionality of the Act of Congress*, 1.

183. "To Protect Game Birds," *Evening Star* (Washington, DC), December 6, 1904, 1.

184. Shiras, *Necessity for and Constitutionality of the Act of Congress*, 1; Smalley with Reeves, *Market in Birds*, 201. In chap. 6, Smalley and Reeves provide a fascinating overview of the ways in which the Weeks–McLean bill illustrated fractures in the coalition of conservationists, bird protection organizations, and sportsmen.

185. Lund, *American Wildlife Law*, 82–83.

186. *Fins, Feathers, and Fur*, Official Bulletin of the Minnesota Game and Fish Department, no. 7 (September 1916): 15, HathiTrust, https://hdl.handle.net/2027/mdp.39015074971402.

187. "Game Laws Conflict," *Washington County News* (Chatom, AL), September 10, 1914.

188. William T. Hornaday to John H. Wallace, March 13, 1919, DC/AC, box SG20188, folder Migratory Bird Treaty Act, F–H, March 1919–February 1920, ADAH.

189. Smalley with Reeves, *Market in Birds*, 204–6. Smalley and Reeves provide a more in-depth look at both cases and opposition from recreational hunters.

190. John H. Wallace to Colonel Stoddard, Sporting Editor, *New York Sun*, July 21, 1919, AC/DC, box SG20187, folder S August–September 1919, ADAH; Smalley with Reeves, *Market in Birds*, 213.

191. For a book-length study of the MBTA and international diplomacy, see K. Dorsey, *Dawn of Conservation Diplomacy*.

192. Smalley with Reeves, *Market in Birds*, 213–14; Lawyer, *Federal Protection of Migratory Birds*, 10–15.

193. See Smalley with Reeves, *Market in Birds*, 212–22.

194. William T. Hornaday to John H. Wallace, March 8, 1919, DC/AC, box SG20188, folder Migratory Bird Treaty Act, F–H, March 1919–February 1920, ADAH. Emphasis in original.

195. John H. Wallace to *American Field*, March 25, 1919, DC/AC, box SG20188, folder Migratory Bird Treaty Act, A–B, April 1919–February 1920, ADAH.

196. For that correspondence, see DC/AC, box SG20188, especially folders titled "Migratory Bird Treaty Act," ADAH.

197. Wallace to Stoddard, July 21, 1919.

198. "John Wallace, Game Commissioner, Dead," *Anniston Star*, January 18, 1922.

199. "I. T. Quinn Named on Federal Board," *Lowndes Signal* (Fort Signal, AL), July 11, 1934.

Chapter 3

1. Charlie Young, "Reminiscences of Charlie Young for Bill Rogers," vertical files, accession number 2001.99.104, THC. To capture Young's voice, accent, and style, I have chosen to transcribe the text as written in the original.

2. Young, "Reminiscences," 15.

3. Young, "Reminiscences," 23.

4. For scholarship that looks extensively at southern tourism in the late nineteenth and early twentieth centuries, see, for example, Silber, *Romance of Reunion*; Youngs, "Lifestyle Enclaves"; McIntyre, "Promoting the South"; and Giltner, *Hunting and Fishing in the New South*.

5. Young, "Reminiscences."

6. Rogers, *Thomas County*.

7. Jule Anderson, Charlie Young's granddaughter, told me that Young and Poe knew each other from Poe's younger years and that after Young retired and became ill, Poe would send a driver to take Young's wife to the store to shop for the couple. Given that Poe was so instrumental in underwriting Rogers's work on the history of Pebble Hill plantation (her estate) and the quail hunting region more generally, it seems very possible she asked Charlie Young to write his own account related to that history. Jule Anderson, interview by author, October 20, 2009, in possession of author.

8. In a 2007 phone call, Professor Rogers told me he did not remember receiving Young's reminiscences. William Warren Rogers, phone conversation with author, September 3, 2007.

9. Historian William D. Bryan pays close attention to how sporting tourism extended arguments about the need for environmental "permanence," language employed by New South boosters and conservation advocates. See chap. 5 in *Price of Permanence*.

10. For the perspective of African American families who labored on northerners' hunting plantations, see Brown and Hadley, *African-American Life on the Southern Hunting Plantation*. Brown and Hadley, whose father and mother worked on Pebble Hill plantation in Thomasville, gathered oral histories of former plantation workers that are excerpted in the book. See also Brock, "Land, Labor, and Leisure," chap. 3.

11. For a full account of the development of a new approach to wildlife and habitat management in the Red Hills region, see Way, *Conserving Southern Longleaf*.

12. Way, *Conserving Southern Longleaf*, 12.

13. Paisley, *From Cotton to Quail*, 77.

14. Campbell, *Georgia History Stories*, 346.

15. Rogers, *Antebellum Thomas County*, 50.

16. Way, *Conserving Southern Longleaf*, 20.

17. T. S. Hopkins, "Better than Florida," *Atlanta Daily Herald*, May 2, 1873.

18. Rogers, *Thomas County*, 146–47.

19. For work on the growth of tourism in and around Asheville, North Carolina, see Starnes, *Creating the Land of the Sky*; for work on Jekyll Island's development for wealthy industrialists, see Harris, *Deep Souths*, 144–48; and McCash, *Jekyll Island Cottage Colony*.

20. *Thomasville (GA) Times-Enterprise*, January 10, 1903.

21. Paisley, *From Cotton to Quail*, 77.

22. Brueckheimer, "Quail Plantations," 44.

23. Way, *Conserving Southern Longleaf*, 39.

24. H. C. S., "A Georgia Quail Country," *Forest and Stream* 42, no. 8 (February 24, 1894), 161.

25. H. C. S., "Georgia Quail Country," 161.

26. Proctor, *Bathed in Blood*, 58.

27. Samuel B. Smith, "Interesting Particular in the Natural History of the Quail," *American Turf Register and Sporting Magazine*, December 1829. See also "The Quail or Partridge," *American Turf Register and Sporting Magazine*, January 1830, 247.

28. Flanagan, "Hunting in Early Illinois," 6.

29. Julius W. Muller, "Industrial Spirit is Improving Hunting," *Savannah Morning News*, November 9, 1902, 8.

30. See Saikku, "Hunting and Wilderness," 116–22.

31. Herman, *Hunting*, 222.

32. See Brinkley, *Wilderness Warrior*.

33. Kelly, *Hunter Elite*.

34. "With Gun and Dog in Georgia," *Forest and Stream* 60, no. 2 (January 10, 1903), 29.

35. E. L. Youmans, "Thomasville as a Winter Resort," *Popular Science Monthly* 28 (December 1885): 190.

36. "Beagles and Bulls and Other Attractions of Thomasville," *Atlanta Weekly-Constitution*, May 2, 1882.

37. *Forest and Stream* 18, no. 18 (June 18, 1882), 376.

38. Young, "Reminiscences," 5.

39. Rogers, *Thomas County*, 116.

40. Young, "Reminiscences," 25.

41. Rogers, *Thomas County*, 289.

42. Young, "Reminiscences," 25.

43. Young, "Reminiscences," 25.

44. "Reports by States with Statistics for Counties," US Census of Agriculture, United States, 1910, 315, US Department of Agriculture, Census of Agriculture Historical Archive, https://agcensus.library.cornell.edu/wp-content/uploads/41033898v6ch3.pdf; chap. 1, "Farms and Farm Property," US Census of Agriculture, United States, 1920, 41, US Department of Agriculture, Census of Agriculture Historical Archive, https://agcensus.library.cornell.edu/wp-content/uploads/1920-Farms_and_Property.pdf.

45. "Reports by States with Statistics for Counties," US Census of Agriculture, 1910, 315; Mauldin, *Unredeemed Land*, 135.

46. Outland, *Tapping the Pines*, Kindle, location 2351; Harris, *Deep Souths*, 120–24. In these pages, Harris notes that Mississippi had a law that restricted corporations in

their accrual of land, but the cotton barons of the Delta got around the law by creating holding companies in neighboring states.

47. D. L. Palmer, "The Sunny South," *Brookings Press*, January 31, 1896.

48. Chalker, "Fitzgerald," 398.

49. John Triplett, "A Colonization Scheme," *Thomasville Times-Enterprise*, April 4, 1896.

50. Rogers, *Thomas County*, 34.

51. Reprinted in the *Thomasville Times-Enterprise*, February 4, 1893.

52. Paisley, *From Cotton to Quail*, 72.

53. Reprinted from the *Green Bay Gazette*, *Thomasville Times-Enterprise*, February 18, 1893.

54. Palmer, "Sunny South."

55. Harris, *Deep Souths*, 36–37.

56. Brueckheimer, "Quail Plantations," 53; Rogers, *Antebellum Thomas County*, 67, 115.

57. Brueckheimer, "Quail Plantations," 54; Rogers, *Thomas County*, 116. Susina remained in the Mason family until 1980; today it is still a private residence.

58. Paisley, *From Cotton to Quail*, 78; "On the River," *Thomasville Times-Enterprise*, March 4, 1893.

59. Brueckheimer, "Quail Plantations," 54.

60. "What a Visitor Says," *Thomasville Times-Enterprise*, February 2, 1893; Paisley, *From Cotton to Quail*, 78.

61. Brueckheimer, "Quail Plantations," 55–56.

62. Brueckheimer, "Quail Plantations," 55–56. For a full history of Pebble Hill plantation, see Rogers, *Pebble Hill*.

63. W. Mitchell, *Landmarks*, 32.

64. Rogers, *Pebble Hill*, 130–31.

65. "What a Visitor Says," *Thomasville Times-Enterprise*, February 2, 1893.

66. W. Mitchell, *Landmarks*, 116–17.

67. Folder 1:1, "1919 March 18," Lula Mae Hamilton Harding Collection, Hargrett Library, University of Georgia, Athens.

68. Young, "Reminiscences," 26.

69. Vivian, *New Plantation World*, 101.

70. Vivian, *New Plantation World*, 18.

71. Rogers, *Transition to the Twentieth Century*, 47.

72. Taken from a talk given by Theo Titus III, May 17, 1987, tape files, THC.

73. D. L. Shepard to H. W. Hopkins, April 26, 1901, box 3010A, folder 1978.010.188, HC, THC.

74. C. S. Hebard to H. W. Hopkins, July 14, 1903, box 3019A, folder 1978.010.269, HC, THC.

75. J. H. Wade to H. W. Hopkins, August 2, 1904, box 3019A, folder 1978.010.269, HC, THC.

76. J. H. Tayler to H. W. Hopkins, May 6, 1907, box 3019A, folder 1978.010.269, HC, THC. Tayler was acting agent for Miss McCartney.

77. Abstract of title, "South half of lot number 94 in the 13th District of Thomas County, State of Georgia," H. J. and A. T. McIntyre to J. H. Wade, 1910, box 3019A, folder 1978.010.269, HC, THC; abstract of title, "Lot 93 in the 13th District of Thomas County, Georgia," H. J. and A. T. McIntyre to J. H. Wade, 1910, box 3019A, folder 1978.010.269, HC, THC.

78. Wade to Hopkins, October 26, 1916, box 3019A, folder 1978.010.269, HC, THC.

79. Folder 1:11, "1919 March 27," Lula Mae Hamilton Harding Collection, Hargrett Library.

80. Palmer, *Some Benefits the Farmer May Derive from Game Protection*, 520.

81. Lueck, "Property Rights," 627–28.

82. Charles M. Chapin to H. W. Hopkins, n.d., box 3020A, folder 1978.010.317, HC, THC.

83. H. W. Hopkins, lease agreement between John Hawkins and Charles Thompson, April 1908, box 3010A, folder 1978.010.177–8, HC, THC.

84. H. W. Hopkins, lease agreement between Mary Eason and John F. Archbold, n.d., box 3019A, folder 1978.010.277, HC, THC.

85. Young, "Reminiscences," 20.

86. Edward Crozer to H. W. Hopkins, February 16, 1914, box 3019A, folder 1978.010.178, HC, THC.

87. Paisley, *From Cotton to Quail*, 94.

88. H. W. Hopkins to Edward Crozer, October 8, 1915, box 3020A, folder 1978.010.330–9, HC, THC.

89. "The Incorporation of the Choctaw Hunting Club," *Weekly Democrat-Times* (Greenville, MS), February 20, 1904; "The Charter of the Incorporation of the Back Bay Hunting and Fishing Club," *Jackson (MS) Daily News*, April 25, 1907; "By Laws of the Macon County Hunting Club," *Tuskegee News*, September 19, 1907; "Selma Fishing and Hunting Club Ready to Build Its Home," *Selma Times-Journal*, September 18, 1920; "Application for Charter," *Union Recorder* (Milledgeville, GA), October 18, 1910; "Fox Hunters Chose Officers and Spin Yarns," *Savannah Morning News*, November 19, 1902.

90. Reiger, *American Sportsmen*, 57–59.

91. Marks, *Southern Hunting in Black and White*, 71.

92. H. W. Hopkins to D. L. Hebard, October 10, 1930, folder 1978.010.326–7, HC, THC; Paisley, *From Cotton to Quail*, 85.

93. Hopkins to Hebard, October 10, 1930.

94. Grady C. Cromartie, interview by Clifton Paisley, January 23, 1970, Clifton Paisley Collection, 1915–68, Special Collections, Archives, and Manuscripts, Florida State University, Tallahassee.

95. Rogers, *Transition to the Twentieth Century*, 215.

96. Rogers, *Transition to the Twentieth Century*, 215.

97. Folder 1:4, "22 March 1919"; folder 1:7, "24 March 1919," Lula Mae Hamilton Harding Collection, Hargrett Library. Emphasis in original.

98. Young, "Reminiscences," 31. Young dated the war incorrectly. It started in 1898.

99. Young, "Reminiscences," 32.

100. See Hayden R. Smith, "Knowledge of the Hunt," in Brock and Vivian, *Leisure, Plantations, and the Making of a New South*, 131–48.

101. Young, "Reminiscences," 8.

102. Raper, *Preface to Peasantry*, 397.

103. Kirby, *Rural Worlds Lost*, 253.

104. Giltner, *Hunting and Fishing in the New South*, 95.

105. Giltner, *Hunting and Fishing in the New South*, 95.

106. Young, "Reminiscences," 26.

107. Giltner, *Hunting and Fishing in the New South*, 23, 81.

108. Giltner, *Hunting and Fishing in the New South*, 82.

109. Giltner, *Hunting and Fishing in the New South*, 115.

110. Young, "Reminiscences," 32–33.

111. Young, "Reminiscences," 2.

112. Young, "Reminiscences," 35.

113. Virginia Anderson, interview by Lee Willis, April 20, 2006, Oral History Collection, THC.

114. For an archaeological study that reveals much about tenant life on a northern hunting plantation, see R. Kilgo, "Life and Labor on the Southern Sporting Plantation," in Brock and Vivian, *Leisure, Plantations, and the Making of a New South*, 177–200.

115. J. J. Healy to Henry W. Hopkins, October 3, 1894, box 3019A, folder 1978.010.256, HC, THC.

116. A. H. Hough, December 14, 1910, box 3019A, folder 1978.010.272, HC, THC.

117. Salary information taken from a letter to C. B. Raymond, May 12, 1911, box 3019A, folder 1978.010.268, HC, THC. Hopkins also acted as manager of Raymond's estate.

118. H. W. Hopkins to C. B. Raymond, March 15, 1910, box 3019A, folder 1978.010.268, HC, THC.

119. H. W. Hopkins to A. H. Hough, December 14, 1910, box 3019A, folder 1978.010.272, HC, THC.

120. Healy to Hopkins, October 3, 1894, HC, THC.

121. Wade to Hopkins, July 28, 1904, box 3019A, folder 1978.010.269, HC, THC.

122. C. S. Hebard to H. W. Hopkins, September 5, 1904, box 3020A, folder 1978.010.327-7, box 3020A, HC, THC.

123. C. S. Hebard to Hopkins, October 25, 1905, box 3020A, folder 1978.010.327-9, HC, THC.

124. Rogers, *Thomas County*, 33.

125. Social Explorer, "Farms of Colored Farmers."

126. *Thirteenth Census of the United States*.

127. "Rent List, Crop 1909," box 3020A, folder 1978.010.320-11, HC, THC.

128. Healy to Hopkins, October 3, 1894, HC, THC.

129. Hough to Hopkins, April 7, 1915, box 3019A, folder 1978.010.272, HC, THC.

130. Hough to Hopkins, n.d., box 3019A, folder 1978.010.272, HC, THC.

131. Ross Johnson to H. W. Hopkins, December 11, 1906, box 3020A, folder 1978.010.320-2, HC, THC.

132. Oscar Zeller to Charles S. Hebard, January 28, 1903, box 3020A, folder 1978.010.327-4, HC, THC.

133. C. S. Hebard to Hopkins, October 25, 1905, HC, THC (emphasis original).

134. Rogers, *Transition to the Twentieth Century*, 62–63.

135. Rogers, *Transition to the Twentieth Century*, 71.

136. *Cairo (GA) Messenger*, June 24, 1904.

137. Rogers, *Transition to the Twentieth Century*, 69, 72–73.

138. *Weekly Thomasville Times-Enterprise and South Georgia Progress*, March 24, 1905, quoted in Rogers, *Transition to the Twentieth Century*, 73–74.

139. "An Open Letter to Mr. Hopkins," *Thomasville Times-Enterprise*, February 14, 1905, box 3012A, folder 1978.010.538, HC, THC.

140. *Cairo Messenger*, June 3, 1904.

141. *Weekly True Democrat* (Tallahassee, FL), July 3, 1914, quoted in Paisley, *From Cotton to Quail*, 84.

142. *Weekly True Democrat*, September 24, 1909, quoted in Rogers, *Foshalee*, 80.

143. *Weekly True Democrat*, January 30, 1920, quoted in Paisley, *From Cotton to Quail*, 84.

144. Rogers, *Thomas County*, 259. Young, "Reminiscences," 40.

145. Young, "Reminiscences," 40.

146. Young, "Reminiscences," 40–41.

147. Hahn, *Roots of Southern Populism*, 58–60.

148. Quoted in Rogers, *Thomas County*, 260.

149. Rogers, *Transition to the Twentieth Century*, 355.

150. Rogers, *Thomas County*, 261.

151. "Index to Register of Posted Lands," 1903, 2–3, Thomas County Clerk of Courts, Thomasville, GA.

152. Young, "Reminiscences," 26.

153. Wade to Hopkins, August 2, 1904, HC, THC.

154. "Memorandum of Accounts Paid by H. W. Hopkins for Account, A. H. Mason, from Sept. 25th, 1909 to May, 1910," box 3020A, folder 1978.010.320-11, HC, THC.

155. Chapin to Hopkins, n.d., HC, THC.

156. C. A. Griscom to A. H. Wade, November 8, 1905, box 3005A, folder "Hunting Rights, Sale of Plantations," HC, THC.

157. Lease for the Iamonia Lake Club, n.d., box 3010A, folder 1978.010.611, HC, THC.

158. C. D. Jordan to H. W. Hopkins, August 2, 1933, box 3025A, folder 1978.010.518, HC, THC.

159. Hopkins served in the state legislature in 1902–4, 1911–12, 1913–14, 1915–16, and 1917–18. "Offices Held by H. W. Hopkins," box 3020A, folder 1978.010.600, HC, THC.

160. Young, "Reminiscences," 17.

161. Way, *Conserving Southern Longleaf*, 160–61.

162. "Offices Held by H. W. Hopkins," HC, THC; Charles H. Arnow to H. W. Hopkins, October 1, 1915, box 3025A, folder 1978.010.516B, HC, THC.

163. *Journal of the House of Representatives of the State of Georgia* (1911), 284, 427; *Acts and Resolutions of the General Assembly of the State of Georgia*, 1911, 137–46.

164. Reynolds, *Game Laws in Brief*, 89.

165. Giltner, *Hunting and Fishing in the New South*, 150–58.

166. W. L. Dorris, "Discussing the Game Laws," *The Jeffersonian*, April 19, 1909, 6–7, Thomas E. Watson Papers Digital Collection, Southern Historical Collection, University of North Carolina, Chapel Hill, https://docsouth.unc.edu/watson/.

167. A Georgia Citizen, "Interesting Facts about the Game Laws," *The Jeffersonian*, February 3, 1916, Thomas E. Watson Papers Digital Collection, Southern Historical Collection, University of North Carolina, Chapel Hill, https://docsouth.unc.edu/watson/.

168. Frances H. Harris, "Criticizes the Georgia Game Law," *The Jeffersonian*, March 6, 1913, 9, Thomas E. Watson Papers Digital Collection, Southern Historical Collection, University of North Carolina, Chapel Hill, https://docsouth.unc.edu/watson/.

169. R. R. Redfearn to H. W. Hopkins, June 20, 1903, folder 1978.010.515-5, HC, THC.

170. Arnow, *Sixth Annual Report of the Department of Game and Fish of Georgia*, 5.

171. Slate, *Seventh Annual Report of the Department of Game and Fish of Georgia*, 5.

172. Young, "Reminiscences," 28; Rogers, *Foshalee*, 112–17.

173. Stoddard, *Bobwhite Quail*, 350–51.

174. Stoddard, *Bobwhite Quail*, 353.

175. Paisley, *From Cotton to Quail*, 104.

176. Way, *Conserving Southern Longleaf*, 226.

177. H. W. Hopkins to C. M. Chapin Jr., July 6, 1933, box 3020A, folder 1978.010.416-4, HC, THC.

178. Young, "Reminiscences," 30.

179. Young, "Reminiscences," 28.

180. Young, "Reminiscences," 30.

181. Paisley, *From Cotton to Quail*, 83.

182. Jule Anderson, interview by author, October 13, 2009, in author's possession.

183. Virginia Anderson interview, April 20, 2006.

184. Jule Anderson interview, October 13, 2009.

185. Jule Anderson interview, October 13, 2009.

186. Aetna Fire Insurance Policy for Walter E. Edge, September 1, 1938, folder 1, "1936–1937," box 16, series 3: Documents and Printed Matter, 1782–1961,Walter E. Edge Papers, Mudd Manuscript Library, Princeton University, Princeton, NJ.

187. Jule Anderson interview, October 13, 2009.

188. Young, "Reminiscences," 21, 39.

189. Young, "Reminiscences," 21.

190. Jule Anderson interview, October 13, 2009.

191. Virginia Anderson interview, April 20, 2006.

192. Jack Hadley, interview by author, October 7, 2009, in author's possession. See also Brown and Hadley, *African-American Life on the Southern Hunting Plantation*.

193. Young, "Reminiscences," 45.

194. Jule Anderson interview, October 13, 2009.

195. *Miller's Thomasville, Ga. City Directory*, vol. 6, 1946–47 (Asheville, NC: Chas. W. Miller, 1947), THC; *Miller's Thomasville, Ga. City Directory*, vol. 8, 1950–51 (Asheville, NC: Chas. W. Miller, 1951), THC.

196. Young, "Reminiscences," 41.

Chapter 4

1. Untitled speech, RG 78: MDWFP, Series 1585: Administrative Files 1930–1943, box 11744, folder Origins of Game and Fish Commission 1930, MDAH. See also "Conservation Convention Comes to a Close," *Greenwood (MS) Commonwealth*, June 16, 1931, 1.

2. "Fish and Game Department Is Needed in Mississippi," *Commercial Appeal* (Memphis, TN), n.d., RG 78: MDWFP, Series 1585: Administrative Files 1930–1943, box 11744, folder Origins of Game and Fish Commission 1930, MDAH.

3. For an important study on transformation in hunting before and after the post–World War II rural exodus in Mississippi, see Prewitt, "Best of All Breathing."

4. Shawhan, *Fannye Cook*, 3–5. The biographical information in this chapter is especially indebted to Libby Hartfield (former director of the Mississippi Museum of Natural Science, founded by Cook), Dorothy Shawhan, and Marion Barnwell, the three women responsible for the only biography of Fannye Cook.

5. Shawhan, *Fannye Cook*, 5–7.

6. Quoted in Shawhan, *Fannye Cook*, 19.

7. "Personal Journal of Fannye A. Cook," RG 78: MDWFP, Series 177: General Files, 1928–1944, box 11827, folder WPA Plant/Animal Survey Conservation Promotion and Survey Project, MDAH.

8. Ancestry.com, 1920 United States Census, Forest, Scott County, Mississippi, digital image s.v. "W. D. Cook."

9. "Personal Journal of Fannye A. Cook," MDAH.

10. "Personal Journal of Fannye A. Cook," MDAH.

11. Shawhan, *Fannye Cook*, 24–25.

12. "Fannye A. Cook," Collections Search Center, Smithsonian Institution, November 20, 2024, https://collections.si.edu/search/results.htm?q=%22Fannye+A.+Cook%22&start=0.

13. Shawhan, *Fannye Cook*, 23; see Hedges, "Alexander Wetmore." For more on the changes in scientific study related to ecology and biology, see Dunlap, *Saving America's Wildlife*, 34–47.

14. "New Lawmakers in Legislature: Three Men and Women Elected to Legislature Last Tuesday," *Winona (MS) Times*, September 4, 1925.

15. Quoted in Shawhan, *Fannye Cook*, 25.

16. Shawhan, *Fannye Cook*, 25.

17. Shawhan, *Fannye Cook*, 29.

18. Helen Goodwin Yerger, "From Day to Day in Mississippi," *Mississippi Sun* (Charleston), October 27, 1927.

19. Yerger, "From Day to Day."

20. "Body Begins to Plan Program," *Greenwood Commonwealth*, November 30, 1927.

21. "Wildlife Is to Be Spared," *Morning Call* (Laurel, MS), February 10, 1929.

22. "Body Begins to Plan Program," November 30, 1927.

23. "Wildlife Is to Be Spared," February 10, 1929.

24. "Game Conservation Association Will Meet in Meridian," *Yazoo Herald* (Yazoo City, MS), July 10, 1928.

25. "Arthur Will Speak," *Greenwood Commonwealth*, July 16, 1929.

26. See Merchant, "George Bird Grinnell's Audubon Society."
27. Unger, *Beyond Nature's Housekeepers*, 92.
28. A. Dorsey, *To Build Our Lives Together*.
29. Rome, "'Political Hermaphrodites.'"
30. Quoted in Rome, "'Political Hermaphrodites,'" 450.
31. Unger, *Beyond Nature's Housekeepers*.
32. Rome, "'Political Hermaphrodites,'" 452.
33. "Dr. Harned Heads New Association," *Semi-Weekly Journal* (McComb, MS), August 17, 1927.
34. Helen Goodwin Yeager, "From Day to Day in Mississippi," *Newton (MS) Record*, December 22, 1927.
35. For more on the fractious politics of Progressive Era Mississippi, see Boschert, "A Family Affair"; and Creswell, *Rednecks, Redeemers, and Race*, chap. 11.
36. Vinson, "Conservation and the South," 270.
37. "Senate Murders House Game and Fish Chapter," *Weekly Clarion-Ledger* (Jackson, MS), March 15, 1906, 8.
38. Whitfield et al., *Mississippi Code of 1906*, 706–11.
39. "Senate Murders House Game and Fish Chapter," 8.
40. Vinson, "Conservation and the South," 271.
41. "Results Achieved in 1907," *Annual Report of the National Association of Audubon Societies for 1907*, 290, HathiTrust, https://hdl.handle.net/2027/uiug.30112111968613.
42. H. H. Kopman, "Birds and Farmer," *Mississippi Union Advocate and Southern Farm and Home*, January 22, 1908, 7.
43. "Rap at Col. Haynie," *Mississippi Union Advocate and Southern Farm and Home*, March 25, 1908, 4.
44. "Fair Play," *Mississippi Union Advocate and Southern Farm and Home*, March 25, 1908, 4.
45. "The Audubon Society," *Jackson Daily News*, February 6, 1909, 7.
46. John Wallace to H. W. Watson, August 8, 1910, DC/AC, box SG20172, folder W 1910 June–August, ADAH; "To Hunters and Fisherman," *Lexington (KY) Advertiser*, February 25, 1910, 5.
47. Pearson, *Adventures in Bird Protection*, 185.
48. "Fish and Game Law," *Jackson Daily News*, February 12, 1912, 3.
49. "Fish and Game Law," 3.
50. Creswell, *Rednecks, Redeemers, and Race*, 227.
51. Broyles died a year later in a violent confrontation with a lessee of his timberlands in Monroe County. See "With Bullet in Heart, Kills Foe," *Port Gibson (MS) Reveille*, September 25, 1913, 6.
52. "Game Commission Bill Defeated," *Jackson Daily News*, February 15, 1912, 1.
53. "Game Commission Bill Defeated," 1, 5.
54. "Norwood Game and Fish Bill," *Jackson Daily News*, January 31, 1912, 5.
55. "Game Commission Bill Defeated," 1, 5.
56. "A Rather Poor Boast," *Jackson Daily News*, March 7, 1917, 4.
57. For a review of the 1922 code, see "S.B. No. 62," *Winona Times*, May 5, 1922, 5.

58. *Laws of the State of Mississippi* (1926), 280. For the entire 1926 code regarding game and fish, see 276–83.

59. *Laws of the State of Mississippi* (1926), 276.

60. See "S.B. No. 62," May 5, 1922; and *Laws of the State of Mississippi* (1926), 274.

61. *Laws of the State of Mississippi* (1926), 276, 281.

62. Mississippi was not alone in southern states to commission a report from the Brookings Institution. The Alabama legislature did so as well, and the report returned similar recommendations regarding consolidation of county executive functions. As in Mississippi, some Alabama politicians railed against the report's finding as being "centralized, bureaucratic, undemocratic, despotic, machine ridden government." See "Brookings Report Rapped by Jarman," *Progressive Age* (Scottsboro, AL), July 28, 1932, 3.

63. Institute for the Government Research of the Brookings Institution, *Report on a Survey of the Organization and Administration of State and County Government in Mississippi*.

64. Brookings Institution, *Report on a Survey*, 616.

65. Brookings Institution, *Report on a Survey*, 923.

66. "Gov. Mike Conner Issues Statement," *Choctaw Plaindealer* (Ackerman, MS), October 20, 1933, 1.

67. Journal Correspondent, "Capitol Weekly News Letter," *Winston County (MS) Journal*, 7.

68. For more on Conner's governorship and political career, see Nash, "Edmund Favor Noel"; Boschert, "Family Affair"; and D. Mitchell, *New History of Mississippi*, 334–35.

69. Spruill, "Nellie Nugent Somerville," 52.

70. Shawhan, *Fannye Cook*, 39.

71. Lucy Somerville Howorth and Constance Myers, June 20, 22, and 23, 1975, Interview G-0028, Southern Oral History Program Collection, University of North Carolina, Chapel Hill, https://docsouth.unc.edu/sohp/G-0028/G-0028.html.

72. Shawhan, *Fannye Cook*, 39.

73. Howorth and Myers interview, June 20, 22, and 23, 1975.

74. Howorth and Myers interview, June 20, 22, and 23, 1975.

75. For particulars of the establishment of refuges in the 1930s in the Delta, see Saikku, *This Delta, This Land*, 244.

76. By Walker Wood over WJDX, "New Mississippi State Game and Fish Law Sets Up a Fine System Building Up the Wild Life of the State," reprinted in *Winona Times*, June 17, 1932, 6.

77. "History," Izaak Walton League of America, accessed November 20, 2024, www.iwla.org/about/history.

78. "An Act to Create a State Game and Fish Commission," prepared and printed by the American Legion, Department of Mississippi, in Co-operation with the Izaak Walton League and the Mississippi Association for the Conservation of Wild Life, RG 78: MDWFP, Series 1585: Administrative Files 1930–1943, box 11744, folder Origin of Game and Fish Commission 1930, 2–5, MDAH.

79. "Act to Create a State Game and Fish Commission," 5–6.

80. "Act to Create a State Game and Fish Commission," 10, 12.

81. "Act to Create a State Game and Fish Commission," 18–19.

82. "Act to Create a State Game and Fish Commission," 18.

83. Draft of "An Act to Create a State Game and Fish Commission," RG 78: MDWFP, Series 1585: Administrative Files 1930–1943, box 11744, folder Origin of Game and Fish Commission, 13, MDAH.

84. Mobley and Mobley, *1938 Supplement to the Mississippi Code of 1930*, 883.

85. Draft of "An Act to Create a State Game and Fish Commission," 6.

86. Draft of "An Act to Create a State Game and Fish Commission," 7.

87. Quinn, *Annual Report* (1936), 6–7.

88. The popularity of restocking programs and "game farming" had national resonance; see Swanson, "Growing Wild," 177–214.

89. *Natural Resources of Georgia*, 7–8.

90. *Natural Resources of Georgia*, 45.

91. Fannye A. Cook to J. Boyd Britton, November 2, 1934, RG 78: MDWFP, Series 187: General Correspondence of Fannye A. Cook, 1929–1941, box 11742, folder Miscellaneous Correspondence S 1932–1935, 2, MDAH. Emphasis in original.

92. Quoted in Shawhan, *Fannye Cook*, 41–42.

93. Shawhan, *Fannye Cook*, 42.

94. "The Mississippi Association for the Conservation of Wild Life: Its Origins and Purpose," n.d., RG 78: MDWFP, Series 177: General Files, 1928–1944, box 11828, folder MS Assoc. for the Conservation of Wild Life, MDAH.

95. Quoted in Cole and Srinivasan, "Eudora Welty and Photography," xxi–xlii.

96. Martha H. Swain and Roger D. Tate Jr., "Great Depression," *Mississippi Encyclopedia*, July 11, 2017, https://mississippiencyclopedia.org/entries/great-depression/.

97. Swain and Tate, "Great Depression."

98. Swain and Tate, "Great Depression."

99. Kirby, *Rural Worlds Lost*, 56. See also Biles, *South and the New Deal*, chap. 6.

100. Frederickson, "South and the State," 399.

101. Frederickson, "South and the State," 400.

102. Rauchway, *Why the New Deal Matters*, 117; Fredrickson, "South and the State," 400. For a specific example of how southerners on the Rules Committee helped propel New Deal experimentation in the first 100 days of Roosevelt's presidency, see Frederickson, *Deep South Dynasty*, 224.

103. G. Wright, "New Deal and the Modernization of the South," 58.

104. Bateman, Katznelson, and Lapinski, *Southern Nation*, 397.

105. Frederickson, *Deep South Dynasty*, 249.

106. Horace F. Rood, "Hunting Fishing," *Brooklyn Times Union*, March 8, 1934, 14.

107. *Hearings before the Special Committee on Conservation of Wildlife*, 8–9.

108. Mississippi State Game and Fish Commission, *Biennial Report* (1933–35), 26–27.

109. See, for example, "S.D. Game Group Is Elated over Wildlife Bills," *Deadwood (SD) Pioneer-Times*, March 22, 1934, 1; "Preparing for a Big Duck Hunting Season," *Williams (AZ) News*, September 21, 1934, 6; and "Duck Stamp Act Finally Passed," *Middlebury (VT) Register*, March 22, 1934.

110. "New Wildlife Legislation," *Outdoor Nebraska* 9, no. 2 (Spring 1934): 7.

111. Mississippi State Game and Fish Commission, *Biennial Report* (1933–35), 27.

112. "Information on Certain Areas in Mississippi Designated as Game Bird, Game Animal and/or Fur-Bearing Animal Refuges and/or Sanctuaries," n.d., RG 78: MDWFP, Series 177: General Files, 1928–1944, box 11829, folder WPA Plant:Animal Survey Animal Sanctuaries, MDAH.

113. Fannye Cook, "Report on a Preliminary Survey Made of Ellisville State School Refuge, May 23, 1934," RG 78: MDWFP, Series 177, box 11829, folder Animal Refuges, MS, 1934, MDAH.

114. "List of Private Hunting Clubs in the State of Mississippi," n.d., RG 78: MDWFP, Series 177: General Files, 1928–1944, box 11828, folder Listings of Private Hunting and Fishing Clubs, MDAH.

115. The evolution of hunting lands (accessed either via private or public land as opposed to common land) illustrates Elizabeth Blackmar's insight that, in the late nineteenth and early twentieth centuries, "the rights of private property and public property expanded together, in both a dialectical and complementary relation." Blackmar, "Appropriating 'the Commons,'" 53.

116. Leopold, *Report on a Game Survey of Mississippi*.

117. Leopold, *Report on a Game Survey of the North Central States*, 5.

118. Lorbiecki, *Aldo Leopold*, 108. On Stoddard's role in managing fellowships, see Aldo Leopold to Paul G. Redington (Chief, US Biological Survey), December 10, 1928, Aldo Leopold Papers, Organizations, Committees, US Biological Survey, UW Digital Collections, University of Wisconsin–Madison Libraries, https://digital.library.wisc.edu/1711.dl/EF3LOH6K3J4BM8S.

119. Leopold, *Game Management*.

120. Shawhan, *Fannye Cook*, 33–34.

121. Memo to Aldo Leopold, n.d., Aldo Leopold Papers, County State and Foreign Files, State: Mississippi–New Jersey, Mississippi–Misc., UW Digital Collections, University of Wisconsin–Madison Libraries, https://digital.library.wisc.edu/1711.dl/X463HCPH6DI6I8F; Fannye A. Cook to Aldo Leopold, January 25, 1929, Aldo Leopold Papers, County State and Foreign Files, State: Mississippi–New Jersey, Mississippi Correspondence, UW Digital Collections, University of Wisconsin–Madison Libraries, https://digital.library.wisc.edu/1711.dl/X463HCPH6DI6I8F.

122. Cook to Leopold, January 25, 1929, Aldo Leopold Papers (emphasis in original).

123. Aldo Leopold to John M. Olin, February 1, 1929, Aldo Leopold Papers, County State and Foreign Files, State: Mississippi–New Jersey, UW Digital Collections, University of Wisconsin–Madison Libraries, https://digital.library.wisc.edu/1711.dl/X463HCPH6DI6I8F.

124. Fannye A. Cook to Aldo Leopold, March 14, 1929, Aldo Leopold Papers, County State and Foreign Files, State: Mississippi–New Jersey, UW Digital Collections, University of Wisconsin–Madison Libraries, https://digital.library.wisc.edu/1711.dl/X463HCPH6DI6I8F; Shawhan, *Fannye Cook*, 34.

125. Cook to Leopold, March 14, 1929, Aldo Leopold Papers.

126. Mississippi State Game and Fish Commission, *Biennial Report* (1933–35), 11.

127. See "Concluding Session Is Held This Morning at Tippah Hunting Club," *Greenwood Commonwealth*, June 16, 1931, 1.

128. I use the term "conservation" broadly here to denote work associated with management of natural resources, but it should be noted that what constituted "conservation" was not agreed upon, even in federal programs; see Maher, *Nature's New Deal*, 168–69.

129. Krause, "Environmental History," 90–92. See also Whatley, "Works Progress Administration."

130. Shawhan, *Fannye Cook*, 47.

131. "Conservation Promotion and Survey Project to Be Sponsored by the State Game and Commission under the Direct Supervision of Fannye A. Cook, Research Director," RG 78: MDWFP, Series 177: General Files 1928–1944, box 11827, folder WPA Plant:Animal Survey Conservation Program and Survey Project, MDAH.

132. "Conservation Promotion and Survey Project to Be Sponsored by the State Game and Commission under the Direct Supervision of Fannye A. Cook, Research Director," MDAH.

133. "Conservation Promotion and Survey Project to Be Sponsored by the State Game and Commission under the Direct Supervision of Fannye A. Cook, Research Director," MDAH.

134. Vivian Cook, "Yearly Accomplishment Report for the Plant and Animal Survey, OP 665-62-3-266, WP 5958, Year-1939," RG 78: MDWFP, Series 177: General Files 1928–1944, box 11829, folder WPA Yearly Accomplishment Report, 1939, MDAH.

135. Vivian Cook to Felix J. Underwood, "Special Report," February 26, 1940, RG 78: MDWFP, Series 177: General Files 1928–1944, box 11829, folder Special Report 1940, MDAH.

136. Cook to Underwood, February 26, 1940, MDAH.

137. Greenberg, *To Ask for an Equal Chance*, 58–59.

138. "List of Workers, W.P.A. Plant and Animal Survey Project No. 5958," RG 78: MDWFP, Series 177: General Files 1928–1944, box 11828, folder Plant and Animal Survey List of Collecting Areas, List of Wardens, 1–4, MDAH.

139. "Daily Field Observations, Wesson Unit, Sheet 2," July 11, 1938, RG 78: MDWFP, Series 177: General Files 1928–1944, box 11829, folder Misc. Field Notes: Reports Adams, Copiah, Lincoln Counties, 1938, MDAH.

140. Cook, "Yearly Accomplishment Report for the Plant and Animal Survey, OP 665-62-3-266, WP 5958, Year-1939," MDAH.

141. R. L. Caylor to Appraisal Supervisor, March 10, 1938, RG 78: MDWFP, Series 1585: Administrative Files 1930–1948, box 11744, folder WPA Plant:Animal Survey, Appraisal of Project 1938–1939 (Report), MDAH.

142. Clytee R. Evans to Appraisal Supervisor, March 11, 1938, RG 78: MDWFP, Series 1585: Administrative Files 1930–1948, box 11744, folder WPA Plant:Animal Survey, Appraisal of Project 1938–1939 (Report), MDAH.

143. "Quail Conservation and Pond Improvement Projects Important," *Yazoo Herald*, August 24, 1937, 1.

144. Werum, "Sectionalism and Racial Politics," 409.

145. "Mississippi List of Schools Tentatively Approved for Vocational Agricultural Aid, 1938–1939," RG 78: MDWFP, Series 177: General Files 1928–1944, box 11828, folder List of Vocational Agricultural Teachers, 1937–1938, MDAH.

146. "Quail Conservation and Pond Improvement Projects Important," 1.

147. Cook, "Yearly Accomplishment Report for the Plant and Animal Survey, OP 665–62-3-266, WP 5958, Year-1939," MDAH.

148. Fannye A. Cook to T. Gilbert Pearson, March 5, 1935, RG 78: MDWFP, Series 187: General Correspondence of Fannye A. Cook, 1929–1951, box 11741, folder National Association of Audubon Societies, MDAH.

149. Greg Case to Mississippi Game and Fish Commission, February 7, 1935, RG 78: MDWFP, Series 177: General Files, 1928–1944, box 11827, folder Conservation Week Reports, MDAH.

150. Malczewski, "Philanthropy and Progressive Era State Building," 371.

151. "Program, First Annual State 4-H Conservation Camp for Negro Boys," September 2–5, 1940, RG 78: MDWFP, Series 177: General Files, 1928–1944, box 11827, folder Conservation Week, MDAH.

152. Lund, *American Wildlife Law*, 85.

153. *Greenwood Commonwealth*, September 23, 1939, 6.

154. Mary Gamble to Miss Fannye Cook, April 28, 1936, RG 78: MDWFP, Series 187: General Correspondence of Fannye A. Cook, 1929–1941, box 11740, folder MS Forests and Parks, MDAH.

155. Lee A. Yeager to Fannie [sic] A. Cooke, August 21, 1939, RG 78: MDWFP, Series 187: General Correspondence of Fannye A. Cook, 1929–1941, box 11742, folder Correspondence Prior to 1941 S, MDAH.

156. "Mississippi Plant and Animal Survey, Read by Fanny A. Cook Before Mississippi Academy of Sciences," February 23, 1940, 7, MDWFP, Series 187: General Correspondence of Fannye A. Cook, 1929–1941, box 11739, folder Mississippi Academy of Sciences, MDAH.

157. Nor were other aspects of state work to enforce environmental change; see Hyman, "Cut and the Color Line."

Afterword

1. Irwin Greenstein, "Finest Afield," *Garden and Gun*, June/July 2017, https://gardenandgun.com/feature/finest-afield/.

2. Durrell Smith, conversation with author, June 11, 2024.

3. Smith conversation, June 11, 2024.

4. According to the results of the 2020 census, 75 percent of southerners live in urban areas. See "Nation's Urban and Rural Populations Shift Following 2020 Census," Census.gov, December 29, 2022, www.census.gov/newsroom/press-releases/2022/urban-rural-populations.html#:~:text=The%20South%20and%20Midwest%20regions,population%20residing%20within%20urban%20areas.

5. Charlie Young, "Reminiscences of Charlie Young for Bill Rogers," 5, vertical files, accession number 2001.99.104, THC.

6. Prewitt, "Best of All Breathing," 37.

7. Kirby, *Rural Worlds Lost*, 353.

8. Daniel, *Breaking the Land*, 60–61; Kirby, *Rural Worlds Lost*, 348–49.

9. For a fuller reflection on southern hunting in the later twentieth century, see James H. Tuten, "New Traditions: Hunting in South Carolina since World War II," in

Lockhart and Tuten, *Southern History of Hunting*; Marks, *Southern Hunting in Black and White*; and Prewitt, "Best of All Breathing."

10. Prewitt, "Best of All Breathing," 131.

11. McGowin, *Department of Conservation, State of Alabama, Report for Fiscal Year* (1953–54), 11.

12. "Private Land Hunting in Georgia," Georgia Department of Natural Resources, accessed March 1, 2024, https://georgiawildlife.com/hunting-permissions.

13. Tina Johannsen, in conversation with author, June 3, 2024.

14. Smith conversation, June 11, 2024.

15. Department of Conservation, State of Alabama, *Report for Fiscal Year* (1964–65), 146.

16. See R. Wright, *History and Evolution*.

17. Johannsen conversation, June 3, 2024. For a synthesis of critiques of the model, see Heister, *Beyond the North American Model of Wildlife Conservation*. For critiques of the ongoing reliance of conservation regimes on Pittman–Robertson, see Casellas Connors and Rae, "Violent Entanglements."

18. Johannsen conversation, June 3, 2024.

19. Department of Conservation, State of Alabama, *Report for Fiscal Year* (1964–65), 80; "Capital Horsemen Also Supporting Patrol Forces," *Selma Times-Journal*, May 8, 1963, 1.

20. Smith conversation, June 11, 2024.

21. Smith conversation, June 11, 2024.

Bibliography

PRIMARY SOURCES
Manuscripts
Athens, GA
    Hargrett Library, University of Georgia
        Lula Mae Hamilton Harding Collection
Jackson, MS
    Mississippi Department of Archives and History
    Mississippi Department of Wildlife, Fisheries, and Parks
Montgomery, AL
    Alabama Department of Archives and History
    Alabama Department of Conservation, Administrative Correspondence
    Governor C. C. Clay Administrative Records
New York City, NY
    National Audubon Society Records
Princeton, NJ
    Mudd Manuscript Library, Princeton University
        Walter E. Edge Papers
Tallahassee, FL
    Special Collections, Archives, and Manuscripts, Florida State University
        Clifton Paisley Collection, 1915–68
Thomasville, GA
    Thomas County Clerk of Courts
    Thomasville History Center
        Hopkins Collection
        Oral History Collection
        Tape files
        Vertical files

Digital
Digital Collections, University of Wisconsin–Madison Libraries
    Aldo Leopold Papers
Southern Historical Collection, University of North Carolina, Chapel Hill
    Southern Oral History Program Collection
    Thomas E. Watson Papers Digital Collection

Periodicals
Alabama Times (Montgomery)
Alexander City (AL) Outlook
American Turf Register and Sporting Magazine
Anniston (AL) Star
Atlanta Constitution
Atlanta Daily Herald
Atlanta Weekly-Constitution
Augusta Herald
The Auk
Banner of the South
Bird Lore
Birmingham News

Brookings County Press
Brooklyn Times Union
Cairo (GA) Messenger
Cherokee Phoenix
Choctaw Plaindealer (Ackerman, MS)
Commercial Appeal (Memphis, TN)
Courtland (AL) Enterprise
Daily Mountain Eagle (Jasper, AL)
Daily Selma Reporter
Deadwood (SD) Pioneer-Times
Edgefield (SC) Advertiser
Evening Star (Washington, DC)
Forest and Stream
Garden and Gun
Greenwood (MS) Commonwealth
Jackson (MS) Daily News
The Jeffersonian
Leighton (AL) News
Lexington (KY) Advertiser
Lowndes Signal (Fort Signal, AL)
Marengo (IL) News
Marion (AL) Standard
Miami News
Middlebury (VT) Register
Mississippi Sun (Charleston)
Mississippi Union Advocate and Southern Farm and Home
Morning Call (Laurel, MS)
Morning Mercury (Huntsville, AL)
Nebraska State Journal
Newton (MS) Record
Popular Science Monthly
Port Gibson (MS) Reveille
Progressive Age (Scottsboro, AL)
Recreation
Rural Carolinian
Savannah Morning News
Selma Times-Journal
Semi-Weekly Journal (McComb, MS)
Southern Cultivator
Spirit of the Times
Tampa Tribune
Thomasville (GA) Times-Enterprise
Times and News (Eufala, AL)
Times-Democrat (New Orleans)
Tuskegee Republican
Union Recorder (Milledgeville, GA)
Washington County News (Chatom, AL)
Weekly Advertiser (Montgomery, AL)
Weekly Clarion-Ledger (Jackson, MS)
Weekly Democrat-Times (Greenville, MS)
Weekly True Democrat (Tallahassee, FL)
Wilcox Progressive Era (Camden, AL)
Winona (MS) Times
Winston County (MS) Journal
Yazoo Herald (Yazoo City, MS)

Articles

Allen, J. A. "The Present Wholesale Destruction of Bird-Life in the United States." *Science* 7 (1886): 191–95. HathiTrust. https://hdl.handle.net/2027/mdp.39015038638550.

Mitchell, Samuel L., MD. "The Progress of the Human Mind from Rudeness to Refinement: Exemplified in an Account of the Method Pursued by Colonel Benjamin Hawkins, under the Authority of the Government of the United States, to Civilize Certain Tribes of Savages within Their Territory." *American Monthly Magazine* 3, no. 5 (September 1818): 357–63. Digital Library of Georgia. https://dlg.usg.edu/record/dlg_zlna_pam011#item.

Books

Campbell, J. Harris. *Georgia History Stories*. New York: Silver, Burdett and Co., 1905.

Elliott, William. *Carolina Sports by Land and Water: Including Incidents of Devil-Fishing, Wild-cat, Deer and Bear Hunting, Etc.* New York: Derby and Jackson, 1859.

Gosse, Philip Henry. *Letters from Alabama*. 2nd ed. Edited by Gary R. Mullen and Taylor D. Littleton. Tuscaloosa: University of Alabama Press, 2013.
Hornaday, William. *Our Vanishing Wildlife: Its Extermination and Preservation*. New York: New York Zoological Society, 1913.
Leopold, Aldo. *Game Management*. Reprint ed. Madison: University of Wisconsin Press, 1986.
———. *Report on a Game Survey of Mississippi: Submitted to the Game Restoration Committee Sporting Arms & Manufacturers' Institute*. February 1, 1929. Edited by Mary P. Stephens. Museum Technical Report no. 61, Mississippi Museum of Natural Science, Mississippi Department of Wildlife, Fisheries and Parks, 2010.
———. *Report on a Game Survey of the North Central States*. Madison, WI, 1931. HathiTrust. https://hdl.handle.net/2027/mdp.39015005807634.
MacIntyre, W. Irwin. *Wiregrass Stories*. 2nd ed. Thomasville: Times-Enterprise, 1913.
Pearson, Thomas Gilbert. *Adventures in Bird Protection: An Autobiography*. New York: D. Appleton-Century, 1937. HathiTrust. https://hdl.handle.net/2027/mdp.39015006891173.
———. *Stories of Bird Life*. Richmond, VA: B. F. Johnson Publishing Company, 1901. HathiTrust. https://hdl.handle.net/2027/uc1.b3271845.
Reynolds, Charles B. *The Game Laws in Brief: A Digest of the Statutes of the United States and Canada Governing the Taking of Game and Fish*. New York: Forest and Stream Publishing, 1911. Internet Archive. www.archive.org/stream/gamelawsinbrief00canagoog#page/n5/mode/2up.
Shiras, George, III. *Necessity for and Constitutionality of the Act of Congress Protecting Migratory Birds*. New York: American Game Protective and Propagation Association, 1914. HathiTrust. https://hdl.handle.net/2027/wu.89034636084.
Stoddard, Herbert L. *The Bobwhite Quail: Its Habits, Preservation, and Increase*. New York: Charles Scribner's Sons, 1932.
Wallace, John H., Jr. *Alabama Bird Day Book*. Montgomery: Alabama Department of Game and Fish, 1908.
———. *The Senator from Alabama—A Romance Treating of the Disfranchisement of the Negro and Including a Scathing Arraignment of the White House Social-Equality Policy*. New York: Neale, 1904.

Government Publications

Acts and Resolutions of the General Assembly of the State of Georgia 1903. Atlanta: Geo. W. Harrison, State Printer, 1903. HathiTrust. https://hdl.handle.net/2027/nyp.33433009067160.
Acts and Resolutions of the General Assembly of the State of Georgia, 1911. Part 1, Title 5. Atlanta: Charles P. Byrd, State Printer, 1911.
Acts of the General Assembly of Alabama, Passed at the Session of 1878–1879. Montgomery: Barrett and Brown, State Printers, 1879. Internet Archive. https://archive.org/details/alabama-acts-1878–1879/Acts_1878_1879/page/n199/mode/2up.
Acts of the General Assembly of Alabama, Passed at the Session of 1880–81. Montgomery: Allred and Beers, State Printers, 1881. Internet Archive. https://archive.org/details/alabama-acts-1880-1881/Acts_1880_1881/page/n143/mode/2up.

Acts of the General Assembly of Alabama, Passed at the Session of 1884–85. Montgomery: Barrett and Co., State Printers and Binders, 1885. Internet Archive. https://archive.org/details/alabama-acts-1884-1885/Acts_1884_1885/page/n321/mode/2up.

Acts of the General Assembly of Alabama, Passed by the Session of 1892–1893. Montgomery: Brown Printing Co., State Printers and Binders, 1893. Internet Archive. https://archive.org/details/alabama-acts-1892-1893/Acts_1892_1893/.

Arnow, Charles Sterling. *Sixth Annual Report of the Department of Game and Fish of Georgia, July 1st, 1916 to June 30th, 1917*. Atlanta: Johnson-Dallis Co. Printers, 1917.

Biennial Report of the Attorney General of Alabama. Montgomery: Brown Printing Company, State Printers, 1894. HathiTrust. https://hdl.handle.net/2027/umn.31951d024254660.

Biennial Report of the Attorney General of the State of Alabama. Montgomery: W. D. Brown and Co., State Printers and Book-Binders, 1884. HathiTrust. https://hdl.handle.net/2027/umn.31951d024254636.

Biennial Report of the Attorney General of the State of Alabama. Montgomery: W. D. Brown and Co., State Printers and Book-Binders, 1887. HathiTrust. https://hdl.handle.net/2027/umn.31951d024254644.

Biennial Report of the Attorney General of the State of Alabama. Montgomery: W. D. Brown and Co., State Printers and Book-Binders, 1889. HathiTrust. https://hdl.handle.net/2027/mdp.35112100939844.

Brickell, Robert C. *Biennial Report of the Attorney General to the Governor of the State of Alabama for the Period from October 1, 1910 to September 30, 1912*. Montgomery: Brown Printing Company, State Printers and Binders, 1912. HathiTrust. https://hdl.handle.net/2027/osu.32437011142474.

———. *Biennial Report of the Attorney General to the Governor of the State of Alabama for the Period from October 1, 1912 to September 30, 1914*. Montgomery: Brown Printing Company, State Printers and Binders, 1914. HathiTrust. https://hdl.handle.net/2027/osu.32437011142177.

———. *Biennial Report of the Attorney General to the Governor of the State of Alabama for the Period from October 1, 1914 to September 30, 1916*. Montgomery: Brown Printing Company, 1916. HathiTrust. https://hdl.handle.net/2027/osu.32437011142128.

Bulletin of the American Game Protective Association 2, no. 2 (December 1, 1913). HathiTrust. https://hdl.handle.net/2027/coo.31924056346509.

Campbell, J. A. P., comp. *Revised Code of the Statute Laws of the State of Mississippi*. Jackson: J. L. Power, State Printer, 1880.

Carter, Clarence Edwin, comp. *The Territorial Papers of the United States*. Vol. 18, *The Territory of Alabama, 1817–1819*. Washington, DC: Government Printing Office, 1952. HathiTrust. https://hdl.handle.net/2027/uc1.31210016047118.

Clark, R. H., T. R. R. Cobb, and D. Irwin. *Code of the State of Georgia*. Macon: J. W. Burke, 1873.

Cobb, Howell, comp. *A Compilation of the General and Public Statutes of the State of Georgia; with the Forms and Precedents Necessary to Their Practical Use*. New York: Printed by Edward O. Jenkins, 1859.

Department of Conservation, State of Alabama, *Report for Fiscal Year, October 1, 1964–September 30, 1965*. Montgomery: Walker Printing Co., 1965. HathiTrust. https://hdl.handle.net/2027/coo.31924056331089.
Digest of the Laws of the State of Alabama: Containing the Statutes and Resolutions in Force at the End of the General Assembly in January, 1823. Cahawba: Published by Ginn and Curtis, J. and J. Harper, Printers, New-York, 1823.
Federal Writers' Project: Slave Narrative Project. Vol. 4, Georgia, Part 1, Adams-Furr. 1936. Library of Congress. www.loc.gov/item/mesn041/.
Federal Writers' Project: Slave Narrative Project. Vol. 9, Mississippi, Allen-Young. 1936. Library of Congress. www.loc.gov/item/mesn090/.
Garber, Alexander M. *Biennial Report of the Attorney General to the Governor of the State of Alabama for the Period from October 1, 1906, to October 1, 1908*. Montgomery: Brown Printing Company, State Printers and Binders, 1908. HathiTrust. https://hdl.handle.net/2027/osu.32437011142375.
———. *Biennial Report of the Attorney General to the Governor of the State of Alabama for the Period from October 1, 1908, to October 1, 1910*. Montgomery: Brown Printing Company, State Printers and Binders, 1910. HathiTrust. https://hdl.handle.net/2027/osu.32437011142425.
Hearings before the Special Committee on Conservation of Wildlife, House of Representatives, Seventy-Third Congress. Washington, DC: Government Printing Office, 1934. HathiTrust. https://hdl.handle.net/2027/mdp.39015063999562.
Hopkins, John L., Clifford Anderson, and Joseph R. Lamar, comps. *Code of the State of Georgia. Adopted December 15, 1895*. Atlanta: Foote and Davies Co., Printers and Binders, 1896.
Institute for the Government Research of the Brookings Institution. *Report on a Survey of the Organization and Administration of State and County Government in Mississippi*. Jackson, MS: The Research Commission of the State of Mississippi, 1931. HathiTrust. https://hdl.handle.net/2027/mdp.39015030830825.
Journal of the House of Representatives of the State of Georgia at the Regular Session of the General Assembly. Atlanta: Charles P. Byrd, State Printer, 1911.
Keyes, Wade, Fern M. Wood, and John D. Roquemore, comps. *Code of Alabama 1876*. Montgomery: Barrett and Brown, Printers for the State, 1877.
Laws of the State of Mississippi. Jackson: Tucker Printing House, 1926. HathiTrust. https://hdl.handle.net/2027/uc1.b3683517.
Lawyer, George A. *Federal Protection of Migratory Birds*. United States Bureau of Biological Survey. Washington, DC: Government Printing Office, 1919. HathiTrust. https://hdl.handle.net/2027/uc1.$b91137.
Marbury, Horatio, and William H. Crawford, comps. *Digest of the Laws of the State of Georgia, from Its Settlement as a British Province, in 1755, to the Session of the General Assembly in 1800, Inclusive*. Savannah: Printed by Seymour, Woolhopter and Stebbins, 1802.
Martin, William L. *Biennial Report of the Attorney General to the Governor of the State of Alabama for the Period from October 1, 1916 to September 30, 1918*. N.p., 1918. HathiTrust. https://hdl.handle.net/2027/osu.32437011142185.

Mayfield, James J., comp. *Constitutions of 1875 and 1901.* 2nd ed. Montgomery: Brown Printing Company, 1918. HathiTrust. https://hdl.handle.net/2027/mdp.35112105447314.

McGowin, Earl M. *Department of Conservation, State of Alabama, Report for Fiscal Year October 1, 1953–September 30, 1954.* Wetumpka: Wetumpka Printing, 1954. HathiTrust. https://hdl.handle.net/2027/mdp.39015069636309.

Mississippi State Game and Fish Commission. *Biennial Report of the State Game and Fish Commission for the Biennial Period October 1, 1933–September 30, 1935.* N.p., n.d. HathiTrust. https://hdl.handle.net/2027/uc1.b3016157.

Mobley, R. T., and Eunice Mobley, comps. *1938 Supplement to the Mississippi Code of 1930.* Atlanta: Harrison Co., 1938.

Natural Resources of Georgia. Georgia Program for the Improvement of Instruction in Public Schools, July 1938, prepared by the State Department of Natural Resources in cooperation with the State Department of Education. HathiTrust. https://hdl.handle.net/2027/uc1.$b46680.

Official Bulletin of the Minnesota Game and Fish Department, no. 7 (September 1916). HathiTrust. https://hdl.handle.net/2027/mdp.39015074971402.

Official Proceedings of the Constitutional Convention of the State of Alabama, May 21st 1901, to September 3, 1901, vol. 2. Wetumpka: Wetumpka Printing Co., 1940. Internet Archive. https://archive.org/details/alabama-constitutional-convention-proceedings-1901-v2/page/n1/mode/2up.

Owen, Thomas M., LLD, comp. *Alabama Official and Statistical Register 1907.* State of Alabama Department of Archives and History. Montgomery: Brown Printing Company, State Printers and Binders, 1907.

Palmer, T. S. *Federal Game Protection: A Five Years' Retrospect.* Reprint from Yearbook of Department of Agriculture, 1905. HathiTrust. https://hdl.handle.net/2027/hvd.32044106196322.

———. *Some Benefits the Farmer May Derive from Game Protection.* Washington, DC: Department of Agriculture, 1905. HathiTrust. https://hdl.handle.net/2027/hvd.32044106196314.

Quinn, I. T. *Annual Report, Department of Conservation of Game, Fish, and Seafoods, October 1, 1935–September 30, 1936.* Montgomery, AL: Department of Conservation, 1936. HathiTrust. https://hdl.handle.net/2027/uc1.b3007983.

———. *First Quadrennial Report, Department of Conservation, State of Alabama, October 1, 1918–September 30, 1922.* Montgomery: Brown Printing Company, State Printers and Binders, 1923. HathiTrust. https://hdl.handle.net/2027/mdp.39015069636283.

———. *Third Quadrennial Report, Department of Game and Fisheries, State of Alabama, October 1, 1926–September 30, 1930.* Montgomery: Wilson Ptg. Co., 1930. HathiTrust. https://hdl.handle.net/2027/uc1.b3007982.

The Revised Code of the Laws of Mississippi in Which Are Comprised All Such Acts of the General Assembly, of a Public Nature, as Were in Force at the End of the Year 1823; with a General Index. Natchez: Printed by Francis Baker, 1824.

Revised Statutes of South Carolina. Columbia: C. A. Calvo Jr., State Printer, 1894.

Slate, Sam J. *Seventh Annual Report of the Department of Game and Fish of Georgia, July 1st, 1917 to June 30th, 1918, State Game and Fish Commissioner*. Atlanta: Johnson and Dallis Co., 1918.

Smith, J. Q. *Biennial Report of the Attorney General to the Governor of the State of Alabama for the Period from October 1, 1918 to September 30, 1920*. N.p., 1920. HathiTrust. https://hdl.handle.net/2027/osu.32437011142235.

Stewart, Ardemus, and John Purdon, comps. *Stewart's Purdon's Digest: A Digest of the Statute L of the State of Pennsylvania from the Year 1700 to 1903*. Philadelphia: George T. Bisel Co., 1905.

Testimony Taken by the Joint Select Committee to Inquire into the Condition of Affairs in the Late Insurrectionary States, Alabama, Volume I. Washington, DC: Government Printing Office, 1872. Internet Archive. https://archive.org/details/reportofjointselo8unit/page/n5/mode/2up.

Testimony Taken by the Joint Select Committee to Inquire into the Condition of Affairs in the Late Insurrectionary States, Mississippi, Volume I. Washington, DC: Government Printing Office, 1872. Internet Archive. https://archive.org/details/insurrectionstate11goverich/page/n5/mode/2up.

Thirteenth Census of the United States. Washington, DC: Government Printing Office, 1900.

Thompson, R. H., et al. *Annotated Code of the General Statute Laws of the State of Mississippi*. Nashville, TN: Marshall and Bruce, 1892.

Wallace, John H., Jr. *First Biennial Report, Department of Game and Fish of the State of Alabama, February 27, 1907–September 30, 1908*. Montgomery: Brown Printing Company, Printers and Binders, 1908. HathiTrust. https://hdl.handle.net/2027/uc1.b3007990.

———. *Fourth Biennial Report, Department of Game and Fish of the State of Alabama, October 1, 1912–September 30, 1914*. Montgomery: Brown Printing Company, Printers and Binders, 1914. HathiTrust. https://hdl.handle.net/2027/hvd.li18yt.

———. *Second and Third Biennial Report of Department of Game and Fish of the State of Alabama, September 30, 1906–September 30, 1912*. Montgomery: Brown Printing Company, Printers and Binders, 1912. HathiTrust. https://hdl.handle.net/2027/hvd.li18yt.

Whitfield, A. H., et al., annotators. *Mississippi Code of 1906 of the Public Statute Laws of the State of Mississippi*. Nashville, TN: Brandon Print. Co., 1907.

Genealogical and Census Resources Published Online

Ancestry.com. 1910 United States Census, Kingdom, Bibb County, Alabama.

———. 1920 United States Census, Forest, Scott County, Mississippi.

FamilySearch.org. Georgia, Chatham County, Superior Court Minutes, 1782–1900, v. 5–7 1799–1808.

Social Explorer. "Farm Ownership Status (Colored Farmers)," 1900. Based on data from US Agricultural Census. www.socialexplorer.com/data/Census1900/metadata?ds=SE&table=T054.

———. "Farm Ownership Status (White Farmers)," 1900. Based on data from US Agricultural Census. www.socialexplorer.com/data/Census1900/metadata ?ds=SE&table=T053.

———. "Farms of Colored Farmers," 1900. Based on data from US Agricultural Census. www.socialexplorer.com/fe79e649a3/view.

———. "Total Population: White, Colored, Chinese, Indian," 1880. Based on data from the US Population Census. www.socialexplorer.com/2e495a7942/view.

US Department of Agriculture. Census of Agriculture Historical Archive. https://agcensus.library.cornell.edu/.

SECONDARY SOURCES

Alston, Lee J., and Kyle D. Kauffman. "Up, Down, and Off the Agricultural Ladder: New Evidence and Implications of Agricultural Mobility for Blacks in the Postbellum South." *Agricultural History* 72, no. 2 (Spring 1998): 267–68.

Anderson, Virginia DeJohn. *Creatures of Empire: How Domestic Animals Transformed Early America*. New York: Oxford University Press, 2004.

Baker, Andrew C. *Bulldozer Revolutions: A Rural History of the Metropolitan South*. Athens: University of Georgia Press, 2018.

Barger, Frank. "History of the Probate Court in Alabama." *Huntsville Historical Review* 46, no. 2 (Fall–Winter 2021): 13–20.

Barrow, Mark V., Jr. *A Passion for Birds: American Ornithology after Audubon*. Princeton, NJ: Princeton University Press, 1998.

Bateman, David A., Ira Katznelson, and John S. Lapinski. *Southern Nation: Congress and White Supremacy after Reconstruction*. Princeton, NJ: Princeton University Press, 2018.

Biles, Roger. *The South and the New Deal*. Lexington: University Press of Kentucky, 1994.

Blackmar, Elizabeth. "Appropriating the 'the Commons'": The Tragedy of Property Rights Discourse." In *The Politics of Public Space*, edited by Setha Low and Neil Smith, 49–80 . New York: Routledge, 2005.

Blevins, Brooks. *Cattle in the Cotton Fields: A History of Cattle Raising in Alabama*. Tuscaloosa: University of Alabama Press, 1998.

Blount, Ben G. "Coastal Refugees: Marginalization of African-Americans in Marine Fisheries of Georgia." *Urban Anthropology and Studies of Cultural Systems and World Economic Development* 29, no. 3 (Fall 2000): 285–313.

Boschert, Thomas Neville. "A Family Affair: Mississippi Politics, 1882–1932." PhD diss., University of Mississippi, 1995.

Braund, Kathryn. *Deerskins and Duffels: The Creek Indian Trade with Anglo-America, 1685–1815*. Lincoln: University of Nebraska Press, 1996.

Brinkley, Douglas. *The Wilderness Warrior: Theodore Roosevelt and the Crusade for America*. New York: Harper Perennial, 2010.

Brock, Julia. "Land, Labor, and Leisure: Northern Tourism in the Red Hills Region, 1890–1950." PhD diss., University of California, Santa Barbara, 2012.

Brock, Julia, and Daniel J. Vivian, eds. *Leisure, Plantations, and the Making of a New South: The Sporting Plantations of the South Carolina Lowcountry and Red Hills Region, 1900–1940.* Lanham, MD: Lexington Books, 2015.

Brown, Ras Michael. *African-Atlantic Cultures and the South Carolina Lowcountry.* New York: Cambridge University Press, 2012.

Brown, Titus, and James "Jack" Hadley. *African-American Life on the Southern Hunting Plantation.* Mount Pleasant, SC: Arcadia Publishing, 2000.

Brownell, Blaine A. "Birmingham, Alabama: New South City in the 1920s." *Journal of Southern History* 38, no. 1 (February 1972): 21–48.

Browning, Judkin, and Timothy Silver. *An Environmental History of the Civil War.* Chapel Hill: University of North Carolina Press, 2020.

Brueckheimer, William R. "The Quail Plantations of the Thomasville-Tallahassee-Albany Regions." In *Proceedings: Tall Timbers Ecology and Management Conference*, February 22–24, 1979, Thomasville, GA.

Bryan, William D. *The Price of Permanence: Nature and Business in the New South.* Athens: University of Georgia Press, 2018.

Cart, Theodore Whaley. "The Lacey Act: America's First Nationwide Wildlife State." *Forest History Newsletter* 17, no. 3 (October 1973): 4–13.

Casellas Connors, John P., and Christopher M. Rae. "Violent Entanglements: The Pittman-Robertson Act, Firearms, and the Financing of Conservation." *Conservation and Society* 20, no. 1 (2022): 24–35.

Cecelski, David S. "The Hidden World of Mullet Camps: African-American Architecture on the North Carolina Coast." *North Carolina Review* 70, no. 1 (January 1993): 1–13.

Chalker, Fussell M. "Fitzgerald: A Place of Reconciliation." *Georgia Historical Quarterly* 55, no. 3 (Fall 1971): 397–405.

Cole, Hunter, and Seetha Srinivasan. "Eudora Welty and Photography: An Interview." In *Eudora Welty: Photographs*, by Eudora Welty, xiii–xxviii. Jackson: University Press of Mississippi, 2019.

Creswell, Stephen. *Rednecks, Redeemers, and Race: Mississippi after Reconstruction.* Jackson: University Press of Mississippi, 2006.

Daniel, Pete. *Breaking the Land: The Transformation of Cotton, Tobacco, and Rice Cultures since 1880.* Champaign: University of Illinois Press, 1986.

Dehler, Gregory. *The Most Defiant Devil: William Temple Hornaday and His Controversial Crusade to Save American Wildlife.* Charlottesville: University of Virginia Press, 2013.

Dorsey, Allison. *To Build Our Lives Together: Community Formation in Black Atlanta, 1875–1906.* Athens: University of Georgia Press, 2004.

Dorsey, Kurkpatrick. *The Dawn of Conservation Diplomacy: U.S.–Canadian Wildlife Protection Treaties in the Progressive Era.* Seattle: University of Washington Press, 1998.

Du Bois, W. E. B. *Black Reconstruction in America: An Essay toward a History of the Part Which Black Folk Played in the Attempt to Reconstruct Democracy.* New York: Harcourt, Brace and Company, 1935.

Dunlap, Thomas. *Saving America's Wildlife*. Princeton, NJ: Princeton University Press, 1988.
Ethridge, Robbie. *Creek Country: The Creek Indians and Their World*. Chapel Hill: University of North Carolina Press, 2003.
Evenden, Matthew D. "The Laborers of a Nature: Economic Ornithology and the Role of Birds as Agents of Biological Pest Control in North American Agriculture, ca. 1880–1930." *Forest and Conservation History* 39, no. 4 (October 1995): 172–83.
Flanagan, John T. "Hunting in Early Illinois." *Journal of the Illinois State Historical Society* 72, no. 1 (February 1979): 2–12.
Flynn, Charles L., Jr. *White Land, Black Labor: Caste and Class in Late Nineteenth-Century Georgia*. Baton Rouge: Louisiana State University Press, 1983.
Forsyth, Craig J., Robert Gramling, and George Wooddell. "The Game of Poaching: Folk Crimes in Southwest Louisiana." *Society and Natural Resources* 11 (1998): 25–38.
Foster, Bucket T. *So Great Was the Slaughter: Market Hunters, Sportsmen, and Wildlife Conservation in Arkansas*. Tuscaloosa: University of Alabama Press, 2025.
Frederickson, Kari. *Deep South Dynasty: The Bankheads of Alabama*. Tuscaloosa: University of Alabama Press, 2022.
———. "The South and the State in the Twentieth Century." In *A New History of the American South*, edited by Fitzhugh Brundage, 392–431. Chapel Hill: University of North Carolina Press, 2023.
Giltner, Scott. *Hunting and Fishing in the New South: Black Labor and White Leisure after the Civil War*. Baltimore: Johns Hopkins University Press, 2008.
———. "Slave Hunting and Fishing in the Antebellum South." In *"To Love the Wind and the Rain": African Americans and Environmental History*, edited by Dianne D. Glave and Mark Stoll, 21–36. Pittsburgh: University of Pittsburgh Press, 2006.
Greenberg, Cheryl Lee. *To Ask for an Equal Chance: African Americans in the Great Depression*. Lanham, MD: Rowman and Littlefield Press, 2009.
Hahn, Steven. "Hunting, Fishing, and Foraging: Common Rights and Class Relations in the Postbellum South." *Radical History Review* 26 (1982): 37–64.
———. *The Roots of Southern Populism: Yeoman Farmers and the Transformation of the Georgia Upcountry, 1850–1890*. Updated ed. New York: Oxford University Press, 2006.
Haley, Sarah. *No Mercy Here: Gender, Punishment, and the Making of Jim Crow Modernity*. Chapel Hill: University of North Carolina Press, 2016.
Harris, J. William. *Deep Souths: Delta, Piedmont, and Sea Island Society in the Age of Segregation*. Baltimore: Johns Hopkins University Press, 2001.
Haveman, Christopher. *Rivers of Sand: Creek Indian Emigration, Relocation and Ethnic Cleansing in the American South*. Lincoln: University of Nebraska Press, 2016.
Hedges, Andrew H. "Alexander Wetmore, the Bear River Marsh, and the Rise of Waterfowl Science, 1914–1916." *Utah Historical Quarterly* 87, no. 1 (Winter 2019): 8–23.
Heister, Anja. *Beyond the North American Model of Wildlife Conservation*. Palgrave Macmillan Animal Ethics Series. New York: Palgrave Macmillan, 2022.

Herman, Daniel Justin. *Hunting and the American Imagination*. Washington, DC: Smithsonian Institution Press, 2001.

Hild, Matthew. *Greenbackers, Knights of Labor, and Populists: Farmer-Labor Insurgency in the Late-Nineteenth-Century South*. Athens: University of Georgia Press, 2007.

Hyman, Owen James. "The Cut and the Color Line: An Environmental History of Jim Crow in the Deep South's Forests." PhD diss., Mississippi State University, 2018.

Jacoby, Karl. *Crimes against Nature: Squatters, Poachers, Thieves, and the Hidden History of American Conservation*. Berkeley: University of California Press, 2014.

Judd, Richard W. *Common Lands, Common People: The Origins of Conservation in Northern New England*. Cambridge, MA: Harvard University Press, 1997.

Kantor, Shawn. *Politics and Property Rights: The Closing of the Open Range in the Postbellum South*. Chicago: University of Chicago Press, 1998.

Kantor, Shawn Everett, and J. Morgan Kousser. "Common Sense or Commonwealth? The Fence Law and Institutional Change in the Postbellum South." *Journal of Southern History* 59 (1993): 201–42.

Kelley, Lucas P. "Clear Boundaries or Shared Territory: Chickasaw and Cherokee Resistance to American Colonization, 1785–1816." *Transactions of the American Philosophical Society* 110, no. 4 (2021): 93–116.

Kelly, Tara Kathleen. *The Hunter Elite: Manly Sport, Hunting Narratives, and American Conservation, 1880–1925*. Lawrence: University of Kansas Press, 2018.

King, J. Crawford, Jr. "The Closing of the Southern Range: An Exploratory Study." *Journal of Southern History* 48, no. 1 (February 1982): 53–70.

Kirby, Jack Temple. *Rural Worlds Lost: The American South, 1920–1960*. Baton Rouge: Louisiana State University Press, 1987.

Knight, Vernon J., Jr. "Document and Literature Review." In *A Draft Report of a Phase I Archaeological Reconnaissance of the Oliver Lock and Dam Project Area, Tuscaloosa, Alabama*, by Lawrence S. Alexander. Report of Investigations No. 33. Tuscaloosa: Office of Archaeological Research, University of Alabama, 1982.

Krause, Robert Edward. "An Environmental History of the New Deal in Mississippi and Florida." PhD diss., University of Mississippi, 2011.

Link, William A. *The Paradox of Southern Progressivism, 1880–1930*. Fred Morrison Series in Southern Studies. Chapel Hill: University of North Carolina Press, 1992.

Lockhart, Matthew A., and James H. Tuten, eds. *A Southern History of Hunting: Essays on South Carolina*. Athens: University of Georgia Press, forthcoming.

Lorbiecki, Marybeth. *Aldo Leopold: A Fierce Green Fire*. Wilderness Society ed. Guildford, CT: Falcon Publishing, 2005.

Lueck, Dean. "Property Rights and the Economic Logic of Wildlife Institutions." *Natural Resources Journal* 35, no. 3 (Summer 1995): 625–70.

Lund, Thomas H. *American Wildlife Law*. Berkeley: University of California Press, 1980.

Maher, Neil M. *Nature's New Deal*. New York: Oxford University Press, 2008.

Malczewski, Joan. "Philanthropy and Progressive Era State Building through Agricultural Extension Work in the Jim Crow South." *History of Education Quarterly* 53, no. 4 (November 2013): 369–400.

Manning, Chandra. "Emancipation as State Building from the Inside Out." In *Beyond Freedom: Disrupting the History of Emancipation*, edited by David W. Blight and Jim Downs, 60–74. Athens: University of Georgia Press, 2017.

Marks, Stuart A. *Southern Hunting in Black and White: Nature, History, and Ritual in a Carolina Community*. Princeton, NJ: Princeton University Press, 1990.

Mauldin, Erin Stewart. *Unredeemed Land: An Environmental History of Civil War and Emancipation in the Cotton South*. New York: Oxford University Press, 2018.

McCash, June Hall. *The Jekyll Island Cottage Colony*. Athens: University of Georgia Press, 1998.

McIntyre, Rebecca C. "Promoting the South: Tourism and Southern Identity, 1840–1920." PhD diss., University of Alabama, 2004.

McIver, Stuart B. *Death in the Everglades: The Murder of Guy Bradley, America's First Martyr to Environmentalism*. Gainesville: University of Florida Press, 2009.

Merchant, Carolyn. "George Bird Grinnell's Audubon Society: Bridging the Gender Divide in Conservation." *Environmental History* 15 (January 2010): 3–30.

Miles, Tiya. *Ties That Bind: The Story of an Afro-Cherokee Family in Slavery*. 2nd. ed. Berkeley: University of California Press, 2015.

Mitchell, Dennis J. *A New History of Mississippi*. Jackson: University Press of Mississippi, 2014.

Mitchell, William R., Jr., *Landmarks: The Architecture of Thomasville and Thomas County, Georgia, 1820–1980*. Thomasville, GA: Thomasville Landmarks, 1980.

Moran, Kelli L., David J. Mallinson, Stephen J. Culver, Eduardo Leorri, and Ryan P. Mulligan. "Late Holocene Evolution of Currituck Sound, North Carolina, USA: Environmental Change Driven by Sea-Level Rise, Storms, and Barrier Island Morphology." *Journal of Coastal Research* 31, no. 4 (July 2015): 827–41.

Nash, Jere. "Edmund Favor Noel (1908–1912) and the Rise of James K. Vardaman and Theodore G. Bilbo." *Journal of Mississippi History* 81, no. 1 (2019): 3–21.

O'Donovan, Susan Eva. *Becoming Free in the Cotton South*. Cambridge, MA: Harvard University Press, 2007.

Outland, Robert B. *Tapping the Pines: The Naval Stores Industry in the American South*. Baton Rouge: Louisiana State University Press, 2004. Kindle.

Ownby, Ted. *Subduing Satan: Religion, Recreation, and Manhood in the Rural South, 1865–1920*. Chapel Hill: University of North Carolina Press, 1993.

Paisley, Clifton. *From Cotton to Quail: An Agricultural Chronicle of Leon County, Florida, 1860–1967*. Gainesville: University of Florida Press, 1968.

Prewitt, Wiley Charles, Jr. "The Best of All Breathing: Hunting and Environmental Change in Mississippi, 1900–1980." MA thesis, University of Mississippi, 1991.

Price, Jennifer. *Flight Maps: Adventures with Nature in Modern America*. New York: Basic Books, 1999.

Proctor, Nicolas W. *Bathed in Blood: Hunting and Mastery in the Old South*. Charlottesville: University of Virginia Press, 2002.

Ransom, Roger L., and Richard Sutch. "One Kind of Freedom: Reconsidered (and Turbo Charged)." Historical Paper 129, National Bureau of Economic Research Working Paper Series on Historical Factors in Long Run Growth (2000). www.nber.org/system/files/working_papers/h0129/h0129.pdf.

Raper, Arthur F. *Preface to Peasantry: A Tale of Two Black Belt Counties*. Atheneum ed. New York: Atheneum, 1968.

Rauchway, Eric. *Why the New Deal Matters*. New Haven, CT: Yale University Press, 2021.

Reiger, John F. *American Sportsmen and the Origins of Conservation*. 3rd. ed. Corvallis: Oregon State University Press, 2000.

Riser, R. Volney. "Disfranchisement, the U.S. Constitution, and the Federal Courts: Alabama's 1901 Constitutional Convention Debates the Grandfather Clause." *American Journal of Legal History* 48, no. 3 (July 2006): 237–79.

Rogers, William Warren. *Antebellum Thomas County, 1825–1861*. Tallahassee: Florida State University Press, 1963.

———. *Foshalee: Quail Country Plantation*. Tallahassee: Sentry Press, 1989.

———. *Pebble Hill: The Story of a Plantation*. Tallahassee: Sentry Press, 1979.

———. *Thomas County, 1865–1900*. Tallahassee: Florida State University Press, 1973.

———. *Transition to the Twentieth Century: Thomas County, Georgia, 1900–1920*. Tallahassee: Sentry Press, 2002.

Rogers, William Warren, Robert David Ward, Leah Rawls Atkins, and Wayne Flynt. *Alabama: The History of a Deep South State*. 2nd ed. Tuscaloosa: University of Alabama Press, 2010.

Rome, Adam. "'Political Hermaphrodites': Gender and Environmental Reform in Progressive America." *Environmental History* 11, no. 3 (July 2006): 440–63.

Rothman, Joshua D. *The Ledger and the Chain: How Domestic Slave Traders Shaped America*. New York: Basic Books, 2021.

Saikku, Mikko. "Hunting and Wilderness in the Creation of National Identities." In *A Field on Fire: The Future of Environmental History*, edited by Mark Hersey and Ted Steinberg, 116–25. Tuscaloosa: University of Alabama Press, 2019.

———. *This Delta, This Land: An Environmental History of the Yazoo–Mississippi Floodplain*. Athens: University of Georgia Press, 2005.

Saunt, Claudio. *Unworthy Republic: The Dispossession of Native Americans and the Road to Indian Territory*. New York: W. W. Norton, 2020.

Sawers, Brian. "Property Law as Labor Control in the Postbellum South." *Law and History Review* 33, no. 2 (May 2015): 351–76.

Shawhan, Dorothy. *Fannye Cook: Mississippi's Pioneering Conservationist*. Edited and with contributions by Marion Barnwell and Libby Hartfield. Jackson: University Press of Mississippi, 2018.

Silber, Nina. *The Romance of Reunion: Northerners and the South, 1865–1900*. Chapel Hill: University of North Carolina Press, 1993.

Silkenat, David. *Scars on the Land: An Environmental History of Slavery in the American South*. New York: Oxford University Press.

Silver, Timothy. *A New Face on the Countryside: Indians, Colonists, and Slaves in South Atlantic Forests, 1500–1800*. New York: Cambridge University Press, 1990.

Smalley, Andrea L., with Henry M. Reeves. *The Market in Birds: Commercial Hunting, Conservation, and the Origins of Wildlife Consumerism, 1850–1920*. Baltimore: Johns Hopkins University Press, 2022.

Spruill, Marjorie Julian. "Nellie Nugent Somerville." In *Mississippi Women: Their Histories, Their Lives*, edited by Martha H. Swain, Elizabeth Anne Payne, and Marjorie Julian Spruill, 39–58. Athens: University of Georgia Press, 2003.

Starnes, Richard. *Creating the Land of the Sky: Tourism and Society in Western North Carolina*. Tuscaloosa: University of Alabama Press, 2005.

Stephens, Deanne Love. *The Mississippi Gulf Coast Seafood Industry: A People's History*. Jackson: University Press of Mississippi, 2021.

Stewart, Mart A. "From King Cane to King Cotton: Razing Cane in the Old South." *Environmental History* 12, no. 1 (January 2007): 59–79.

———. *"What Nature Suffers to Groe": Life, Labor, and Landscape on the Georgia Coast, 1680–1920*. Athens: University of Georgia Press, 1996.

Swanson, Drew. "Growing Wild: Visions of Wildlife Management as Agricultural Science in American Forests and Fields." *Agricultural History* 97, no. 2 (May 2023): 177–214.

Taylor, Dorceta E. *The Rise of the American Conservation Movement: Power, Privilege, and Environmental Protection*. Durham, NC: Duke University Press, 2016.

Taylor, Mark T. "North Carolina Fisheries in the Old and New South." *North Carolina Review* 69, no. 1 (January 1992): 1–36.

Thompson, E. P. *Whigs and Hunters: The Making of the English Working Class*. New York: Pantheon, 1975.

Tober, James A. *Who Owns the Wildlife? The Political Economy of Conservation in Nineteenth-Century America*. Westport, CT: Praeger, 1981.

Unger, Nancy C. *Beyond Nature's Housekeepers: American Women in Environmental History*. New York: Oxford University Press, 2012.

Vinson, Frank B. "Conservation and the South, 1890–1920." PhD diss., University of Georgia, 1971.

Vivian, Daniel J. *A New Plantation World: Sporting Estates in the South Carolina Lowcountry, 1900–1940*. New York: Cambridge University Press, 2018.

Wadewitz, Lissa. "Are Fish Wildlife?" *Environmental History* 16, no. 3 (July 2011): 423–27.

Warren, Louis. *The Hunter's Game: Poachers and Conservationists in Twentieth-Century America*. New Haven, CT: Yale University Press, 1997.

Way, Albert G. *Conserving Southern Longleaf: Herbert Stoddard and the Rise of Ecological Land Management*. Athens: University of Georgia Press, 2011.

Werum, Regina. "Sectionalism and Racial Politics: Federal Vocational Policies and Programs in the Predesegregation South." *Social Sciences History* 21, no. 3 (Autumn 1997): 399–453.

Whatley, Larry. "The Works Progress Administration in Mississippi." *Journal of Mississippi History* 30 (February 1968): 35–50.

Wolfe, Patrick. "Settler Colonialism and the Elimination of the Native." *Journal of Genocide Research* 8, no. 4 (2006): 387–409.

Wright, Gavin. "The New Deal and the Modernization of the South." *Federal History*. Discussion Papers 08-042, Stanford Institute for Economic Policy Research (2010): 58–73.

———. *Old South, New South: Revolutions in the Southern Economy since the Civil War*. Baton Rouge: Louisiana State University Press, 1986.

Wright, Robert E. *The History and Evolution of the North American Wildlife Conservation Model*. New York: Palgrave Macmillan, 2022.

Youngs, Larry. "Lifestyle Enclaves: Winter Resorts in the South Atlantic States, 1870–1930." PhD diss., Georgia State University, 2001.

Ziegler, Edith. *Schools in the Landscape: Localism, Cultural Tradition, and the Development of Alabama's Public Education System, 1865–1915*. Tuscaloosa: University of Alabama Press, 2010.

Index

Agricultural Wheel, 50
Aiken, South Carolina, 46, 81
Alabama Constitutional Convention of 1901, 52–55
Alabama Constitution of 1901, 36, 50
Alabama Department of Conservation, 124
Alabama Department of Game and Fish, 58–61
Alabama Game and Fish Protective Association, 55
Alcorn A&M College, 140
American Forestry Association, 125
American Game Protective Association, 72, 74
American Ornithologists' Union, 30–31, 39, 41–44, 46
Anderson, Jule, 114–16
Anderson, Virginia, 114, 116
Archbold, John D., 90
Archbold, John F., 93, 113
Auburn University, 156

Bankhead, John, Jr., 74, 139
Bankhead-Jones Farm Tenant Act (1937), 139
Bartsch, Paul, 122–23
bears, 10, 19, 82, 127
Beretta USA, 158
Bibb County, Alabama, 65
biological surveys: in Mississippi, 141–43, 147–48
bird protection movement, 41–43. *See also* American Ornithologists' Union
Black Act, 15
black powder shells, 106, 129
Black Warrior River, 10
Boone, Daniel, 16–17
Boone and Crockett Club, 72
Bradley, Guy, 46
Breton Island Bird Reservation, 47

Brookings Institution, 131–32
Bureau of Biological Survey, 30–31

Cairo, Georgia, 104
Carter, Neal, Jr., 153, 159
Centre, Alabama, 1
Chapin, Charles M., 86, 89, 91, 93, 96, 108, 111
Charleston, South Carolina, 10, 46, 61
Chatham County, Georgia, 15, 48
Cherokee Nation, 11, 14
Chickasaw Nation, 10–11, 13
Choctaw Nation, 10–11, 13
Clay, Clement C., 13
commons, 71, 107, 156, 165n5, 167n23; erosion of, 4, 7, 9, 13–15, 17, 21, 26, 33, 34. *See also* open range
Conner, Mike, 131–32
Conservation Week, 149
Cook, Fannye A., 8, 118, 120, 154; conservation work, 144–50; early life and education, 120–23; and Mississippi Association for the Conservation of Wild Life, 123; and Mississippi Game and Fish Commission, 137
Cook, Vivian, 145–46
Creek hunters, 10–12
Creek Nation (Muscogee [Creek] Nation), 10–14, 80
Creek War (1813–14), 10, 12
Crystal Springs, Mississippi, 121, 142, 151

Dallas County, Alabama, 15
deer, 10, 16, 24, 26, 29, 51, 122, 124, 169n87; and Black Act, 15; as "game," 131; open seasons for, 127; populations of, 11, 154; as "trophy" animal, 82
deer hunting, 12, 15
deerskins, 10, 11, 14

209

Delta State Teacher's College (Delta State University), 148
doves, 31, 48, 82; dove hunts, 1–2
Ducks Unlimited, 159
economic ornithology, 30–31
Ellisville, Alabama, 1

enclosure, 3, 4, 6, 7, 10, 11, 25–27, 66, 86, 107, 118; and race, 28; of Red Hills region, 86–96
environmental change, 22
extension laws, 13

factory system, 11
Farmer's Alliance, 50
fence laws, 25–26, 107
firearms, 6, 9, 10, 28, 34, 83, 95, 107; and enslaved hunters, 18–21; manufacturers of, and Alabama game and fish laws, 57; and Migratory Bird Treaty Act, 131; and race, 22–23, 129
fishing: as leisure activity, 91; and licenses, 135; as livelihood, 63; as part of game laws, 57; and seining, 57, 62, 127; and traps, 19, 60, 63
Florida Audubon Society, 46
forestry, 5, 55, 56, 68, 126, 133, 136, 141, 156; and Mississippi game and fish laws, 134, 144; and segregated 4-H clubs, 150; and women, 125
4-H Clubs, 144, 148, 150
fox hunts, 50, 84, 96, 118
Fugler, Madge Quin, 133

game laws: and camp hunting, 26, 29, 33, 169n86; and class, 16–17, 61, 79, 95–96, 110–11, 129; and closed seasons, 2, 26, 31, 37, 48, 51, 56, 61, 70, 73, 75, 93, 109, 127, 129–31, 134, 150, 152, 169n86–87; convictions for violating, 31–33, 65–68; and dynamiting streams, 48, 57, 169n86; and fire hunting, 26; and gender, 124–26, 133–34, 137; and landowners, 16, 26, 29, 33, 58–61, 65–70, 108, 109, 111, 129, 131, 136, 155; penalties for violating, 33, 51, 56–57, 66, 130, 135, 136; and poll tax, 135; and pollution, 57; and property rights, 66; racial motivations for, 25–28, 36, 58–59, 129; resistance to, 4, 32–33, 110; role of probate judges in, 57, 62–63, 175n130; and slave code, 18–19; and Sunday hunting, 22, 26, 33; and trespass, 4, 7, 66–67
game wardens, 2, 6, 38, 43, 45–47, 48, 57, 59, 60, 75, 106–8, 124, 126, 129, 133, 135, 137, 143, 149, 158; monthly reports of, 63–64; salaries of, 59, 130, 135
Geer v. Connecticut (1896), 60, 65, 73, 74
General Federation of Women's Clubs, 124
Georgetown, South Carolina, 46, 90
Georgia Audubon Society, 47–48
Georgia Department of Game and Fish, 68–71, 108–9
Georgia Department of Natural Resources, 155
Georgia–Florida Shooting Dog Handlers' Club, 153, 155, 159
Gosse, Philip Henry, 15
Grady County, Georgia, 104–5

Hall, Minna B., 42
Hanna, H. M., 89
Hanna, Mark, 89
hawks, 30, 47, 48, 142
Hemenway, Harriet Lawrence, 42
hogs, 14, 15, 17–18, 26, 28, 33
Hopkins, Henry W., 83–86, 90–95, 100–111; and northern estate owners, 100–102
Hornaday, William, 38, 73–75
Houk, L. Seely, 58
house sparrow, 41
Howorth, Lucy Somerville, 133
hunters: Black, 5, 18, 28, 33, 59, 60, 97, 99, 106–7, 111, 135; enslaved, 18–21; as "game hogs," 37; market, 4, 16, 39, 45–47, 48, 55, 63, 131, 165n5; as "pothunters," 4, 17, 37, 38, 60, 129; as

"sportsmen," 3, 5, 6, 16, 17, 34, 37, 42, 43, 69, 83, 110, 146, 156
hunting: colonial commercial, 10–12; and masculinity, 8, 16, 20–21, 82–83; and racial customs, 6, 97; and racial violence, 22–24; for sustenance, 1, 4, 11, 12, 17, 19, 20, 22, 29, 30, 37, 60, 110, 111, 168n48
hunting clubs, 80, 87, 94, 133, 136, 141, 154
hunting dogs, 17, 20, 29, 94, 102, 107, 114, 115, 118; and fox hunting, 96; and game laws, 22–23; and quail hunting, 82–86, 94–96; and slave codes, 18; training of, 98–100, 153
hunting labor, 97–100
hunting lands, 10–11, 13
hunting laws. *See* game laws
hunting licenses, 6, 45, 58, 60, 65, 70, 129–131, 158; and "aliens," 58; cost of, 62, 109, 128, 135; and free people of color, 18; and poll tax, 135; resistance to, 110, 130; and tenants, 111; and violations of game law, 66

Interstate Sportsmen's Protective Association, 74
Izaak Walton League, 134

Jackson, Andrew, 12
Jackson, Mississippi, 121
Jeanes Fund, 150
Jim Crow laws, 7, 35, 135, 158; and disenfranchisement, 35, 50, 52–53
Johannsen, Tina, 157–58
Jones, J. Wyman, 85–86, 87
Joseph T. Robinson National Forest Refuge Act (1934), 140

Ku Klux Klan, 22–23

Lacey Act (1900), 43
land consolidation, 79–82, 86–89, 92, 141; resistance to, 103–6
land leases, 92–94

land tenure system, 21, 24–25, 102–3
Lauderdale County, Alabama, 48, 169n85
League of American Sportsmen, 43
Leopold, Aldo, 141–43
Louisiana Audubon Society, 47, 127
Louisiana Department of Conservation, 124

Macon County, Alabama, 17, 64
Madison County, Alabama, 48, 52, 54, 169n85
Marion, Alabama, 29
Marion County, Alabama, 64, 169n85
Mason, A. H., 85, 89, 102, 103, 108
Massachusetts Audubon Society, 42
Masury, John W., 87, 88, 90
Meridian, Mississippi, 23
Migratory Bird Hunting and Conservation Stamp Act (1934), 140
Migratory Bird Treaty Act (1918), 2, 37, 74, 120, 131, 137–39
Miller, Frank M., 47, 127
Mississippi A&M (Mississippi State University), 123
Mississippi Academy of Sciences, 150
Mississippi Association for the Conservation of Wild Life, 119, 123–24, 126, 131, 133–34, 137, 140–42
Mississippi Audubon Society, 127–29
Mississippi Game and Fish Commission, 120, 133–39, 141, 143, 145, 148, 150, 152
Mississippi State College for Women (Mississippi University for Women), 121, 140
Mississippi State Wildlife Museum (Mississippi Museum of Natural Science), 152
Model Law, 41–44, 46–48, 51, 61, 127, 129
Montgomery, Alabama, 32, 33, 53

National Association of Audubon Societies, 36, 38–48, 56, 72, 127–28, 149
National Association of Colored Women's Clubs, 125
National Wild Turkey Federation, 125

Native dispossession, 12–13
natural history museums, 122, 144–48, 152
New Deal, 6, 8, 120, 126, 134; and conservation work, 137–40
Nineteenth Amendment, 133
North American Model of Wildlife Conservation, 156
North Carolina Audubon Society, 44–46, 129

open range, 13–15, 17, 26–27, 86. See also commons
opossums, 19, 131, 147
owls, 30, 47, 48, 131

Palmer, T. S., 39, 43–44, 47, 51, 55–58, 68, 92
partridges, 19, 20, 41, 82. See also quail
Pearson, Thomas Gilbert, 38, 43, 55, 68, 70, 129, 149; and game laws in southern states, 44–48
Pelican Island, Florida, 46
Perry County, Alabama, 64, 169n85
pheasants, 30, 41
Pheasants Forever, 159
Pittman-Robertson Act (1937), 150, 157–58
poachers, 15, 108
Poe, Elisabeth (Pansy), 78, 178n7
Populist movement, 35, 50, 52
posted lands, 2, 15, 66, 69, 106–7, 110
Progressive Era, 2–6, 7, 53, 56, 59, 129, 158; and conservation, 3, 35, 109, 112, 126; and race, 35, 71, 111; and state consolidation, 34, 76; and women, 120–21, 124, 126
property laws, 6–7, 21; changes to, in post–Civil War South, 25–26, 29, 31, 34, 118
property rights, 5, 8, 9, 128, 133, 152
public lands, 12, 80, 133–34, 141, 154, 155

quail, 8, 19, 31, 41, 46, 48, 55–56, 60, 80, 85, 94, 99, 102, 103, 109, 127, 129, 147, 153, 156; and conservation, 111–13; hunting of, after Civil War, 82–83, 94–96, 106; sanctuaries for, in Mississippi, 140, 148–49
Quinn, I. T., 65, 75, 124, 135, 136

raccoons, 19, 131
Raper, Arthur F., 97
Reconstruction, 7, 22–24, 27, 29, 81, 105
Red Hills region, 80–82; hunting colony in, 86–96
Rogers, William Warren, 78
Rome, Georgia, 1
Roosevelt, Franklin D., 134, 138, 139
Roosevelt, Theodore, 46, 47, 72, 73, 83

Shields, G. O., 43
Smith, Ashley, 158
Smith, Durrell, 153, 155, 157, 158
Smith-Hughes Act (1917), 148
Smith-Lever Act (1914), 148
smokeless shells, 106, 107
Society for the Prevention of Cruelty to Animals, 48
songbirds, 3, 30, 42, 48, 73
South Carolina Audubon Society, 45–46
Sporting Arms and Ammunition Institute Game Restoration Committee, 141
squirrels, 15, 19, 22–23, 62, 123, 130, 131, 147
state ownership of wildlife, 36, 60–61, 65, 73, 127. See also Geer v. Connecticut
stock laws, 4, 25–28, 31, 54. See also enclosure
Stoddard, Herbert, 112–13, 142
Sumter County, Alabama, 31, 169n86

Thayer Fund, 43–44
Thomasville, Georgia, 20, 77–78
Thompson, Lewis S., 93, 100, 111, 113, 114, 142
Top, Mildred Spurrier, 133
trapping, 17, 106, 109–111, 123, 131, 135
trespass, 2, 18, 21, 22, 25–26, 28–29, 33, 65
turkeys, 15, 19, 24, 41, 48, 56, 82, 103, 127
Tuscaloosa County, Alabama, 10, 12–13

University of Alabama, 23
University of Mississippi, 140
US Department of Agriculture, 30–31, 39, 43, 73, 92, 121, 137, 139
US Fish and Wildlife Service, 156

Van Duzer, S. R., 87, 89

Wade, J. H., 90–92, 96, 101, 107
Wallace, John H., Jr., 1, 7, 35, 37, 39; and creation of the Alabama Department of Game and Fish, 58–61; early life, 48; and migratory bird protection, 72–76; as novelist, 50
Watson, Thomas E., 110
Weeks-McClean Act (1913), 72–73
Welty, Eudora, 121, 138
Wetmore, Alexander, 123

wildlife management, 80, 125, 142, 152, 154, 158
wildlife management areas, 155
wildlife refuges, 123, 130, 134, 137, 139–41, 143
Wilson, Woodrow, 74
Winston County, Alabama, 33
Winston County, Mississippi, 23
Works Progress Administration, 138, 143; and conservation work in Mississippi, 143–49
World War II, 1, 25, 90, 103, 139, 154

Young, Charlie, 7, 77–79; and hunting labor, 83–84, 96–100, 113–17; and love of hunting, 97, 100, 118; and observations of historical change, 77–78, 84–86, 107–8

www.ingramcontent.com/pod-product-compliance
Lightning Source LLC
Chambersburg PA
CBHW030735250426
43671CB00035B/405